AN AMERICAN HARVEST

Readings in
American
History

Volume 2

AN AMERICAN HARVEST

Readings in American History

Volume 2

J. R. Conlin
California State University, Chico

C. H. Peterson
California State University, Chico

Harcourt Brace Jovanovich, Publishers

San Diego   New York   Chicago   Atlanta   Washington, D.C.
London   Sydney   Toronto

Copyright © 1986 by Harcourt Brace Jovanovich, Inc.

ISBN: 0-15-502305-5
Library of Congress Catalog Card Number: 85-80083
Printed in the United States of America

to
G. D. Lillibridge,
generous friend

Preface

Montaigne said that historians spoil everything because "they chew our meat for us." He was right, of course. The task of historians is to study the documents—the primary sources, the meat of history—and to make of these a coherent, truthful representation of the past, as historians understand it, for those without the time or inclination to do so themselves.

Nowhere is the meat more thoroughly chewed than in survey courses in the history of the United States. How could it be otherwise? There are only a few weeks in every course, a few hundred pages in any textbook, in which to negotiate the complex experience of several hundred million Americans over nearly four centuries. Each instructor, each author must tell the story as swiftly and as simply as he or she can, wanly hoping that what is served up contains more than individual opinion.

It is only a minor improvement to supplement this fare by dragging in the "conflicting interpretations" of other historians. Two or three historians' truths undoubtedly make better grist for grinding than those of one. But if the historian's craft is worthwhile, why not present students with a few untouched portions on which to feast for themselves?

It is in the belief that the examination of primary sources can be a useful exercise in survey courses in American history that we have prepared *An American Harvest*. Although it can be used alone in courses organized around "problems" or "issues" and in classes that are blessedly small, we have arranged the reading material in ten sections corresponding to the periods into which American history is usually divided so that *An American Harvest* may be assigned in conjunction with any of the standard textbooks.

Within each section are five or six documents focusing on major questions of public policy. We have elected to include comparatively few documents, in part because of the crush of information and scarcity of time in survey courses and in part because this arrangement has permitted us to add more than the usual few words of sketchy introduction. In a foreword to each document we explain its historical context. In an afterword we comment on its subsequent history and significance. It bears emphasis that these auxiliary remarks are not pre-chewing. Their purpose is only to avoid the self-defeating consequences of presenting students with a document cold. They supply whatever information is required to permit students to understand the document in its own terms and to think about it for themselves.

In selecting the documents to be included in *An American Harvest* we have aimed to provide staple fare. Here are notable or representative documents that illuminate major questions of public policy in American history. Absent are essays on the social, cultural, religious, literary, or private lives of the American people, or of the many groups into which they have been divided, each with urgent concerns of its own. The broad questions of economic and social development included here are those which have engaged most Americans most of the time and around which they have organized their political efforts.

As editors our goal has been to provide readable texts useful to modern students. Therefore, especially in the earlier readings, we have modernized spelling, and here and there we have altered punctuation, whenever we believed the result would be a clearer version of the author's meaning. These are not, then, critical editions of the texts, especially since the limitations of space have prevented our using the whole of any but a few of them. But we have scrupulously respected the language of the originals. The words are the authors' own; difficult or obscure phrases are explained in the footnotes; omissions are indicated by ellipses; and, in the few cases where we have inserted a word, it is enclosed in brackets.

We thank Professor Jay Coughtry, University of Nevada, Las Vegas, for his helpful review of our manuscript.

J. C.
C. P.

Contents

AN AMERICAN HARVEST

Readings in
American
History

Volume 2

PART 1

✿ ✿ ✿

Government and Economy
1862–1905

1

William McKee Dunn

✦ ✦ ✦

Speech on the Transcontinental Railroad

1862

*I*n 1850, with more than 9000 miles
of track crisscrossing the states east of the Mississippi, the United States was
already the world's premier railroading nation. Americans had taken so
enthusiastically to the "Iron Horse," steaming along on "two streaks of rust
and a right of way," because the railroad deftly conquered the natural
obstacles that had hindered economic development from the beginning:
the harsh winters that froze rivers and canals over much of the country,
rendering them useless several months a year; and the formidable
Appalachians which, running in nearly unbroken ridges, precluded
canals connecting East with West or extensive use of horse- and ox-drawn
overland transportation. Now, after 1850, with the territorial prizes of the
Mexican War attached to the Union, there were the far more formidable
Rocky Mountains and the Sierra Nevada; the broad, forbidding deserts
of the Southwest; and, simply, the vast, intimidating distances of the
continental republic. A wagon train needed six months to cross from
Independence, Missouri, to Sacramento, about as long as a ship rounding
South America to California.

SPEECH ON THE TRANSCONTINENTAL RAILROAD   From House of Representatives,
meeting as a Committee of the Whole, April 17, 1862, *Congressional Globe*, 1701.

It is no surprise, therefore, that as soon as California won statehood in 1850, prominent politicians began to speak of building a railroad across the continent. Both Whigs, with their long tradition of advocating federally financed internal improvements, and Democrats, traditionally hostile to such improvements, urged this project on. Both southerners and northerners spoke out in favor of it. Indeed, support for so glorious a national undertaking encouraged moderates on the slavery question to hope that the transcontinental railroad would distract both anti-slavery and pro-slavery extremists from the bitter antipathy that, in 1850, almost split the Union in two.

That was not to be. Instead, the transcontinental railroad was itself soon snarled in the sectional conflict as leaders of North and South argued that the line's eastern terminus should lie within the section from which they hailed. In 1853, the "Gadsden Purchase" of land from Mexico (southern Arizona and New Mexico below a line drawn roughly from Yuma to El Paso) was engineered by Secretary of War and future president of the Confederate States of America, Jefferson Davis, in order to encourage adoption of the southern route: the purchase tract allowed the projected railroad to flank the Rocky Mountains to the south. Stephen Douglas' Kansas-Nebraska Bill, introduced in Congress in January 1854, a month after the Gadsden Purchase, was designed to put the "Central Route," which benefitted Douglas's Chicago, back in the competition by establishing territorial law in what had been Indian country.

It was not Douglas' ambitions for Chicago, but the resurrection of the issue of the legality of slavery in lands north of the Missouri Compromise line (see Volume 1, Part 5, Reading 3), which has earned the Kansas-Nebraska Act its place in history. So increasingly bitter did the slavery issue become after Kansas-Nebraska that some historians have seen an inevitable progression from that Act to Fort Sumter and the great Civil War.

However true that may have been, the 1850s saw virtually no further progress towards a transcontinental railroad. Even proposals that two transcontinental lines be built simultaneously, one in the North, the other in the South, received scant attention. It was only after the South had seceded, the war had begun, and the North had become the Union in its entirety, that an internal improvement could be imbued with the fervent nationalism of Indiana Congressman William McKee Dunn.

❀ Mr. Chairman, the construction of a railroad which shall unite the waters of the Atlantic with those of the Pacific, will be the consummation of the great idea which filled the mind of Columbus when he discovered a new world. It will unite this continent, and all western and commercial Europe with the richest trade of the world, by a more direct route than it is possible to secure in any other way.[1] It will place our Goverment in a just and merited position among the leading nations of the earth, by compelling them to pay a tribute to it for the enjoyment of a commerce, which is the chief source of their wealth. And as we are about to suppress a rebellion by which perfidious traitors have sought to overthrow and destroy our Government, and thus demonstrate our great military power, and the stability of our institutions, it seems to me to be an appropriate time to organize this great enterprise. It will be most fit that we should crown our victories of war with this higher and nobler victory of peace.

It is not a wild fancy to suppose that Providence has reserved us for such a destiny and such a history as this. No people on earth have been so blessed by God's protecting care as we have. There is nothing, or scarcely anything, which is or can be made the source of wealth, prosperity, or happiness which we do not possess. All the varieties of soil, climate, and production are ours; and while the tide of rebellion is now rolling back before the march of our gallant armies, we should be untrue to ourselves if we did not stretch forth our hands to seize upon a commerce for which the world has struggled from the time when the Middianitish merchants brought their spices and myrrhs of the East across the plains of Asia.

The time is not inappropriate in another sense. England and France, the acknowledged rivals for years which exceed in number the age of our nation, are employing all the agency which wealth and diplomacy can furnish to obtain a direct route to India, not only for the purpose of securing the wealth of India, China, and Japan, but to retain a controlling influence over the commerce of the world. English enterprise has projected a railroad from the eastern shores of the Mediterranean to the Euphrates, but it has met with a check in the unflinching enmity of the Arab tribes who roam the plains where the flocks of the patriarchs were fed. England already owns and occupies several unfortified points on the Red sea, and both she and France are struggling to overcome the impediments which nature has thrown in the way of accomplishing the great idea which filled the mind of Alexander when he built the city of Alexandria, that of uniting the waters of the Red sea with those of the

---

[1] Columbus, of course, was seeking to open up the East Asian trade when he made his American landfall. The allure of Oriental goods and the huge Asian market continued (and continues) to enamor American business.

Mediterranean, by canal.[2] Their habitual and long-cherished jealousy has thus far prevented the concentration of their united energies in the work, until each nation is afraid to invest its capital alone in so uncertain and hazardous an enterprise.

At such a time as this, and when all the nations of Europe are agitated with political complications, which it may be that the sword alone can cut, it is most appropriate for us to assert our true position in the world of commerce, and by putting forth our energies in the construction of this great highway, become, as I trust it is our destiny to be, the greatest nation of the earth.

These are only a few of the foreign aspects of the question, and are referred to only to show that the present condition of the world is such as to make that which is manifestly our interest also an imperative duty, unless there is some domestic difficulty in the way. Such difficulties have been stated, but are they well founded? Even those who have heretofore been most noted for what they call a strict construction of the Constitution, admit that we have an undoubted power to build such a road if it is a military necessity. And who can doubt that such a necessity now exists in a far greater degree than it ever existed in any nation before? Our internal security demands that we should tie together with iron bands our Atlantic and Pacific shores, not only that we may be enabled to defend every portion of our soil against foreign invasion, if it shall ever come, but against all such domestic foes as those who have rendered their names accursed by the present iniquitous rebellion.

A question of great moment is that growing out of the present condition of our finances, when we are just inaugurating a new scheme of taxation, which will put the patriotism and patience of our people to the severest test.[3] But, properly considered, this objection is not insurmountable, for the plain reason that the present bill does not propose to raise a dollar by taxation for the purpose of constructing the road. An accurate and careful examination of the scheme will show that it is a self-sustaining one; and that although the Government lends it credit—which is the representative of its wealth—it is not required to draw the money from the pockets of the people. The only question, in this connection, which is to be

---

[2]The Suez Canal, which shortened sea travel from Europe to Asia by weeks, had been under construction for three years when Dunn's speech was delivered. It was completed in 1869, the same year as the transcontinental railroad.

[3]The first federal income tax was enacted in 1862. It levied a three percent rate on incomes between $600 and $10,000 and five percent on incomes above $10,000. The tax was allowed to die in 1872.

considered is, whether or no the road can be constructed upon a line and through a portion of the country where it will secure, during the progress of its construction, a sufficient amount of trade and transportation to produce revenue equal to the interest upon the cost of construction; for it is conceded on all hands that if it does, when completed, it must, from the nature of things, secure an amount of business sufficient to make it the source of profit to those by whose energy and enterprise it shall be built. While, when this result has been attained, it may not run all our great ocean steamers from the sea, yet this road must, by the irresistible laws of trade, draw to it so much of what they now transport as to add vastly to its receipts. The freights of the ocean once made Spain the most prosperous nation upon earth, and when the superior energy and enterprise of neighboring nations wrested these freights from her, she sank down to inferiority, if not decay. Holland built her dykes into the sea, and erected cities upon them, by these freights; and even England herself, with all her boasted superiority, would have lost much of her power and supremacy, if the wealth of her East India Company had not gone to swell her coffers. If we can succeed, as undoubtedly we shall by building this road, to draw a large share of these freights to this great thoroughfare, we will have opened a mine of wealth far richer than the mines of California and Australia combined.

❂ ❂ ❂

The secession of the southern states did not end all controversy concerning the transcontinental railroad. Congressman Dunn, for example, turned from his eloquent generalities to a partisan plea for the route that would feed western commerce through Chicago, and then into Indiana and the eastern states. There was also disagreement as to how and when the railroad should be financed. Undoubtedly, private capital alone was not up to the task. It was some 2400 miles from the Missouri River to California. To lay tracks over the Sierra Nevada and the Rockies would cost up to $48,000 a mile. Because there were virtually no potential customers already settled along the right of way, it would be years—until the line was completed—before the transcontinental would begin to return revenues worth noticing. With many other attractive investments beckoning during the 1860s, few capitalists were interested.

The solution was federal finance and, as Dunn made clear, there were any number of political and strategic, as well as economic, reasons to justify public subsidy. However, with the Civil War already straining the national treasury, tax revenues, and government credit, there was little cash to be spared. Consequently, some congressmen urged that the project be shelved until after the war was won.

The majority of the congressional Republicans would hear nothing of this. They would subvent the construction of the railroad with the one commodity in which the federal government was fabulously rich: land. The Pacific Railway Act of July 1, 1862 authorized a grant of public domain to two great companies—the Union Pacific (building east to west), and the Central Pacific (west to east)—of ten alternate sections (square miles) of land for each mile of railroad the companies actually completed. In addition to capital raised by selling this land, the Union Pacific and Central Pacific were authorized to borrow from the federal coffers.

By 1864, railroad fever had reached such heights that the land grant was doubled, and the government agreed that the railroads' debt would be secured by a second mortgage, which encouraged banks to make additional loans. To the Northern Pacific Railroad, which was commissioned to build a second transcontinental line in 1864, the grant of land in the territories was up to forty alternate sections for each mile of track laid. That is, in a swath of land eighty miles wide across present-day Washington, Montana, and North Dakota, the Northern Pacific Railroad was to own precisely half!

By the time the giveaway ended in 1877, some 131 million acres of public domain (and 45 million acres of state land) had been given to a handful of huge corporations. Until the 1870s, few Americans objected to this generosity. The land seemed unending. Big business seemed unambivalently an agent of progress. With the exception of the odd romantic, virtually everyone shared the vision of Congressman Dunn.

2

Johnson Newlon Camden

❖ ❖ ❖

The Standard Oil Company
1883

*T*he railroads were the nation's first
big businesses. During the 1870s and 1880s they were joined by dozens of
other multimillion-dollar firms, conducting business on a national scale
and manufacturing a variety of products familiar to millions of American
households. Gradually, during the last quarter of the nineteenth century,
the multitude of small, independent local producers who had hitherto
conducted the nation's business were replaced by giant corporations,
some of which achieved a virtual monopoly in their industries.

Some of these firms grew great by pioneering new methods of
machine production that swamped their competitors. High-volume,
continuous-process machinery permitted almost limitless production
which quickly saturated local markets and forced its owners to build
aggressive national marketing and distributing organizations. By the 1880s
Diamond matches, American Tobacco cigarettes, Pillsbury flour, Quaker
oats, Heinz canned foods, Campbell soups, Borden condensed milk,
Colgate and Procter and Gamble soap, and Eastman-Kodak film had
become household words.

Similarly a few firms employed the new technique of mechanical

THE STANDARD OIL COMPANY   From J. N. Camden, "The Standard Oil Company,"
North American Review (February 1883), CXXXVI, 182–90.

refrigeration to market products whose perishable nature required control of all stages of production from manufacturing to distribution. Thus the Swift and Armour companies wiped out innumerable local butchers and meat wholesalers, and Pabst, Schlitz, and Anheuser-Busch replaced many of the nation's independent brewers.

These were examples of firms which won their commanding position by internal growth, the development of advanced technologies, and superior marketing skills. In the case of other giants which appeared in the 1870s and 1880s, greatness was achieved by the more direct means of buying up or merging with other competitors until only a single firm remained to monopolize its industry.

The single most urgent reason for the wave of mergers which swept through the American business community during the last quarter of the nineteenth century was the uncontrolled productivity of the American economy—often far in excess of any immediate remunerative demand. Such overproduction had become chronic in the nation's staple commodities by the 1870s, including petroleum, wheat, and cotton, to name a few. But it was also true of the manufacturing industries, which it afflicted with special force.

In an economy of small producers, such as Adam Smith had described, trial-and-error market competition may have been a satisfactory way to keep supply and demand in balance. In enterprises requiring only a small capital, there were always thousands of producers, some of them less skillful and efficient than others. When supply exceeded demand, they were the ones who were driven out of business at no great cost to society and perhaps some gain in efficiency. It was far to the contrary in the case of modern industries where businessmen had invested heavily in expensive, highly specialized machinery. Rather than lose the capital they had invested, such businessmen might continue to produce for long periods, even if at a loss while the supply of unsold goods mounted higher and prices continued to fall. The gravity of the problem may be seen from the fact that the nation's wholesale price index on all commodities fell from 151 in 1870 to 82 by 1886. Was it any wonder that businessmen complained bitterly of the "ruinous" competition to which they were exposed by these unprecedented circumstances?

The only practical way to control production and maintain acceptably high prices was for businessmen to stop competing against each other and instead form producers' associations or "pools." The members of such associations agreed to divide the business between themselves, setting production quotas and allocating specific markets to each member. During the 1870s pools came to be the normal way of conducting business in most American industries.

It was, however, a highly imperfect arrangement. Because pools were not legally binding upon their members, their enforcement depended wholly upon shifting considerations of self-interest. In the steel industry, for example, Andrew Carnegie routinely entered into pooling arrangements in the 1870s and just as cheerfully broke them when it suited his advantage. Outright merger was a far more reliable way of eliminating competition between firms. Thus in the 1880s the trust appeared.

The first businesses to achieve a commanding lead in this manner were found in the nation's refining and distilling industries—petroleum, sugar, and whiskey, among others. In these industries the chaotic and uncontrollable production of the basic commodities which they processed made it all the more essential for the processor to intervene to arrest declining prices.

In petroleum John D. Rockefeller organized the first pool among the oil refiners in 1872. In order to make it stick he negotiated preferential rates with railroads which only association members in good standing could qualify for. By 1880 the 40 members of the pool controlled 90 percent of the refining capacity of the nation. Two years later ingenious company lawyers worked out a way by which their ownership could be combined under a single board of managers. Thus the Standard Oil Company became the granddaddy of the trusts.

Johnson N. Camden was a lawyer and pioneer oil man from Parkersburg, West Virginia and one of the first to bring his firm into Rockefeller's combination. When he wrote the following article for the *North American Review* he was serving the first of two terms in the United States Senate. Senator Camden's essay was one of the very rare occasions in which someone associated with Standard Oil attempted to explain the character of its business to the public. While it is not free of factual misrepresentations, it makes the generally persuasive case followed by apologists for the company ever since.

❀ Few things in fiction are more wonderful than the history of petroleum since the opening of the first oil-well in Pennsylvania, on August 28, 1859. Four years before that time, Jonathan Watson, who owned a tract of land on Oil Creek, noticed oil flowing from a spring. He took a bottle of it to Hartford, Conn., to have it analyzed by a well-known chemist. This authority pronounced it an artificial product and not a natural one. Had any person then predicted that North-western Pennsylvania and West Virginia would be found to contain vast reservoirs of this oil, and that it would in a score of years have added $1,000,000,000 to the wealth of the nation, he would have been considered insane. Yet such a prediction would have fallen short of the truth. There are to-day more than 20,000 wells producing this oil, and over 100,000 persons are exclusively engaged in handling it. Railroads have been built to transport it, while through a net-work of over 4,000 miles of iron pipes[1], running over mountains, beneath rivers, and through cultivated fields, streams of it pulsate continually. Oil from the wells in Pennsylvania lights the streets of South American cities, cathedrals in Europe, the mosques of Asia, the shop-windows of Jerusalem, and it is known and used over the whole civilized world.

These surprising results are by no means due to the simple discovery, in 1859, that oil could be obtained by drilling for it. Petroleum was no new thing in 1859. It has been known in Europe and Asia since the earliest ages of the world. Kerosene was extracted from the cannel coals of England in 1694. . . . It is produced in the north of Italy, and was used there for illuminating purposes before attention was called to it in this country in 1859. It is also found in Germany, France, Russia, India, in the Island of Trinidad, and in Canada.

It is plain, therefore, that it is to neither priority of discovery nor monopoly of the world's supply that the overwhelming preeminence of American petroleum is due. Quite as much as from the native superiority of the article, this preeminence results from our peculiar national genius and capacities in respect to both mechanics and commerce. The following example will serve to illustrate the difference between American and other methods in this industry. In 1735 an oil field was discovered in Alsace. It proved a profitable investment, and oil—used there principally for lubricating purposes—is still obtainable in paying quantities. The striking peculiarity is that the working of this field has been developed to the extent of only four wells in one hundred and fifty years, while the same crude methods for obtaining it are in use now that were used in the beginning. . . . Still more striking comparisons could be made with other and less civilized countries where petroleum has been obtained in greater or less quantities for ages.

It may be admitted, then, that to our national characteristics is to be largely attributed the unprecedented development of the American petroleum industry. The specific agency through which this development has been mainly effected is the organization known as the Standard Oil Company, which may be defined to be

---

[1]After 1879 Standard constructed a vast system of long-distance pipelines to replace the refiners' earlier dependence on far more expensive railroad transportation. The development necessitated the further concentration of refining at a few strategically located points and inspired the reorganization of the company as a trust in 1882.

an association of business houses united under one management in such a manner as to insure harmony of interests, and a consolidation of capital adequate to any possible business emergency, yet each retaining its individuality, and even competing sharply with the others.

In order to appreciate what the Standard Oil Company has achieved, it is first necessary to glance at the condition of the oil industry at the time when this company entered it. All the circumstances surrounding the first production of petroleum tended to make it an unbusiness-like enterprise. The novelty of the article, the romance of the search for it in the wilderness, the sudden and fabulous wealth that rewarded success—all these attracted especially the unsettled and adventurous elements of the community, and made the oil regions, in 1865, almost the counterpart of California fifteen years before. Truth, stranger than fiction, turned men's heads. Sober business was neglected. The one idea was to obtain a fortune by speculation or by a fortunate turn of the drill. . . .

In such a condition of affairs the state of the oil industry was, of course, deplorable, from a business stand-point. The universality of speculation; the utter disregard of the laws of supply and demand, aggravated by the haste of each landowner to multiply his wells and get as large a share as possible of the underlying oil pool which his neighbors were sucking up; the lack of handling facilities, resulting in prodigal waste; the apparent instability of the whole business, which was hourly expected to vanish, and in many instances did vanish as suddenly as it had appeared—all this conspired to make the oil regions a pandemonium of excitement and confusion, and the simple statement of a man's connection with oil was a severe blow to his credit. The refining of oil at this early period was on a basis but little better than that of its production. Processes were extremely crude, and their product would to-day be unmerchantable for illuminating purposes. Still the demand for it was great and growing, and refineries multiplied. The competent and the incompetent rushed into the business in shoals, until the refining capacity of the country was more than three times the demand for consumption. Reaction, failures, and demoralization were the inevitable consequences.

The refiners recognized the dangerous and demoralized condition into which the excessive capacity of the refineries had brought them. The world would take only so much refined oil as it needed for immediate consumption, and no more; and the manufactured article, unlike the crude, could not be stored for any length of time. Various efforts were made to correct this evil of overproduction, through pools and running arrangements, restricting capacity; but pools were broken, and agreements were ineffectual, until the lowest ebb in the oil business was reached. By this time bankruptcy had overtaken a large portion of the refining interest, and was threatening all. Such in general was the situation out of which was developed the Standard Oil Company, as a necessity, to arrest the conditions which were driving all connected with the business to bankruptcy and ruin. To limit production was impossible. The extent of the oil-field was a matter of conjecture, while the number of persons who would engage in boring wells and in prospecting for new territory was without limit. Leaving production, therefore, to take care of itself, the labors of the Standard Company were concentrated upon the refining interest, with the object of stopping the disastrous overproduction of the manufactured products. Without entering into the details of their progress,—how the principal refining interests were first united under the management of the Standard Company, and how others gradually came into coöperation, whilst those less hopeful of the future of the business were bought out for money; how ineligibly located or poorly equipped refineries were dismantled and others better adapted to their purposes were improved,—it is only necessary to state that their success was such as to vindicate the wisdom of their broad plans and to establish the superiority of their business methods.

It did more than this. . . . While a commanding position in refining was thus being won, the Standard managers were equally active in the mechanical and chemical departments of the business. Under their direction the process of refining was improved more rapidly than ever before. Oils grew better, cheaper, and more uniform, and as the problems of distribution were grasped and solved, the market for these products widened continually. In a word, the phenomenal genius for organization, which all concede to the Standard, produced its natural results throughout the entire business, and from being one of the most irregular and unprofitable of American industries, oil refining and selling became thoroughly systematized; and in the train of system followed economy and success. . . .

In view of this state of facts it might reasonably be supposed that the Standard Oil Company would have been entitled in some degree to public commendation for what it has accomplished, and the beneficial results produced—not that it has any claim on the score of philanthropy. It has not. It was organized and is operated to do in the best manner the largest possible amount of business.

But the fact that philanthropy is not the mainspring of its corporate action cannot destroy the other fact that great public benefit has resulted from the Standard's work; greater, unquestionably, than could ever have been brought about by the use of even equal capital and equivalent energy, divided between a score or a hundred disconnected and unfriendly organizations.

In place, however, of the approbation which has been referred to, the Standard Oil Company has for some years been the target for unlimited abuse and misrepresentation. . . .

There was no lack of unsuccessful oil-men, sensational writers,[2] and persons with grievances, to help give utterance to the anti-Standard cry. The bitterest grievances were those of the small refiners, whose real complaint was that the Standard, with its improved processes and immense product, had too greatly cheapened the cost of manufacturing and marketing refined oil. As it would not do, however, for them to complain that the public was getting its oil too low, they, too, raised a clamor against the "monopoly." A class of politicians, adopting what is known amongst themselves as "the Anti-Monopoly racket," were anxious to inflame the public mind against all large corporations. The Standard seemed most vulnerable. It could not be denied that it was a corporation, that it was rich, busy, and little given to talk; and as it paid no attention to attacks, its enemies insisted that this was a guilty silence. . . .

Whether its indifference to public accusations was the best course under the circumstances, it would be fruitless to discuss. Perhaps it was, as all calumny eventually dies of itself. And in the oil regions, where the hostile feeling had its birth, it is indeed practically at an end. Many, however, may still be surprised to learn that the Standard Oil Company is not the monster that it has been represented; that it has never had a contract with a railroad company which a fair-minded man could pronounce to be against public policy, good morals or good business principles;[3] that it has never broken an agreement nor committed an act of treachery; that it is not a speculator nor a manipulator of speculative prices, as has been so often charged; that it is not a monopoly,[4] and never can become

---

[2]Two years earlier Henry Demarest Lloyd had published the first of many articles attacking "the monopoly of light." See Lloyd in "Our Criminal Rich," in Part 2.

[3]Many critics would have argued, on the contrary, that the special rates negotiated between Standard and the railroads were in flagrant violation of the railroads' legal responsibilities as common carriers.

[4]By common definition the possession of two-thirds of a market constitutes a monopoly. When Camden wrote, Standard controlled about 90 percent of the nation's domestic kerosene business and equivalent proportions of its refining capacity and export oil trade.

one, despite its present great preponderance in the trade; in short, that this great bugbear is nothing more nor less than an organization of laborious, painstaking men, who, with great abilities and great opportunities, have made a great success by legitimate means, in a legitimate business.

❀ ❀ ❀

The subsequent history of the Standard Oil is quickly told. In 1882 shareholders of the various firms in the combination had vested their stock in a board of nine trustees composed of Rockefeller and his closest associates. In 1890 the Ohio Supreme Court ruled that Standard Oil of Ohio, the largest of the firms, had violated its state charter by placing control of the company in out-of-state hands and ordered it to withdraw from the trust. Similar action by other states made the trust agreement useless as a tool for industrial mergers after 1891.

Even so, because the same nine persons owned a controlling interest in the various firms, their management continued as before. But the possibility of the death of any of them made some more permanent arrangement desirable. New Jersey came to their rescue with a novel general incorporation law which permitted companies to hold stock in out-of-state corporations. Therefore, in 1899 the combination incorporated as the Standard Oil Company of New Jersey, a single holding company owning the other firms outright.

In 1906 the federal government brought suit against the New Jersey corporation under the Sherman Antitrust Act of 1890. In 1911 the Supreme Court ordered it dissolved, and within the year it had been broken up into 38 separate companies which were forbidden to have any officers or directors in common.

Federal antitrust proceedings, however, scarcely restored the nation's oil industry to the competitive conditions of the mid-nineteenth century. After 1911 the industry continued to be dominated by about twenty very large companies, many of them former members of the Rockefeller combination. After many metamorphoses the petroleum industry had arrived at a kind of organization typical of twentieth-century business—not a monopoly, but an oligopoly, an arrangement by which a few dominant firms erect an umbrella over an industry which shields it from destructive competition.

The consolidation of business, of which Standard Oil had been one pioneer, permanently transformed the American economy. Federal census figures on the eve of World War I revealed that only 4 percent of the nation's manufacturing firms accounted for 68 percent of its production, and 20 percent of the firms did 93 percent of the business. The day of the small entrepreneur was over.

3

Adolph Strasser

❖ ❖ ❖

Testimony on Labor-Capital Relations

1883

*T*he relationship between employer and employee is by its nature unequal. Employers own property and have the economic independence and security, the social standing, and the political power property endows. Employees, however, depend for their living upon the availability of jobs and the sufferance of their employers; their social standing and political influence derive from that dependence. This relationship is obvious in advanced industrial societies where goods are produced and services rendered, for the most part, by men and women with varying degrees of skill, expertise, responsibility, and authority employed by large private corporations (that is, the shareholders) or by government agencies (that is, the public). These things were also true in preindustrial society when journeymen, apprentices, and laborers worked in small groups, with hand tools or very simple machines, for a master craftsman. The wages, hours, and conditions under which such preindustrial workers labored were determined by guilds that the masters dominated.

However, preindustrial employees possessed some controls over the conditions of their employment that, individually, employees of large modern organizations lack. The rarity of the artisans' hard-won

TESTIMONY ON LABOR-CAPITAL RELATIONS   From United States Senate, Committee on Education and Labor, *Report on the Relations Between Labor and Capital* (Washington, 1885), I, 459–62, 465–66.

skills prevented employers from dealing with them too capriciously. (The master cobbler with orders to fill could not afford to lose the services of his journeyman cobblers for trivial reasons or over minor disagreements; he could not find someone on the streets to fill a place left vacant at the bench.) Because preindustrial workshops and communities were typically small, employers, employees, and townspeople were apt to know one another personally. The respect an employer commanded, and the esteem in which the community held him, depended as much upon how he used his wealth and power as the fact that he possessed them.

It would be a foolish mistake to romanticize preindustrial relations between employers and employees, as a great many people of the nineteenth century did. There were plenty of cruel and exploitative masters, plenty of suffering workers, before the age of the machine and the thousand-employee factory. However, the diminution of skills required to manufacture goods, which was the very purpose of machinery; the extraordinary growth of the units of production which machines made possible (the factories); and the size of the huge combinations which dominated the economy virtually destroyed the capacity of individual employees to affect their conditions of work. An obstreperous unskilled worker could be dismissed on a foreman's whim. There were many others outside the gates to take his place. The national character of the new industrial economy and the impersonality built into the structure of the corporation insulated shareholders from the actual workplace both because of their numbers and because of the tiers and tiers of supervisors inserted between "employer" and "employee." This meant that the owners of stock in, say, the meat-processing companies of Philip D. Armour and Gustavus Swift, needed to feel no responsibility (could hardly feel responsibility!) for the manner in which employees of those companies were treated in far-off Chicago. Unionism was the workers' response to their plight.

The crux of unionism is *collective* bargaining. Helpless to bargain individually with their employers because they were each expendable, unable to appeal to the better instincts of their employers because they did not really know who their employers were, workers turned to the only weapon they had: their collective numbers. If all the bricklayers in a city refused to work until satisfactory wages, hours, and conditions were established, employers had to bargain or else try to destroy the unity of the bricklayers. If the entire workforce of a factory maintained solidarity and struck the factory until the bosses came to terms with their union representatives, work went undone, orders went unfilled, and profits ceased until the strike was successful or was crushed. Unhappy workers meant the same instability that impelled big business organizers to eliminate competition.

It was not easy to organize a union, of course, nor to maintain solidarity among members during the crisis. Effective collective bargaining required individual sacrifice—most obviously, staying off the job and giving up wages for the good of all. What made the situation more difficult for union pioneers like Adolph Strasser of the Cigar Makers' Union, was that radicals and revolutionaries in the union movement often tried to persuade members to fight not just for better wages, hours, and conditions, but for a new kind of society, socialistic or anarchistic, in which capitalists would be divested of their property, profits, and power. With this accomplished, the workers, or the people as a whole, would own and administer industry for the good of all. Such agitators, Strasser believed, frightened the many working people who did not object to the system but wanted only a better life. Moreover, the sight of the red flag of revolution among working people steeled employers in their resolve to destroy unions and encouraged the government to intervene in industrial disputes on the employers' side. When he was called to testify before a Senate Committee on Education and Labor in 1883, Strasser determined to impress on government and employers alike that he represented a conservative form of unionism that accepted the system and aimed to be part of it.

Sen. Blair: It occurs to me to ask you whether it is in contemplation, as one of the ultimate purposes of the trades unions, that their funds shall be accumulated so that if, in order to prevent a panic by the excess of products being thrown upon the market, they can in future lessen production by suspending labor for a time, and maintain the laborers meanwhile out of the accumulated fund. Have your trades organizations any such idea as that?—A. The trades unions try to prevent panics, but in fact they cannot prevent them, because panics are governed by influences beyond their control.[1]

Q. Panics result, do they not, largely from overproduction?— A. The trades unions try to make their members better consumers, thereby enlarging the home market, and at the same time to make them better producers. If we can make the working people generally better consumers we shall have no panics.

Q. But if the increase of the power of production goes on by the improvement of machinery and all that, will not your efforts be

---

[1]In the nineteenth century, the word *panic* was used much as we use the word *depression* today. It refers to the sudden collapse of values—for example, in a stock market crash—that almost inevitably precipitated the wave of bankruptcies, factory closures, unemployment, and contraction of demand for goods and services (thus setting off the cycle all over again) that creates an economic depression.

counteracted in that way?—A. Then we propose a reduction of the hours of labor. That will decrease production and will increase consumption. We hold that a man who works but eight hours a day will demand a better home than a man who works longer hours; he will not be willing to live in one or two squalid rooms; he will demand better clothes, better food, more books, more newspapers, more education, more of the commodities that labor provides, more of the world's wealth, and that will bring about a better distribution of wealth and will consequently check panics to a certain extent. . . .

Sen. Pugh: Q. You are seeking to improve home matters first?—A. Yes, sir; I look first to the trade I represent; I look first to cigars, to the interests of men who employ me to represent their interests.

Sen. Blair: I was only asking you in regard to your ultimate ends.

Strasser: We have no ultimate ends. We are going on from day to day. We are fighting only for immediate objects—objects that can be realized in a few years.

Sen. Call: Q. You want something better to eat and to wear, and better houses to live in?—A. Yes; we want to dress better and to live better, and become better off and better citizens generally.

Sen. Blair: I see that you are a little sensitive lest it should be thought that you are a mere theorizer. I do not look upon you in that light at all.

Strasser: Well, we say in our constitution that we are opposed to theorists, and I have to represent the organization here. We are all practical men. . . .

Sen. Pugh: Q. You have furnished us with a very valuable fund of information. Have you any further statement to make of any other facts connected with this labor question?—A. Well, I have not yet proposed any remedies.

Q. We shall be glad to hear your views on that subject.—A. Well, we propose—

1. That trades unions shall be incorporated.[2] At present there are a great many of the States that do not protect our funds. It is simply a breach of trust to use our funds improperly and we have

---

[2]Under English common law, often observed in American courts, unions were defined as conspiracies and, therefore, illegal. In *Commonwealth* v. *Hunt* (1842), the Supreme Court held that labor unions were lawful institutions so long as their objects were legal and their methods "honorable and peaceful." Nevertheless, state legislatures beholden to employer interests soon concocted formulas by which they could find labor unions guilty of "malicious mischief" and suppress them. Strasser's plea for a positive recognition of union legitimacy, through the granting of corporate charters, was essential to escape sporadic government harassment.

lost considerable money in that way. . . . Therefore, we request that the Committee on Education and Labor of the Senate report . . . a bill for the incorporation of the trades unions, giving them legal rights and allowing them to have headquarters wherever they deem most fit or practicable. This, we hold, will give our organization more stability, and in that manner we shall be able to avoid strikes by perhaps settling with our employers, when otherwise we should be unable to do so, because when our employers know that we are to be legally recognized that will exercise such moral force upon them that they cannot avoid recognizing us themselves.

2. The next demand we make, one which we think will benefit labor, is the enforcement of the eight-hour law and its extension to the operation of all patents granted by the Government. By that I mean that if the Government grants a patent to anybody for any kind of invention, it shall be with the stipulation that the labor performed under that patent shall not be more than eight hours a day.

3. Our third demand is this: We claim that it is necessary to obtain information in regard to such questions as those which this committee is now investigating, and to that end we believe there is a necessity for a national bureau of labor statistics. . . .[3] We hold that such a national bureau of labor statistics would give our legislators a great deal of information which will be very valuable to them as legislators, and we hold further that it would be a benefit, not only to labor, but, also, even greater benefit to capital, to have all this information compiled annually and distributed generally. . . .

Sen. George: Q. What is the feeling on the part of wage receivers generally towards their employers; is it a feeling of amity and confidence or is it a feeling of distrust?—A. In places where men receive good wages there is general good feeling; where they receive poor wages—starvation wages—there is generally bad feeling. The feeling between labor and capital depends largely on the employers. If they treat their men well and pay them fair wages, there is generally good feeling. If the employers treat their men badly and pay starvation wages, there is generally bad feeling. It depends wholly upon the employer. He has the power to encourage good feeling or the reverse.

Q. Mr. Lenz, the editor of a paper called Capital and Labor, expressed an opinion here that there was a growing socialistic feel-

---

[3]The Bureau of Labor was founded within the Department of the Interior in 1884. In 1888, it became an independent executive department (without cabinet rank) and included a Bureau of Labor Statistics which is now one of six bureaus within the full-fledged Department of Labor.

ing among the members of the trades unions; what is your observation in regard to that?—A. It is not so in the Cigar Makers' International Union. That organization does not inquire into the private opinions of a member; it takes in Democrats and Republicans, or anybody else so long as they are workers at the trade; that organization aims at practical measures, and will not allow any vague theories to be foisted upon it.

Q. Then you deny Mr. Lenz's statement so far as it relates to your organization?—A. As regards the Cigar Makers' International Union, I positively deny it. The members of that organization are simply practical men, going for practical objects that can be accomplished in a few years. . . .

❂ ❂ ❂

In effect, Strasser laid out the strategy of the first successful national labor organization in the United States, the American Federation of Labor. Organized in 1886, the A.F. of L. was headed by Strasser's close associate in the Cigar Makers' Union, Samuel Gompers. Elected president of the A.F. of L. annually (with the exception of one year) until his death in 1924, Gompers steered the American labor movement away from independent political action and radical ideologies of all kinds. He also insisted that member unions be organized along craft lines rather than by industry, and he urged A.F. of L. unions to admit only skilled workers to membership.

The young Gompers was an eminently "practical man." At first, he espoused these policies because they were realistic. Over and over, the American two-party system had survived and crushed third party challenges. Repeatedly, employers used the socialistic or anarchistic programs of some labor unions to whip up hostility against them and to ensure the intervention of local, state, and federal government on the employers' side. In the 19th century, it was eminently realistic to believe that unskilled workers could not strike effectively because a ready supply of labor from Europe and China made it easy for employers to hire scab workers to take the strikers' places.

As Gompers aged, however, his hardheaded policies became dogmas. He battled against socialist unions even when they showed they could operate efficiently within the system and could claim the active support of a large number of people. He clung to the ideal of craft unionism in the face of the fact that advancing industrialization made the crafts increasingly obsolete. He railed against admitting unskilled workers to unions even though they proved that they could maintain solidarity and win strikes. So earnestly did Gompers court the approbation of the corporations with assurances of the A.F. of L.'s conservatism that

A.F. of L. unions came to be far less flexible, far less able to adjust to changing conditions in the economy and society as a whole, than the large corporations.

The American labor movement is unique in that, in principle as well as in practice, it is an integral and working partner in the capitalistic system. This cannot be said of any other nation's unions. What is more remarkable, the most important organization in the history of American labor set out to play this role from the beginning. Strasser's words could be uttered—and are regularly uttered—by the most important union leaders today.

4

The Supreme Court
❖ ❖ ❖

The Wabash Case
1886

*T*he first American railroad companies were small, regional in their purview, and even specialized in function. The earliest lines often hauled only one or two commodities between two points: for example, granite from New Hampshire quarries to the harbor at Portsmouth. Even those lines that hauled whatever freight was brought to them were usually metropolitan in scope; they tapped the hinterland as a service to the city's commercial and industrial interests. *Systems*, trunk line railroads that bound vast regions together in a busy, noisy exchange of products, came to dominate the American railroad scene only in the 1860s.

There was the transcontinental, tying the Pacific states to the rest of the Union. In the Midwest there was the Illinois Central, also constructed with the help of government subsidies. And in the East, the Baltimore and Ohio, the Pennsylvania, the New York Central, and the Erie each operated hundreds of miles of track. At first, almost everyone, particularly western farmers, welcomed the trunk line railroad as an economic stimulus comparable to banking. By bringing the huge markets of the Atlantic seaboard to within a few days' haul of the cornfields and feedlots of Illinois, Iowa, and the other states in the Mississippi Valley, the steam locomotive

---

THE WABASH CASE   From *Wabash, St. Louis, and Pacific Railroad Company* v. *Illinois*, 118 U.S. 557, 1886.

made it possible for farmers to concentrate on growing the single crop to which their lands were best suited, to sell it for the cash with which to expand or, simply, to enjoy the cornucopia of goods turned out by American and European factories and shops.

By the early 1870s, however, midwestern farmers learned that the haulers of their produce did not define themselves as benefactors of the husbandman. With maximization of profit the guiding principle, regional trunk lines like the Wabash, St. Louis, and Pacific Railway often charged their shippers all they could squeeze out of them. The cause of this injustice, as the farmers saw it, was bigness: the monopoly of a single railroad in some counties, the railroad pool in areas where a multiplicity of railroads might have meant competition. In several states, a farmers' social lodge, the Patrons of Husbandry, or Grange, called for members to unite politically in order to elect representatives who would bring the corporate monsters to heel by regulating the rates they could charge in the shippers' interest.

The Grangers were most successful in Illinois, where they controlled the state legislature and passed a series of laws including one that set a limit on what railroad companies could charge farmers for storing their grain. The railroads challenged this law in the courts on the ground that the grain was to be sold in other states and was therefore a part of interstate commerce which Congress alone could regulate. The railroads' lawyers also claimed that the Fourteenth Amendment to the Constitution prohibited states from depriving any "person," by which was meant corporations as well as people, of their property "without due process of law." In limiting what the owners of grain elevators might charge for the use of them, the railroads argued, the Granger Laws deprived those owners of the free use of their property in ways such as other "persons" were not deprived.

In the case of *Munn* v. *Illinois*, which reached the Supreme Court in 1877, Chief Justice Morrison C. Waite spoke for all but one of his colleagues in declaring that the state of Illinois had the right to regulate the rates railroads charged for shipment or storage of grain within the state. Quoting a seventeenth-century British jurist, Waite held that "when private property is 'affected with a public interest, it ceases to be *jus privati* only.'" That is, businesses involved in serving the public in matters vital to the public were subject to regulation in the public interest.

Although he appeared to agree with the railroads' contention that a corporation was entitled to the rights of persons under the Fourteenth Amendment, Waite chose not to address the question in *Munn* v. *Illinois*. However, in several cases involving California's Southern Pacific Railroad, argued before the Court in 1882 and 1886, Waite agreed with Southern Pacific counsel Roscoe Conkling, who had helped write the Fourteenth Amendment, that this had indeed been among the intentions of the amendment. It was this doctrine that set the stage for the Wabash Case of 1886.

❋ The general subject of the power of the State legislatures to regulate taxes, fares, and tolls for passengers and transportation of freight over railroads within their limits has been very much considered recently . . . and the question how far such regulations, made by the States . . . are valid or void, as they may affect the transportation of goods through more than one State, in one voyage, is not entirely new here.

The supreme court of Illinois, in the case now before us, conceding that each of these contracts was in itself a unit, and that the pay received by the Illinois railroad company was the compensation for the entire transportation from the point of departure in the State of Illinois to the city of New York, holds that, while the statute of Illinois is inoperative upon that part of the contract which has reference to the transportation outside of the State, it is binding and effectual as to so much of the transportation as was within the limits of the State of Illinois and undertaking for itself to apportion the rates charged over the whole route, decides that the contract and the receipt of the money for so much of it as was performed within the State of Illinois violate the statute of the State on that subject.[1]

If the Illinois statute could be construed to apply exclusively to contracts for a carriage which begins and ends within the State, disconnected from a continuous transportation through or into other States, there does not seem to be any difficulty in holding it to be valid. . . .

[And it] cannot be denied that the general language of the court in [several previous cases, including *Munn* v. *Illinois*] upon the power of Congress to regulate commerce, may be susceptible of the meaning which the Illinois court places upon it. . . . Whatever may be the instrumentalities by which the transportation from one point to the other is effected, it is but one voyage, as much so as that of the steamboat on the Mississippi River.

It is not the railroads themselves that are regulated by this act of the Illinois legislature so much as the charge for transportation, and . . . if each one of the States through whose territories these

---

[1]The Illinois state law under consideration by the Court prohibited a railroad practice known as "the long and short haul." That is, it was common for railroads in the Midwest to charge farmers what the market would bear. In some cases, a shipper living nearer to the market than others paid higher freight charges per mile because there were no alternative means of transportation to which they might turn, whereas in the case of farmers living farther away, the railroad was obligated to compete for business with other lines or river transportation. The Illinois statute held that all railroads doing business in the state were obligated to charge all shippers the same per mile rate.

goods are transported can fix its own rules for prices, for modes of transit, for times and modes of delivery, and all the other incidents of transportation to which the word "regulation" can be applied, it is readily seen that the embarrassments upon interstate transportation, as an element of interstate commerce, might be too oppressive to be submitted to. "It was," in the language of the court cited above, "to meet just such a case that the commerce [commercial] clause of the Constitution was adopted."

It cannot be too strongly insisted upon that the right of continuous transportation, from one end of the country to the other, is essential, in modern times, to that freedom of commerce from the restraints which the States might choose to impose upon it, that the commerce clause was intended to secure. This clause, giving to Congress the power to regulate commerce among the States, and with foreign nations, as this court has said before, was among the most important of the subjects which prompted the formation of the Constitution. And it would be a very feeble and almost useless provision. . . . if, at every stage of the transportation of goods and chattels through the country, the State within whose limits a part of this transportation must be done could impose regulations concerning the price, compensation, or taxation, or any other restrictive regulation interfering with and seriously embarrassing this commerce. . . .

We must therefore hold that it is not, and never has been, the deliberate opinion of a majority of this court that a statute of a State which attempts to regulate the fares and charges by railroad companies within its limits, for a transportation which constitutes a part of commerce among the States, is a valid law.

Let us see precisely what is the degree of interference with transportation of property or persons from one State to another which this statute proposes. A citizen of New York has goods which he desires to have transported by the railroad companies from that city to the interior of the State of Illinois. A continuous line of rail over which a car loaded with these goods can be carried, and is carried habitually, connects the place of shipment with the place of delivery. He undertakes to make a contract with a person engaged in the carrying business at the end of this route from whence the goods are to start, and he is told by the carrier: "I am free to make a fair and reasonable contract for this carriage to the line of the State of Illinois, but when the car which carries these goods is to cross the line of that State, pursuing at the same time this continuous track, I am met by a law of Illinois which forbids me to make a free contract concerning this transportation within that State, and subjects me to certain rules by which I am to be governed as to the charges which the same railroad company in Illinois may make, or has made, with reference to other persons and other places of delivery." So that while that carrier might be willing to carry these goods from the city of New York to the city of Peoria at the rate of fifteen cents per hundred pounds, he is not permitted to do so, because the Illinois railroad company has already charged at the rate of twenty-five cents per hundred pounds for carriage to Gilman, in Illinois, which is eighty-six miles shorter than the distance to Peoria.[2]

So also, in the present case, the owner of corn, the principal product of the country, desiring to transport it from Peoria, in Illinois, to New York, finds a railroad company willing to do this at the rate of fifteen cents per hundred pounds for a car-load, but is compelled to pay at the rate of twenty-five cents per hundred pounds, because the railroad company has received from a person residing at Gilman twenty-five cents per hundred pounds for the transportation of a car-load of the same class of freight over the same line of road from Gilman to New York. This is the result of the statute of Illinois, in its endeavor to prevent unjust discrimination, as construed by the supreme court of that State. . . .

Of the justice or propriety of the principle which lies at the foundation of the Illinois statute it is not the province of this court to speak. As restricted to a transportation which begins and ends within the limits of the State, it may be very just and equitable, and it certainly is the province of the state legislature to determine that question. But when it is attempted to apply to transportation through an entire series of States a principle of this kind, and each one of the States shall attempt to establish its own rates of transportation, its own methods to prevent discrimination in rates, or to permit it, the deleterious influence upon the freedom of commerce among the States, and upon the transit of goods through those States, cannot be overestimated. That this species of regulation is one which must be, if established at all, of a general and national character, and cannot be safely and wisely remitted to local rules and local regulations, we think is clear from what has already been said. And if it be a regulation of commerce, as we think we have demonstrated it is, and as the Illinois court concedes it to be, it must

---

[2]The state of Illinois had, in effect, said that having charged shippers from Peoria (the "long haul") the lower rate, the Wabash Railroad could not charge shippers from Gilman (the "short haul") the higher rate. In order to dramatize its point, the Supreme Court turned the tables, showing that the Illinois law could result in a raising of rates for shippers from Peoria.

be of that national character; and the regulation can only appropriately exist by general rules and principles, which demand that it should be done by the Congress of the United States under the commerce clause of the Constitution.

❖ ❖ ❖

Because the Court addressed somewhat different questions in the *Munn* and *Wabash* cases, regulation of rates charged for storage of grain in *Munn* and regulation of a stream of commerce that crossed state lines in *Wabash*, it is not quite correct to say that the latter case "reversed" the Court's findings in the former. The ancient legal principle that government possesses the right to regulate businesses involved in affairs of vital interest to the public has remained a basic law to this day. Indeed, the most important political consequence of *Wabash* was to bring pressure on Congress to create the Interstate Commerce Commission for the purpose of regulating the interstate stream of commerce *Wabash* removed from state competence.

However, what the Court specifically stated in the Wabash Case is not so important as the drift its decision illustrated. Quite unlike its temper in the *Munn* decision, in *Wabash* the Court indicated its accommodation to the reality and desirability of big business. What had changed was the personnel of the Court. Of the seven Justices who concurred in Waite's opinion in *Munn* in 1877, four were gone from the Court in 1886. Of the four men who replaced them, all but one voted with the "pro-railroad" majority in the *Wabash* case. In 1877, only Stephen J. Field disagreed with Waite's "anti-big business" decision. In 1886, he was part of a six to three "pro-big business" majority, with Waite and Joseph P. Bradley, another holdover, in the minority. The agrarian republic for which they stood was no more; corporate America was.

5

Andrew Carnegie

❀ ❀ ❀

Wealth

1889

Great Britain was the foremost manufacturing nation in the world in the early nineteenth century. This achievement was largely due to its successful development of power-driven machinery to replace the ages-old tedium of spinning thread and weaving cloth by hand. During the second half of the nineteenth century Britain's manufacturing lead was overtaken by the United States, in part as a result of American preeminence in another of the major achievements of the industrial revolution—the substitution of stronger, more durable, and more versatile metals for traditional wood and stone as the universal building materials of the modern world.

Of all metals, iron is by far the most readily abundant, even though it is never found in its pure state. The techniques of smelting common iron oxides, using carbon-rich fuels like charcoal to take off the oxygen, had been known for thousands of years. The problem was to get the right amount of carbon in the smelted iron; there was always either too much of it, or not enough. At low temperatures, traditional smelting produced an almost carbon-free iron. This was called wrought iron because it was finished up by hammering at the forge. However, if the ore being smelted were heated to its melting point, the molten metal suddenly sucked up carbon from the fuel like a sponge and became cast iron when it cooled. Wrought iron was soft, ductile, and easily hammered but neither strong

WEALTH   From Andrew Carnegie, "Wealth," *North American Review* (June 1889), CXLVII, 653–64.

nor long wearing. Cast iron was strong and hard but brittle. Subjected to sudden stress, it shattered.

To be truly useful, iron needs a carbon content between these extremes, combining both strength and resilience. Such iron is called steel, and it was very difficult to make. One common method was to assemble small sandwiches of wrought iron and carbon and heat them for days in sealed containers until the iron absorbed enough carbon to make steel. So costly was this process that the use of steel was limited to the manufacture of small high-priced items like knives, razor-blades, and surgical instruments.

Meanwhile the early railroad builders, among others, were wrestling with the problem of inadequate structural materials. Their first experiments with wooden rails were quickly abandoned, but the wrought-iron rails they subsequently used wore out in two or three years. The thousands of wooden bridges they erected were a continual headache because of the ease with which they were destroyed by flood or fire. Cast-iron bridges laid up like stonework were tried, but they collapsed at an alarming rate. Wrought iron was better, but it sagged and bent under ever-heavier loads.

Around 1855 the Englishman Henry Bessemer hit on one of the great inventions of the nineteenth century. He had the idea to make steel the other way around, not by adding carbon to wrought iron, but by burning off the carbon in cast iron. He introduced a blast of cold air to molten cast iron in a chamber which he called a "converter." The result was a "veritable volcano" as the oxygen in the air combined with the carbon in the iron to leave a residue of beautiful molten "mild" steel with a carbon content perfectly suited for steel rails, beams, and other structural uses. Previously, it had taken two weeks and a small mountain of fuel to make 50 pounds of steel. A Bessemer converter could make 5 tons of steel in twenty minutes using no fuel whatsoever!

From the beginning the Bessemer steel industry in the United States enjoyed a leg up on its competitors because of the almost simultaneous discovery of the greatest iron ore deposits in the world along the shores of Lake Superior. Here were found not only the low-phosphorus ores required by the Bessemer process (the British had to import theirs from Sweden and Spain), but also—as in the fabulous Mesabi Range—soft ores of almost pure iron oxide thinly covered by only a few inches of topsoil. Almost overnight the cost of digging a ton of ore fell from 3 dollars to 5 cents!

By 1900 the United States was making more than a third of the world's steel, and the greatest steelmaster on earth was a transplanted Scot whose mills in Pittsburgh, Pennsylvania, produced half as much steel as all the mills in Great Britain put together. Andrew Carnegie decided soon after the Civil War to give his full attention to the steel business. "Put all your eggs in one basket," was his favorite advice, "and *watch that basket.*" Confident that lower production costs justified almost any expenditure for new equipment, Carnegie made his Edgar Thomson Steel Works, opened in 1875, the most modern and efficient Bessemer steel plant in the world.

To the newest technology he added one of the leanest, most efficient business organizations in America. Shares in the Carnegie Steel Company were never traded on Wall Street. Carnegie hated stock speculations and conducted his business as a limited partnership in which he was careful always to own the majority interest. In this way (much to the frustration of his other partners) he could avoid declaring dividends and plow almost all the profits back into the firm. "Take care of costs," Carnegie often said, "and profits will take care of themselves." They did. Edgar Thomson, for instance, almost paid for itself and its site during its first year of operation. "Was there ever such a business?" Carnegie happily exclaimed. When he retired in 1901, his interest in his company was worth $225 million.

The essay which follows was written by Carnegie in 1889 when he was already one of the richest men in the world. In that year Carnegie Steel earned profits of $3.5 million on a capitalization of about $7 million. In his essay Carnegie attempted to defend the accumulation of such vast wealth in so few hands.

❀ The problem of our age is the proper administration of wealth, so that the ties of brotherhood may still bind together the rich and poor in harmonious relationship. The conditions of human life have not only been changed, but revolutionized, within the past few hundred years. In former days there was little difference between the dwelling, dress, food, and environment of the chief and those of his retainers. . . . The contrast between the palace of the millionaire and the cottage of the laborer with us today measures the change which has come with civilization.

This change, however, is not to be deplored, but welcomed as highly beneficial. It is well, nay, essential for the progress of the race, that the houses of some should be homes for all that is highest and best in literature and the arts, and for all the refinements of civilization, rather than that none should be so. . . . The "good old times" were not good old times. Neither master nor servant was as well situated then as today. A relapse to old conditions would be disastrous to both—not the least so to him who serves—and would sweep away civilization with it. But whether the change be for good or ill, it is upon us, beyond our power to alter, and therefore to be accepted and made the best of. It is a waste of time to criticize the inevitable. . . .

The price we pay for this salutary change, is, no doubt, great. We assemble thousands of operatives in the factory, in the mine, and in the counting-house, of whom the employer can know little or nothing, and to whom the employer is little better than a myth. All intercourse between them is at an end. Rigid castes are formed, and, as usual, mutual ignorance breeds mutual distrust. Each caste is without sympathy for the other, and ready to credit anything disparaging in regard to it. Under the law of competition, the employer of thousands is forced into the strictest economies, among which the rates paid to labor figure prominently, and often there is friction between the employer and the employed,[1] between capital and labor, between rich and poor. Human society loses homogeneity.[2]

The price which society pays for the law of competition, like the price it pays for cheap comforts and luxuries, is also great; but the advantages of this law are also greater still, for it is to this law that we owe our wonderful material development, which brings improved conditions in its train. But, whether the law be benign or not, we must say of it: . . . It is here; we cannot evade it; no substitutes for it have been found; and while the law may be sometimes hard for the individual, it is best for the race, because it insures the survival of the fittest[3] in every department. We accept and welcome, therefore, as conditions to which we must accommodate ourselves, great inequality of environment, the concentration of business . . . in the hands of a few, and the law of competition between these, as being not only beneficial, but essential for the future progress of the race . . . .

---

[1]Carnegie's own labor record was mixed. In 1877 Edgar Thomson became the first steel mill in the country to substitute an 8-hour day for the murderous 12-hour shifts customary in the industry. Carnegie hoped that his example would force other manufacturers to follow suit. Ten years later, however, none had, and Carnegie was compelled by competitive pressures to reintroduce the 12-hour day. Subsequently he advocated state intervention to force businessmen to adopt the 8-hour standard. Moreover, as he explained in a series of *Forum* essays in 1886, he had no objection in principle to the organization of trade unions. He viewed them as the counterpart to the pooling arrangements customary among capitalists themselves. On the other hand, the Carnegie plant at Homestead was the scene in 1892 of one of the most savagely fought strikes in American labor history.

[2]The English Social Darwinist philosopher Herbert Spencer taught that the development of civilization followed a universally progressive law, true both in physics and society, according to which "heterogeneity" evolved from originally "homogeneous" materials. Carnegie was an enthusiastic fan of the "Victorian Aristotle," and sponsored his celebrated American tour in 1882.

[3]Another phrase of Spencer's, based on the Darwinian struggle for survival among members of a species.

Objections to the foundations upon which society is based are not in order, because the condition of the race is better with these than it has been with any others which have been tried. Of the effect of any new substitutes proposed we cannot be sure. The Socialist or Anarchist who seeks to overturn present conditions is to be regarded as attacking the foundation upon which civilization itself rests, for civilization took its start from the day that the capable, industrious workman said to his incompetent and lazy fellow, "If thou dost not sow, thou shalt not reap," and thus ended primitive Communism by separating the drones from the bees. One who studies this subject will soon be brought face to face with the conclusion that upon the sacredness of property civilization itself depends—the right of the laborer to his hundred dollars in the savings bank, and equally the legal right of the millionaire to his millions. To those who propose to substitute Communism for this intense Individualism the answer, therefore, is: The race has tried that. All progress from that barbarous day to the present time has resulted from its displacement. Not evil, but good, has come to the race from the accumulation of wealth by those who have the ability and energy that produce it . . . .

We start, then, with a condition of affairs under which the best interests of the race are promoted, but which inevitably gives wealth to the few. Thus far, accepting conditions as they exist, the situation can be surveyed and pronounced good. The question then arises— and, if the foregoing be correct, it is the only question with which we have to deal—What is the proper mode of administering wealth after the laws upon which civilization is founded have thrown it into the hands of the few? And it is of this great question that I believe I offer the true solution. . . .

There are but three modes in which surplus wealth can be disposed of. It can be left to the families of the decedents; or it can be bequeathed for public purposes; or, finally, it can be administered during their lives by its possessors. Under the first and second modes most of the wealth of the world that has reached the few has hitherto been applied. Let us in turn consider each of these modes. The first is the most injudicious. In monarchical countries, the estates and the greatest portion of the wealth are left to the first son, that the vanity of the parent may be gratified by the thought that his name and title are to descend to succeeding generations unimpaired. The condition of this class in Europe today teaches the futility of such hopes or ambitions. . . . Why should men leave great fortunes to their children? If this is done from affection, is it not misguided affection? Observation teaches that, generally speaking, it is not well for the children that they should be so burdened. Neither is it well for the state. . . . It is no longer questionable that great sums bequeathed oftener work more for injury than for the good of the recipients. . . .

As to the second mode, that of leaving wealth at death for public uses, it may be said that this is only a means for the disposal of wealth, provided a man is content to wait until he is dead before it becomes of much good in the world. Knowledge of the results of legacies bequeathed is not calculated to inspire the brightest hopes of much posthumous good being accomplished. . . . Besides this, it may fairly be said that no man is to be extolled for doing what he cannot help doing, nor is he to be thanked by the community to which he only leaves wealth at death. Men who leave vast sums in this way may fairly be thought men who would not have left it at all, had they been able to take it with them. . . .

The growing disposition to tax more and more heavily large estates left at death is a cheering indication of the growth of a salutary change in public opinion.[4] The State of Pennsylvania now takes . . . one-tenth of the property left by its citizens. The budget presented in the British Parliament the other day proposes to increase the death-duties; and, most significant of all, the new tax is to be a graduated one. Of all forms of taxation, this seems the wisest. . . . By taxing estates heavily at death the state marks its condemnation of the selfish millionaire's unworthy life. . . .

There remains, then, only one mode of using great fortunes; but in this we have the true antidote for the temporary unequal distribution of wealth, the reconciliation of the rich and the poor— a reign of harmony—another ideal, differing, indeed, from that of the Communist in requiring only the further evolution of existing conditions, not the total overthrow of our civilization. . . . Under its sway we shall have an ideal state, in which the surplus wealth of the few will become, in the best sense, the property of the many, because it is administered for the common good, and this wealth, passing through the hands of the few, can be made a much more potent force for the elevation of our race than if it had been distributed in small sums to the people themselves. Even the poorest can be made to see this, and to agree that great sums gathered by some of their fellow-citizens and spent for public purposes, from which the masses reap the principal benefit, are more valuable to them than if

---

[4]Consistent with his principles, Carnegie favored confiscatory inheritance taxes, but he was furiously opposed to the income tax.

scattered among them through the course of many years in trifling amounts. . . .[5]

This, then, is held to be the duty of the Man of Wealth: First, to set an example of modest, unostentatious living, shunning display of extravagance; to provide moderately for the legitimate wants of those dependent upon him; and after doing so to consider all surplus revenues which come to him simply as trust funds, which he is called upon to administer . . . in the manner which, in his judgment, is best calculated to produce the most beneficial results for the community—the man of wealth thus becoming the mere agent and trustee for his poorer brethren, bringing to their service his superior wisdom, experience, and ability to administer, doing for them better than they would or could do for themselves. . . .

In bestowing charity, the main consideration should be to help those who will help themselves; to provide part of the means by which those who desire to improve may do so; to give those who desire to rise the aids by which they may rise. . . . Neither the individual nor the race is improved by alms-giving. . . . The amount which can be wisely given . . . [to] individuals is necessarily limited, . . . for in alms-giving more injury is probably done by rewarding vice than by relieving virtue.

The rich man is thus almost restricted to following the examples of Peter Cooper, Enoch Pratt of Baltimore, . . . Senator Stanford,[6] and others, who know that the best means of benefiting the community is to place within its reach the ladders upon which the aspiring can rise—parks, and means of recreation, by which men are helped in body and mind; works of art, certain to give pleasure and improve the public taste, and public institutions of various kinds, which will improve the general condition of the people—in this manner returning their surplus wealth to the mass of their fellows in the forms best calculated to do them lasting good.

Thus is the problem of Rich and Poor to be solved. The laws of accumulation will be left free; the laws of distribution free. Individualism will continue, but the millionaire will be but a trustee for the poor; intrusted for a season with a great part of the increased

---

[5] Among the greatest accomplishments of nineteenth-century physics were the general laws of thermodynamics, which Social Darwinists also applied to social phenomena. According to the law of the "dissipation of force," as Spencer called it, useful forms of energy in the universe are ultimately dissipated as useless heat. Great concentrations of wealth, therefore, represented a hoard of social "force" potentially far more useful than their random dissipation, or entropy.

[6] Peter Cooper was an early American iron manufacturer who founded the Cooper Institute in New York in 1857 to provide free scientific education. Enoch Pratt, another iron manufacturer, gave Baltimore its Enoch Pratt Free Library in 1886. The railroad builder Leland Stanford founded Stanford University in 1885.

wealth of the community, but administering it for the community far better than it could or would have done for itself. The best minds will thus have reached a stage in the development of the race in which it is clearly seen that there is no mode of disposing of surplus wealth . . . save by using it year by year for the general good. The day already dawns. But a little while, and . . . the man who dies leaving behind him millions, . . . which was his to administer in life, will pass away "unwept, unhonored, and unsung," no matter to what uses he leaves the dross which he cannot take with him. Of such as these the public verdict will then be: "The man who dies thus rich dies disgraced."

Such, in my opinion, is the true Gospel concerning Wealth, obedience to which is destined some day to solve the problem of the Rich and the Poor, and to bring "Peace on earth, among men Good-Will."

❖ ❖ ❖

By temperament Andrew Carnegie was the most sanguine of men—in Wordsworth's phrase, "a man of cheerful yesterdays and confident tomorrows." Carnegie's essay exudes the optimism of a man whose personal motto was "All is well, since all grows better." He was opinionated, as the rich tend to be, but he was also astonishingly well-read and articulate, a source of endless fascination to a world more accustomed to millionaires whose celebrated drive could not carry them successfully to the end of a sentence. He was also unusually cosmopolitan, spending half of every year in Great Britain, the other half in New York. Once he even seriously proposed that England and Scotland be admitted to statehood. Always an enemy of class and privilege, the main point of his book *Triumphant Democracy* was that the more like the United States Britain became, the better it would be. Our "Star-Spangled Scot," someone remarked.

In "Wealth" Carnegie proclaimed the duty of the millionaire to give his money away before he died, and he was true to his word. When he sold his business to the United States Steel Corporation in 1901, he retired at the age of 65 with a quarter of a billion dollars worth of 5 percent U.S. Steel bonds. (A special vault was constructed in Hoboken, New Jersey, to hold them all.) Over the next ten years, having first settled comparatively modest trusts on his wife and daughter, he gave it all away. When it was all over he said it had been ten times as much work to distribute his fortune as to acquire it. About $60 million went to build nearly 3,000 free public libraries throughout the English-speaking world. Among other major philanthropies there was $25 million for the Carnegie Institution of Washington for the purpose of scientific research, $10 million for the

Carnegie Foundation for the Advancement of Teaching (it improved standards almost overnight in American colleges and universities), and another $10 million for the Carnegie Endowment for International Peace. In 1911 he gave his last $125 million to the Carnegie Corporation, instructing its trustees to carry on the kinds of philanthropic activities he had begun. A confirmed anti-imperialist (when the United States acquired the Philippines in 1898 he offered to buy it for $20 million so that he could set it free), Carnegie devoted his busy pen and his last years to the faltering cause of world peace.

6

George Washington Plunkitt
❂ ❂ ❂

Machine Politics
1905

*B*ig business grew and government
aided the growth because, in the nineteenth century, many Americans
believed that greater transportation networks, industries, and banks were
not only agents of economic progress (that is, a better material life for all),
but they were also agents of moral and political progress. There were
dissenters. (Some of them are the subjects of Part 2.) But the spirit of the
age was swept up in its extraordinary economic growth. Bigger was better.
The great railroaders, John D. Rockefeller and Andrew Carnegie, were the
era's heroes, not their competitors who fell by the wayside.

No titan of industry ever condoned illegal or corrupt acts as means
to the ends they exalted. But the growth of the American economy was so
explosive—between 1865 and 1900, the gross national product grew from
$2 billion to $13 billion—and the cooperation of government so necessary
that some corruption was inevitable. The builders of the Union Pacific
Railroad, for example, saw to it that both cash and shares in the Crédit
Mobilier, a company set up to construct the line, found their way into the
pockets of many of the congressmen who voted for the acts that granted
so much public land to the Union Pacific.

Among those who benefitted from the U.P.'s largesse was future
President James A. Garfield. That he could be elected President after it
was revealed he had accepted such favors—indeed, be considered a
comparatively "clean" politician—illustrates the fact that many Americans

MACHINE POLITICS   From William L. Riordan, *Plunkitt of Tammany Hall* (New York:
McClure, Phillips and Co., 1905), pp. 3–11, 54–62.

were unsure about where the perquisites of government office ended and corruption began. In another example, the railroads were seldom criticized for routinely providing free passes to members of state legislatures, their families, and others for whom the politicians requested them.

This ambiguity was most dramatic not on the national or state levels of government but in the nation's metropolises. Cities grew even faster than the economy during the late nineteenth century. The greatest of all, New York, grew from 1.8 million people in 1880 to 3.4 million in 1900. Philadelphia ranked second to New York in 1880 with 847,000 people. In 1900, William Penn's "Greene countrie towne" was the crowded, frantic home of 1.3 million. At that, Philadelphia had slipped to third place behind the hub of the national railroad network, Chicago, which in the same twenty years grew from 500,000 to 1.7 million! The same was true of Boston, St. Louis, Baltimore, Cincinnati, Pittsburgh, Cleveland, and Buffalo.

Such growth created, on a somewhat miniaturized scale, the same opportunities for personal gain as growth in the nation at large. Bald thievery was common. It was estimated that the "Tweed Ring," a circle of brigands that controlled the government of New York City during the 1860s, reduced the municipal treasury by at least $30 million and perhaps by as much as $200 million.

William Marcy "Boss" Tweed's machine for keeping control of New York was Tammany Hall, a tightly knit political club which dominated the city's Democratic Party. After Tweed was exposed and prosecuted, Tammany "sachems" (as leaders were called) became rather more circumspect in their grafting. Indeed, according to George Washington Plunkitt, a second-rank leader of Tammany during the 1890s and 1900s, Tammany did not "steal" at all. The sachems merely used their control of government to enrich themselves well within the law.

Honest Graft and Dishonest Graft

❁ Everybody is talkin' these days about Tammany men growin' rich on graft, but nobody thinks of drawin' the distinction between honest graft and dishonest graft. There's all the difference in the world between the two. Yes, many of our men have grown rich in politics. I have myself. I've made a big fortune out of the game, and I'm gettin' richer every day, but I've not gone in for dishonest graft—blackmailin' gamblers, saloon-keepers, disorderly people, etc.—and neither has any of the men who have made big fortunes in politics.

There's an honest graft, and I'm an example of how it works. I might sum up the whole thing by sayin': "I seen my opportunities and I took 'em."

Just let me explain by examples. My party's in power in the city, and it's goin' to undertake a lot of public improvements. Well, I'm tipped off, say, that they're going to lay out a new park at a certain place.

I see my opportunity and I take it. I go to that place and I buy up all the land I can in the neighborhood. Then the board of this or that makes its plan public, and there is a rush to get my land, which nobody cared particular for before.

Ain't it perfectly honest to charge a good price and make a profit on my investment and foresight? Of course, it is. Well, that's honest graft. . . . It's just like lookin' ahead in Wall Street or in the coffee or cotton market. It's honest graft, and I'm lookin' for it every day in the year. I will tell you frankly that I've got a good lot of it, too.

I'll tell you of [another] case. They were goin' to fix up a big park, no matter where. I got on to it, and went lookin' about for land in that neighborhood.

I could get nothin' at a bargain but a big piece of swamp, but I took it fast enough and held on to it. What turned out was just what I counted on. They couldn't make the park complete without Plunkitt's swamp, and they had to pay a good price for it. Anything dishonest in that? . . . I seen my opportunity and I took it. I haven't confined myself to land; anything that pays is in my line.

For instance, the city is repavin' a street and has several hundred thousand old granite blocks to sell. I am on hand to buy, and I know just what they are worth.

How? Never mind that. I had a sort of monopoly of this business for a while, but once a newspaper tried to do me. It got some outside men to come over from Brooklyn and New Jersey to bid against me.

Was I done? Not much. I went to each of the men and said: "How many of these 250,000 stones do you want?" One said 20,000, and another wanted 15,000, and another wanted 10,000. I said: "All right, let me bid for the lot, and I'll give each of you all you want for nothin'.

They agreed, of course. Then the auctioneer yelled: "How much am I bid for these 250,000 fine pavin' stones?"

"Two dollars and fifty cents," says I.

"Two dollars and fifty cents!" screamed the auctioneer. "Oh, that's a joke! Give me a real bid."

He found the bid was real enough. My rivals stood silent. I got the lot for $2.50 and gave them their share. That's how the attempt to do Plunkitt ended, and that's how all such attempts end. . . .

Another kind of honest graft. Tammany has raised a good many salaries. There was an awful howl by the reformers, but don't you know that Tammany gains ten votes for every one it lost by salary raisin'?

The Wall Street banker thinks it shameful to raise a department clerk's salary from $1500 to $1800 a year, but every man who draws a salary himself says: "That's all right. I wish it was me." And he feels very much like votin' the Tammany ticket on election day, just out of sympathy.

Tammany was beat in 1901 because the people were deceived into believin' that it worked dishonest graft.[1] They didn't draw a distinction between dishonest and honest graft, but they saw that some Tammany men grew rich, and supposed they had been robbin' the city treasury or levyin' blackmail on disorderly houses, or workin' in with the gamblers and lawbreakers.

As a matter of policy, if nothing else, why should the Tammany leaders go into such dirty business, when there is so much honest graft lyin' around when they are in power? Did you ever consider that? . . . I want to say that I don't own a dishonest dollar. If my worst enemy was given the job of writin' my epitaph when I'm gone, he couldn't do more than write:

"George W. Plunkitt. He Seen His Opportunities, and He Took 'Em."

On "The Shame of the Cities"

I've been readin' a book by Lincoln Steffens on "The Shame of the Cities."[2] Steffens means well but, like all reformers, he don't know how to make distinctions. He can't see no difference between honest graft and dishonest graft and, consequent, he gets things all mixed

---

[1] Tammany was defeated in the municipal elections of 1901 by an alliance of Republicans and reform Democrats headed by former Brooklyn mayor and well-to-do merchant Seth Low. Despite considerable accomplishments, Low's reformers were defeated by Tammany in 1903.

[2] See Lincoln Steffens, "The Shame of the Cities," in Part 2.

up. There's the biggest kind of a difference between political looters and politicians who make a fortune out of politics by keepin' their eyes wide open. The looter goes in for himself alone without considerin' his organization or his city. The politician looks after his own interests, the organization's interests, and the city's interests all at the same time. See the distinction? For instance, I ain't no looter. The looter hogs it. I never hogged. I made my pile in politics, but, at the same time, I served the organization and got more big improvements for New York City than any other livin' man. And I never monkeyed with the penal code.

A big city like New York or Philadelphia or Chicago might be compared to a sort of Garden of Eden, from a political point of view. It's an orchard full of beautiful apple trees. One of them has got a big sign on it, marked: "Penal Code Tree—Poison." The other trees have lots of apples on them for all. Yet, the fools go to the Penal Code Tree. Why? For the reason, I guess, that a cranky child refuses to eat good food and chews up a box of matches with relish. I never had any temptation to touch the Penal Code Tree. The other apples are good enough for me, and O Lord! how many of them there are in a big city! . . .

Now, a few words on the general subject of the so-called shame of cities. I don't believe that the government of our cities is any worse, in proportion to opportunities, than it was fifty years ago. I'll explain what I mean by "in proportion to opportunities." A half a century ago, our cities were small and poor. There wasn't many temptations lyin' around for politicians. There was hardly anything to steal, and hardly any opportunities for even honest graft. A city could count its money every night before goin' to bed, and if three cents was missin', all the fire-bells would be rung. What credit was there in bein' honest under them circumstances? It makes me tired to hear of old codgers back in the thirties or forties boastin' that they retired from politics without a dollar except what they earned in their profession or business. If they lived to-day, with all the existin' opportunities, they would be just the same as twentieth century politicians. There ain't any more honest people in the world just now than the convicts in Sing Sing. Not one of them steals anything. Why? Because they can't. See the application?

Understand, I ain't defendin' politicians of to-day who steal. The politician who steals is worse than a thief. He is a fool. With the grand opportunities all around for the man with a political pull, there's no excuse for stealin' a cent. The point I want to make is that if there is some stealin' in politics, it don't mean that the politicians of 1905 are, as a class, worse than them of 1835. It just means that the old-timers had nothin' to steal, while the politicians now are surrounded by all kinds of temptations and some of them naturally—the fool ones—buck up against the penal code.

❁ ❁ ❁

Plunkitt's frank and comical, if not cynical, description of "practical politics" in the Gilded Age has been compared to Machiavelli's *The Prince*. But one might as well compare it to James Madison's *Federalist* because the analogy is invalid. Plunkitt was not writing a treatise on what government should be, nor even, primarily, an analysis of American government as it was, as Alexis DeTocqueville and Lord Bryce had done. He was boasting of his personal success in his chosen business, which was precisely how Plunkitt and many other successful politicians of the era viewed the profession of politics.

By the time of Tammany Hall, holding public office was no longer a sacred trust accepted selflessly by "natural aristocrats" like Adams and Jefferson as their duty to society. Nor was it a position of power sought in the interest of an ideal, or even to represent the interests of a particular electorate. Public office was an "opportunity" for self-improvement to be seized and exploited by the alert, ambitious, and energetic, like a coal mine or a mechanical invention. Plunkitt's belief that he got "more improvements for New York City than any other livin' man" was to him as sufficient a social justification for his personal success as Commodore Vanderbilt's pride in creating an orderly, efficient transportation network for the Northeast, or John D. Rockefeller's pride in providing a reliable flow of cheap kerosene, or Carnegie's socially beneficial distribution of his wealth.

On the face of it, Plunkitt and his colleagues in urban machine politics were not as philosophical nor as articulate as Carnegie, and so they have come down to us as rogues and scoundrels despite the charm of their Irish wit. And yet, in the closing paragraphs of this disquisition, Plunkitt ventures a historical observation which many critics of "politics as business" failed to appreciate. The Great Barbecue of the late nineteenth century (whether in industry and finance, or in government) was not the consequence of the sudden introduction of men of inferior morality, but of the opportunities created and repeatedly regenerated by America's amazing growth. The opportunities were there to be taken, and they were.

PART 2

❋ ❋ ❋

Tensions and Conflicts

1880–1904

1

George William Curtis
❖ ❖ ❖

Civil Service Reform
1880

*T*he Founding Fathers and the second generation of American political leaders under the Constitution believed that the republic should be governed by what Thomas Jefferson and John Adams called its "natural aristocracy." Definitions of this platonic elite were usually vague. Few were so precise (or forthright) as James Madison and Alexander Hamilton in recognizing that the possession of property in some considerable quantity was necessary for talent to show itself, education to be acquired, and leisure time for the task of governing to be had. Therefore, it was the economically privileged, and their associates in the professions, who would guide the government. Thus property ownership became the minimum first index by which to identify "the best men."

By the Reconstruction period, this ideal was badly tattered. The heirs of society's former arbiters discovered that their "old wealth" was dwarfed by fortunes newly made in transportation and manufacturing. In society, they were bypassed by the likes of Cornelius Vanderbilt, the richest man of his time, who had the manners of the New York ferryman he had been at the outset of his career, or by crude socialites like Harry Lehr, who at an elegant soiree shouted drunkenly at the genteel Mrs. Hamilton Fish and her cortege, "You Fishes can't come in here. You're not rich enough."

CIVIL SERVICE REFORM From "Address to the Independent Republicans," Chickering Hall, New York, May 20, 1880. Charles E. Norton, ed., *Orations and Addresses of George William Curtis*, (New York: Harper, 1894), II, 149–50, 160–66.

In politics, the displacement of the old elite was carried out on the municipal level by the ambitious likes of George Washington Plunkitt. In Washington during the presidency of Ulysses S. Grant (1869–1877), similarly uncouth, grasping "men on the make" blatantly stole from the public treasury and viewed holding public office, at best, as a career—a way to advance themselves. Henry Adams, grandson of one president, great-grandson of another, was so appalled by the vulgarity and frank self-serving of the politicos who swarmed in Washington that, in an age that worshiped progress, he was inspired to devise a historical theory of regression.

Feeling himself defiled, Adams retreated to private life in aloof (and declining) Boston and Cambridge, Massachusetts. George William Curtis, a splended essayist and political editor of *Harper's Magazine*, an organ of the American intelligentsia, attempted to work "within the system." As head of the Civil Service Commission under Grant between 1871 and 1875, his cause was to revive the ideal of public office as public service by ridding government of the "Spoils System." This was the practice of appointing to government posts, and therefore to government salaries, loyal and working members of the party in power, regardless of their fitness for the office or the worthiness and credits of the people of other political persuasions who had to be dismissed in order to make room for them.

The palpable purpose of the spoils system was not good government but the strengthening of the party, the creation of a self-perpetuating agency of reward and advancement for those who were active on its behalf. Staunch Republicans like Curtis pointed out that the spoils system had its origins with the election in 1828 of the Democrat Andrew Jackson. At that time hundreds of federal office holders were dismissed simply because they had been supporters of Jackson's predecessor, John Quincy Adams. "To the victors belong the spoils of war," said a prominent Jackson man, William Marcy, when the appointment of a professional politician to be Minister to Great Britain was questioned in Congress. Curtis and his genteel associates were likewise not surprised by the cynical use of public office for purely partisan purposes when it was practiced by corrupt Democratic municipal machines like Tammany Hall.

But it seemed a profanation of the high ideals Curtis attributed to Republicanism that members of his own party, particularly under Grant, should have used public office with the same cynicism. In 1875, Curtis resigned his position in disgust. Between 1877 and 1881, when Rutherford B. Hayes was President, the number of purely political appointments declined. However, honest, efficient, and businesslike government was threatened by Hayes's unpopularity among Republican spoilsmen.

By May of 1880, when Curtis delivered the speech reproduced in part below, the head of the Republican machine in New York, "Stalwart" Roscoe Conkling, had already begun a campaign to win the Republican presidential election for his patron and protege, former President, Ulysses S. Grant.

❊   The most startling fact in our present political situation is that the party is ceasing to be an agency of the people. A system is rapidly developing itself which usurps the political initiative—the vital point of popular government—and which rules in the name of the party, as the meanest king was said to rule by the grace of God. This system is known as the machine. The machine is an oligarchy, a ring or clique of professional politicians, that is, of men who live by the emoluments of official place, and who give their lives to politics. They are not formally organized, but there is a common and instinctive understanding among them. Their object is the maintenance of their own power for their own advantage, by means of the party organization and of the party spirit which keeps party men faithful to the regular party action. The machine has no public purpose, no faith in private honor or integrity or patriotism. Its cry is that all is fair in politics. . . .

The source of the power of the machine . . . is official patronage. It is the command of millions of the public money spent in public administration; the control of the vast labyrinth of place, with its enormous emoluments; the system which makes the whole Civil Service, to the least detail and most insignificant position, the spoils of party victory; which perverts necessary party organization into intolerable party despotism. It is upon this that the hierarchy of the machine is erected. Strike at this system strongly, steadily, persistently, and you shiver the machine to pieces.

The tale is familiar, but it cannot be heard too often. The wrong of slavery was always old and the story never new, but it took thirty years of endlessly reiterated argument and agitation to arouse the heart of the people and elect an antislavery President. The spoils system, the basis of the machine both in State and national politics, is a vast and elaborate structure. It rises in regular graduation from the poor old women who scrub the floors of public buildings, and the pages who run errands, and the messengers who sit at office-doors, and the coal-heavers who feed fires, each place in order dependent, not upon merit or service, but wholly upon a higher personal favor. It rises to chief appointing officers, to governors, heads of departments, and superintendents, to collectors and postmasters who dispose of thousands of places. The national spoils system culminates in the Senate, in which usurpation of the executive functions is decently veiled under the phrase of "the courtesy of the Senate,"[1] by which senators from a State control the national

---

[1]The practice of "senatorial courtesy" illustrates why reformers like Curtis (and machine politicians) spoke of a machine. While the President signed commissions for all federal appoint-

patronage within it as a perquisite of their position, and which makes the cardinal question, upon confirming a nomination of the President, not the fitness of the candidate, but his acceptability to the senator from the State.

Naturally under this system public officers multiply uselessly that there may be more rewards for political and personal service. Primaries, caucuses, conventions are controlled by the promise and expectation of a chance of plunder which the machine distributes. Of course the sentiment of loyalty in the recipient is not to the government; it is that of a dog to his master who throws him a bone. The messenger at the door, the clerk at his desk, has not the legitimate pride of honorable service; he is in dread of the frown of his superior, and forced to avert it at any price. His tenure corrodes his manhood and his self-respect. Men who were serving their country, in civil positions, as honestly and efficiently as any "boy in blue"[2] ever served in the field, have come to me with tears of shame in their eyes to tell me of political duties assigned to them which they would rather cut off their hands than do, but which they did rather than take the bread from the mouths of their families. . . .

The number of persons officially employed in the New York custom-house is somewhat more than one thousand, and the annual amount of salaries paid is a little more than a million and a half of dollars. Now, under the patronage system this is virtually a bribery fund at the disposition of the collector,[3] and as, under the party usage in this State, the collector is usually—not now—one of the chief machine managers, this great sum of the public money, paid in salaries at a single public office, is spent for the advantage of the party machine, and serves to maintain and confirm its power. In the same way the wanton waste, arising from the incessant change of officers, is due to the necessities of the machine. The late collector

---

ments, he could not possibly know what individuals "deserved"—that is, had worked hard enough for the party to warrant—appointment to such minor positions as postmasterships, clerkships in federal bureaus, and so on. Senators and congressmen, active in the politics of their states, could. So, as a "courtesy," the president accepted lists from supporters in the Senate, of appointees. Rewarded, the postmasters, et al. supported their Senator, the Senator his President. Thus fueled, the machine milled its product, federal jobs.

[2]The "boys in blue" were, of course, the Union soldiers in the Civil War. It was virtually mandatory for Republican orators, whatever their subject, to make reference to the great cataclysm in which the Republican party was forged.

[3]The Collectorship of the Port of New York was the juiciest plum in the federal patronage. Not only did the Collector control so many jobs, but, before 1874, his salary was augmented by one-half of all duties he collected by catching importers attempting to evade the tariff. In one case, soon-to-be President Chester A. Arthur split $135,000 with two other officials—all quite legally. Naturally, he was expected to contribute generously from such windfalls to party campaign funds. After 1874, the salary of the Collector was set at $12,000, a munificent wage in the 19th century.

of the port states that, under his immediate predecessors, more than a fourth of the persons employed were removed every year. The reports of Congressional committees state more in detail that, during three years of one of these predecessors, out of 903 officers he removed 830. Another made 338 removals in eighteen months, and another made 510 removals in sixteen months. For a period of six years, therefore, more than 230 persons out of an aggregate of about 1000 were removed in the custom-house every year. This incredible change was made, not because the officers were inefficient and dishonest and therefore deserving removal, nor for the advantage of the service, nor for any public reason whatever, but solely to consolidate and strengthen the machine. . . .

To destroy this malign power, which degrades our politics and demoralizes the national life and character; which insinuates its slime into every part of the public administration, however remote from party politics, so that political influence retains drunken nurses in hospitals and brutal overseers in asylums; to overthrow a usurpation which has already seized so much of their own power from the people, the destruction of the spoils system of the Civil Service is indispensable. . . .

Reform of the Civil Service, by abolishing patronage, effectually stops the machine, by compelling it to empty its own pockets and not to pick those of the public to pay its way. It is in the truest sense the people's reform. It restores the public service and the political control of the country to the great mass of the people. It asserts the essentially American doctrine that public offices are public trusts and not personal perquisites. It demands that the public business shall be done upon business principles; that the vast multitude of places in the public service, which are merely administrative and clerical and in no sense political, shall be absolutely non-political; that they shall be filled solely upon consideration of fitness, ascertained in a definite and reasonable manner, free from all political influence; and that the tenure shall be faithful, efficient, and economical discharge of duty, whether that tenure be for a day or for fifty years. This is the great conservative movement of American liberty, good government, and honest politics. It is the rapidly increasing demand of the American people. The issues of the last generation are fast disappearing, and the party of the future is the party of Civil-Service reform.

❖ ❖ ❖

Grant was denied the Republican nomination in 1880. The candidate, however, was far from satisfactory to Curtis and his fellows. James A. Garfield was a Republican "half-breed." That is, he did not stalwartly defend the spoils system like Conkling, who called Curtis a "snivel service reformer" and a "man milliner," a sissy, but he believed in using the patronage—public appointments—to reward his political friends. In making 390 appointments during his first four months in office, Garfield dismissed 89 officeholders, to the great distress of the Independents. Then, on July 2, 1881, Garfield was shot and fatally wounded by an office seeker he had not accommodated. A President who, alive, had been a frustration to the civil service reformers became, in death, a martyr.

Public opinion, to which Curtis had previously appealed with little response, hastened Congress in the Pendleton Act of 1883 to establish a Civil Service Commission which drew up examinations to determine the qualifications of applicants for some non-political government jobs, administer the tests, and protect those people who had demonstrated their merit. At first, only 10,000 very low-level federal positions were "protected" under the Pendleton Act. Disappointed, Curtis remained busy on behalf of civil service reform until his death in 1892. However, the Act empowered the President to add job classifications to the civil service list without the specific approval of Congress. By 1900, among non policy-making government positions, all but a few were removed from the patronage. In many states and most large cities, however, effective civil service reform had to wait until the progressive era after the turn of the century.

2

Henry Demarest Lloyd
❖ ❖ ❖

Our Criminal Rich
1881

*D*elmonico's on 44th Street was the restaurant to which New Yorkers in the late nineteenth century resorted when they wished to put on the dog. Here in December, 1876, a gathering of notables convened to fête the eighteenth-century economist Adam Smith in observance of the 100th anniversary of the publication of *The Wealth of Nations.* The father of economics would doubtless have been astonished to find himself in a place like Delmonico's, but in truth he had helped to make it possible. Smith had taught the world the "laws" of economic competition according to which each individual, by seeking only his own self-interest, efficiently contributed to the wealth of the whole community. Thus when "Commodore" Cornelius Vanderbilt celebrated his eighty-first birthday in 1875, he boasted he had made a million dollars for every year of his life, but he also estimated that it had been worth "three times that to the people of the United States."

Ever since the Protestant Reformation, poverty had been no virtue in the world, merely a misfortune, and material riches were a sign of God's blessing. "To secure wealth," said a famous nineteenth-century preacher, "is an honorable ambition, and is one great test of a person's usefulness to others." The Americans were a religious people, if church attendance on Sunday mornings was any indication, and, judging by the nightly crowd at Charlie Delmonico's, they were also very usefully occupied. "Captains of Industry," Thomas Carlyle had called the business elite of the industrial revolution, "the ultimate genuine Aristocracy of this Universe."

Our Criminal Rich   From H. D. Lloyd, "Story of a Great Monopoly," *The Atlantic Monthly,* (March 1881), XLVII, 317–34.

In the 1870s and 1880s Americans began to have their doubts.
Charles Francis Adams, Jr., writing some of the best prose of the century,
exposed the stock manipulations by which Daniel Drew and Jay Gould
wrecked the Erie Railroad, transforming a great trunk line into "the Scarlet
Woman of Wall Street." The scandals of the Grant administration gave the
nation a glimpse of business leaders less worthy of a place in the pantheon
than in the penitentiary. Mark Twain dubbed the 1870s "the Gilded
Age"—a name which stuck—and peopled it with hilariously flatulent
businessmen who were no better than confidence artists. Carl Schurz called
them "Robber Barons," another name which stuck. Critics derided their
fanciful granite and marble palaces going up along Fifth Avenue, and
when John Rockefeller refused to build one, they condemned him for his
stinginess. William Allen White suggested that fashionable Americans
grew beards in the 1870s "to hide their naked shame." So great had this
flood of recrimination become by the end of the century that it worried
even Theodore Roosevelt. He was reminded, he said, of the man with the
muckrake in Bunyan's *Pilgrim's Progress*, who could never look up from the
filth on the floor to see the celestial crown which was offered him.

One of the first, and perhaps the greatest, of the muckrakers was
Henry Demarest Lloyd, who began his career as a reform journalist in
1873 on the staff of the *Chicago Tribune*. Between 1881 and 1884 Lloyd
published a series of powerfully written articles in the *Atlantic Monthly* and
the *North American Review*, indicting "the criminal rich" for a variety of
business abuses harmful to the public and helpful only to themselves. In
the first (excerpted below) he described the way in which the manipulation
of railway rates permitted John D. Rockefeller to destroy his competitors
and create the Standard Oil monopoly. The article was a sensation.
Reprinted six times, it fixed Standard Oil in the public mind as "the
whipping boy among the Trusts" for the rest of the century. A subsequent
article called attention to the way that speculators on the nation's
commodities exchanges ("thugs of the Board and Produce Exchange")
depressed farm prices, raised food costs, and caused artificial famine on
the other side of the earth ("they rob the world of its daily bread"). A third
identified more than fifty monopolies at work in the American economy,
by which the prices of everything from kitchen matches to coffins were
rigged, production curtailed, and the public deprived of the potential
benefits of modern industry. "In a society which has the wherewithal to
cover, fatten, and cheer every one," Lloyd wrote, "Lords of Industry are
acquiring the power to pool the profits of scarcity and to decree famine."

✿ When Commodore Vanderbilt[1] began [in] the world he
had nothing, and there were no steamboats or railroads. He was

---

[1]Cornelius Vanderbilt (1794–1877) made a fortune in steam shipping before he turned to railroads and organized the New York Central, one of the nation's great trunk lines.

thirty-five years old when the first locomotive was put into use in America. When he died, railroads had become the greatest force in modern industry, and Vanderbilt was the richest man of Europe or America, and the largest owner of railroads in the world. He used the finest business brain of his day and the franchise of the state to build up a kingdom within the republic, and like a king he bequeathed his wealth to his eldest son. Bancroft's *History of the United States*[2] and our railroad system were begun at the same time. The history is not yet finished, but the railroads owe on stocks and bonds $4,600,000,000—more than twice our national debt, . . . and [they] tax the people annually $490,000,000—one and a half times more than the government's revenue last year. . . . More than any other class, our railroad men have developed the country, and tried its institutions. . . . Violations of trust by Crédit Mobiliers,[3] Jay Gould's wealth and the poverty of Erie stockholders, such corruption of legislatures as . . . nicknamed New Jersey "the State of Camden and Amboy," are sins against public and private faith on a scale impossible in the early days of republics and corporations. . . .

Our treatment of "the railroad problem" will show the quality and calibre of our political sense. It will go far in foreshadowing the future lines of our social and political growth. It may indicate whether the American democracy, like all the democratic experiments which have preceeded it, is to become extinct because the people had not wit enough or virtue enough to make the common good supreme. . . .

Kerosene has become, by its cheapness, the people's light the world over. In the United States we used 220,000,000 gallons of petroleum last year. It has come into such demand abroad that, . . . after articles of food, this country has but one export, cotton, more valuable than petroleum. . . . In the United States, in the cities as well as the country, petroleum is the general illuminator. We use more kerosene lamps than Bibles. The raw material of this world's light is produced in a territory beginning with Cattaraugus County in New York, and extending southwesterly through eight or nine counties of Pennsylvania, making a belt about one hundred and fifty miles long, and twelve or fifteen miles wide. . . .

---

[2]George Bancroft (1800–1891) published the first volume of his famous *History* in 1834, the tenth in 1874.

[3]Crédit Mobilier refers to a great scandal, discovered in 1872, in the construction of the Union Pacific.

Very few of the forty millions of people in the United States who burn kerosene know that its production, manufacture, and export, its price at home and abroad, have been controlled for years by a single corporation—the Standard Oil Company. This company began in a partnership, in the early years of the Civil War, between Samuel Andrews and John Rockefeller in Cleveland. Rockefeller had been a bookkeeper in some interior town in Ohio, and had afterwards made a few thousand dollars by keeping a flour store in Cleveland. Andrews had been a day laborer in refineries, and so poor that his wife took in sewing. He found a way of refining by which more kerosene could be got out of a barrel of petroleum than by any other method, and set up for himself a ten-barrel still in Cleveland, by which he cleared $500 in six months. Andrews' still and Rockefeller's savings have grown into the Standard Oil Company. It has a capital, nominally $3,500,000, but really much more, on which it divides among its stockholders every year millions of dollars of profits. . . .

The four quarters of the globe are partitioned among the members of the Standard combinations. . . . The Standard produces only one fiftieth or sixtieth of our petroleum, but dictates the price of all, and refines nine tenths. . . . There is not today a merchant in Chicago, or in any other city in the New England, Western, or Southern States, dealing in kerosene, whose prices are not fixed for him by the Standard. . . . This corporation has driven into bankruptcy, or out of business, or into union with itself, all the petroleum refineries of the country except five in New York, and a few of little consequence in Western Pennsylvania. Nobody knows how many millions Rockefeller is worth. Current gossip . . . puts his income last year at a figure second only . . . to that of Vanderbilt. . . .

Their great business capacity would have insured the managers of the Standard success, but the means by which they achieved monopoly was by conspiracy with the railroads. Mr. Simon Sterne, counsel for the merchants of New York in the New York investigation, declared that the relations of the railroads to the Standard exhibited "the most shameless perversion of the duties of a common carrier to private ends that has taken place in the history of the world." The Standard killed its rivals, in brief, by getting the great trunk lines to refuse to give them transportation. Commodore Vanderbilt is reported to have said that there was but one man— Rockefeller—who could dictate to him. Whether or not Vanderbilt said it, Rockefeller did it. The Standard has done everything with the Pennsylvania legislature, except refine it. . . .

The contract is in print by which the Pennsylvania Railroad agreed with the Standard, under the name of the South Improvement Company, to double the freights on oil to everybody, but to repay the Standard one dollar for every barrel of oil it shipped, and one dollar for every barrel any of its competitors shipped. . . . Rockefeller . . . effected secret arrangements with the Pennsylvania, the New York Central, the Erie, and the Atlantic and Great Western. . . . Vanderbilt . . . has given the Standard special rates and privileges. He has paid it back in rebates millions of dollars, which have enabled it to crush out all competitors. . . .

When Mr. Vanderbilt was questioned by Mr. Sterne . . . about these and other things, his answers were, "I don't know," "I forget," "I don't remember," to 116 questions out of 249 by actual count. . . . Mr. Roger Sherman, of counsel for the complainants in the suit brought by the State of Pennsylvania, hunted through the officers of the Pennsylvania Railroad to find someone who knew what rebates the Standard was getting. Most of the officers knew as little as Mr. Vanderbilt. Finally, Mr. Cassatt[4] was put on the stand. He testified . . . that . . . the public rate for transporting crude oil was $1.40 a barrel, but the Standard paid only eight-eight and a half cents, and finally but ten cents. . . . The rebates given the Standard extend to nearly every State in the Union. These rebates are about equal to the average value of the oil at the wells. The railroads of the United States virtually give the Standard its raw material free. . . .

It seems incredible that Americans should have been willing to do what the Standard, by means of these special privileges from the railroads, did to its competitors. The refineries at New York had often to lie idle while the oil was running on the ground at the wells, because they could not get transportation. . . . There was apparently no trick the Standard would not play. It delivered its competitors inferior oils when they had ordered the high-priced article, out of which alone they could manufacture the fancy brands their customers called for. . . . Hundreds and thousands of men have been ruined by these acts of the Standard and the railroads; whole communities have been rendered desperate, and the peace of Pennsylvania imperiled more than once. . . . If we turn to the experience of the refiners we find they fared as badly as the producers. The handful of New York refiners who survived the conspiracy against them testify that they had to keep their capacity limited and to do

---

[4]Identified by Lloyd as a vice-president of the Pennsylvania.

as little as they could. . . . Mr. Alexander, of Cleveland, tells how he was informed by Rockefeller, of the Standard, that if he would not sell out he should be crushed out. . . . D. P. Reichardt tells us how the agents of the Standard came to him with the threat that if he did not come into their combination they would drive him to the wall. The Standard called upon this free man to choose between financial ruin and joining them on these terms: he was to refine only half as much as he had been doing, and was to pay them a tribute of one cent a gallon, a tax of five to twelve per cent. . . .

Today, in every part of the United States, people who burn kerosene are paying the Standard Oil Company a tax on every gallon amounting to several times its original cost to that concern. . . . A family that uses a gallon of kerosene a day pays a yearly tribute to the Standard of $32, the income from $800 in four per cents. . . .

It is the railroads that have bred the millionaires who are now buying newspapers, and getting up corners in wheat, corn, and cotton, and are making railroad consolidations that stretch across the continent. By the same tactics that the railroads have used to build up the Standard, they can give other combinations of capitalists the control of the wheat, lumber, cotton, or any other product of the United States. . . .

One mind invented the locomotive, established the railroad, and discovered the law of this new force. All railroad history has been a vindication of George Stephenson's[5] saying that where combination was possible competition was impossible. Today, wherever in this country there is a group of railroads doing business at a common point, you will find a pool. These pools are nothing more mysterious than combinations to prevent competition. . . .

These pools must be either dispersed, . . . or controlled. . . . The cat must be killed or belled. In either case, it must be confronted by a power greater than itself. . . . In less than the ordinary span of a life-time, our railroads have brought upon us the worst labor disturbance, the greatest of monopolies, and the most formidable combination of money and brains that ever overshadowed a state. The time has come to face the fact that the forces of capital and industry have outgrown the forces of our government. . . . Our strong men are engaged in a headlong fight for fortune, power, precedence, success. Americans as they are, they ride over the people like Juggernaut to gain their ends. The moralists have preached

---

[5]The English engineer George Stephenson (1781–1848) built the first steam locomotive in 1815.

to them since the world began, and have failed. The common people, the nation, must take them in hand. . . . When monopolies succeed, the people fail; when a rich criminal escapes justice, the people are punished; when a legislature is bribed, the people are cheated. There is nobody richer than Vanderbilt except the body of citizens; no corporation more powerful than the transcontinental railroad except the corporate sovereign at Washington. The nation is the engine of the people. They must use it for their industrial life, as they used it in 1861 for their political life. The States have failed.[6] The United States must succeed, or the people will perish.[7]

✿ ✿ ✿

The walls of Henry Lloyd's study were hung with portraits of the great Victorian moralists—Emerson, Carlyle, and Ruskin. Their influence could be felt even in the aphoristic style of his essays. Moral spokesmen for the middle class, they—Lloyd among them—led an important attack upon the laissez-faire economic theories of Adam Smith and his successors which helped to pave the way for the twentieth-century welfare-state in Britain and the United States. It was Carlyle who first called classical economics "the dismal science." Lloyd was one of the earliest Americans to conclude that Smith's principle of economic competition was "one of the historic mistakes of humanity." It is "a fallacy," he said, to think that the self-interest of the individual is an adequate guide to the welfare of society. "There is no other field of human associations in which any such rule of action is allowed. The man who should apply in his family or his citizenship this . . . theory as it is practically professed and operated in business would be a monster . . . [on] a short road to the penitentiary or the gallows." In 1882 Lloyd published an informative essay in the *Atlantic Monthly* which introduced American readers to a growing body of British economic thought critical of the classical school. Three years later the American Economic Association was formed by a number of younger American economists whose platform declared that the doctrine of laissez-faire was unsafe in politics, unsound in morals, and unfounded in science.

---

[6]Beginning in 1870, the legislatures of several midwestern states had attempted to regulate railroads, an effort eventually doomed to defeat by the intervention of the courts (see "The Wabash Case," in Part 1).

[7]Public clamor compelled Congress in 1887 to pass the Interstate Commerce Act, which prohibited, among other practices, rebates and pools. It was, however, not very effectively enforced during the first twenty years after its passage.

Therefore, when Lloyd called attention to the growth of giant, competition-destroying monopolies like Standard Oil, it was not in the hope of restoring competitive business conditions. "We have given competition its own way," he wrote, "and have found that we are not good enough or wise enough to be trusted with this power of ruining ourselves in the attempt to ruin others." Competition had destroyed itself. The Trusts were here to stay, and the only defense against the predations of the monopolists was the intervention of government to regulate their behavior in the public interest. "When capitalists combine irresistibly against the people, the Government, which is the people's combination, must take them in hand."

3

The People's Party, "the Populists"
❂ ❂ ❂

The Omaha Platform
1892

*I*n no part of American society did
the fabulous growth of the late nineteenth century have a greater impact
than on the farm. Stimulated by the increase of urban population and
the railroad's integration of the economy, emigrants from the older states
and Europe brought more virgin land under cultivation between 1870
and 1900 than had been domesticated during the previous 270 years of
American history. Each year for thirty years, an average 14.4 million acres
of new farmland were brought under the plow. New methods of farming
and new kinds of machines enabled the farm work force, which had nearly
doubled in size, to increase its production of cotton, corn, wheat, and pork
by 150 percent.

However, agriculture's finest hour proved to be a nightmare for
many farmers. As production soared, the wholesale price of every staple
crop—the price at which farmers sold to processors—plummeted. By
1896, when agricultural discontent peaked in near-rebellion, a grower of
corn or wheat or cotton had to produce twice as much as he had a quarter
century before in order to enjoy the same standard of living. Many farmers
were doing just that. Many others were not. And a declining standard of
living, increased debt and foreclosures on mortgages, put much of the
farm belt in an ugly mood.

Some leaders of farmer organizations recognized that
overproduction was an essential part of the farmer's woes. Others

THE OMAHA PLATFORM   From Edward McPherson, *A Handbook of Politics for 1892*
(Washington: James J. Chapman, 1892), 269 ff.

took jaundiced note of widespread deprivation in the cities and asked if there were a glut of food there. They blamed artificial impediments to consumption, the middlemen who stood between farmers and consumers, for the nation's plight. Foremost among these sinister forces "at work like thieves in the night" were railroaders and bankers. After the decision in the *Wabash* case, railroad companies seemed to have the prerogative to deal with customers as they chose. Bankers were attacked for working through the federal government to reduce the amount of money in circulation. This deflation benefited the lenders of money while damaging the borrowers: farmers had to pay back loans in currency that was worth more, and therefore more difficult to earn, than the inflated currency which they had borrowed a few years earlier.

At Ocala, Florida, in 1890, two regional farmers' organizations joined together to form the People's, or Populist, Party. This movement was consecrated to taking control of the government of the United States from the hands of "special interests," the big businessmen and bankers whom the Populists held responsible for the corruption of America's promise, and returning it to ordinary men and women, to the people who actually produced wealth, the farmers and industrial workers.

There was an evangelical fervor to Populism that alarmed many Americans. A reporter described the July 1892 convention of the Populists in Omaha, Nebraska as an orgy of hysterics. When the platform was adopted, "cheers and yells . . . rose like a tornado . . . and raged without cessation for thirty-four minutes, during which women shrieked and wept, men embraced and kissed their neighbors, locked arms, marched back and forth, and leaped upon tables and chairs in the ecstasy of their delirium." This spirit shines through the Populists' 1892 platform and declaration of sentiments. The preamble was written by Ignatius Donnelly, a former Radical Republican from Minnesota. The Populists' comprehensive program for reform drew on the protests that farmers, industrial workers, and social critics had been lodging against industrial America for a generation.

Preamble

The conditions which surround us best justify our co-operation; we meet in the midst of a nation brought to the verge of moral, political, and material ruin. Corruption dominates the ballot-box, the Legislatures, the Congress, and touches even the ermine of the bench. The people are demoralized; most of the States have been compelled to isolate the voters at the polling places to prevent universal intimidation and bribery.[1] The newspapers are largely subsidized or muzzled, public opinion silenced, business prostrated, homes covered with mortgages, labor impoverished, and the land concentrating in the hands of capitalists. The urban workmen are denied the right to organize for self-protection, imported pauperized labor beats down their wages, a hireling standing army,[2] unrecognized by our laws, is established to shoot them down, and they are rapidly degenerating into European conditions. The fruits of the toil of millions are boldly stolen to build up colossal fortunes for a few, unprecedented in the history of mankind; and the possessors of these, in turn, despise the Republic and endanger liberty. From the same prolific womb of governmental injustice we breed the two great classes—tramps and millionaires. . . .

Assembled on the anniversary of the birthday of the nation, and filled with the spirit of the grand general and chief who established our independence, we seek to restore the government of the Republic to the hands of the "plain people," with which class it originated. We assert our purposes to be identical with the purposes of the National Constitution; to form a more perfect union and establish justice, insure domestic tranquility, provide for the common defence, promote the general welfare, and secure the blessings of liberty for ourselves and our posterity. . . .

Platform

We declare, therefore—

First.—That the union of the labor forces of the United States this day consummated shall be permanent and perpetual; may its

---

[1]Polling place procedures in some states allowed those present to know how an individual voted. For example, the parties would print ballots for their candidates on paper of distinctive color so that a voter's preference was immediately known. The secret, or "Australian," ballot was already employed in some parts of the United States, and the Populists called for its universal adoption.

[2]Some railroads and manufacturers hired "guards" from private agencies such as the Pinkerton and Burns agencies. These armed, sometimes uniformed officers often specialized in harassing and even beating union organizers and malcontents and served in effect as "armies" during labor disturbances.

spirit enter into all hearts for the salvation of the Republic and the uplifting of mankind.

Second.—Wealth belongs to him who creates it, and every dollar taken from industry without an equivalent is robbery. "If any will not work, neither shall he eat." The interests of rural and civil labor are the same; their enemies are identical.

Third.—We believe that the time has come when the railroad corporations will either own the people or the people must own the railroads. . . .

FINANCE.—We demand a national currency, safe, sound, and flexible issued by the general government only, a full legal tender for all debts, public and private. . . .

1. We demand free and unlimited coinage of silver and gold at the present legal ratio of 16 to 1.

2. We demand that the amount of circulating medium be speedily increased to not less than $50 per capita.

3. We demand a graduated income tax.

4. We believe that the money of the country should be kept as much as possible in the hands of the people, and hence we demand that all State and national revenues shall be limited to the necessary expenses of the government, economically and honestly administered.

5. We demand that postal savings banks be established by the government for the safe deposit of the earnings of the people and to facilitate exchange.[3]

TRANSPORTATION.—Transportation being a means of exchange and a public necessity, the government should own and operate the railroads in the interest of the people. The telegraph and telephone, like the post-office system, being a necessity for the transmission of news, should be owned and operated by the government in the interest of the people.

LAND.—The land, including all the natural sources of wealth, is the heritage of the people, and should not be monopolized for speculative purposes, and alien ownership of land should be prohibited. All land now held by railroads and other corporations in

---

[3]Because of their antipathy toward banks, and the fact that many banks would not accept small accounts, the Populists and labor unions both in the United States and abroad urged the Post Office to institute a savings program.

excess of their actual needs, and all lands now owned by aliens should be reclaimed by the government and held for actual settlers only.

Expression of Sentiments

1. RESOLVED, That we demand a free ballot, and a fair count in all elections, and pledge ourselves to secure it to every legal voter without Federal intervention, through the adoption by the States of the unperverted Australian or secret ballot system.

2. RESOLVED, That the revenue derived from a graduated income tax should be applied to the reduction of the burden of taxation now levied upon the domestic industries of this country.

3. RESOLVED, That we pledge our support to fair and liberal pensions to ex-Union soldiers and sailors.

4. RESOLVED, That we condemn the fallacy of protecting American labor under the present system, which opens our ports to the pauper and criminal classes of the world and crowds out our wage-earners; and we denounce the present ineffective laws against contract labor, and demand the further restriction of undesirable emigration.

5. RESOLVED, That we cordially sympathize with the efforts of organized workingmen to shorten the hours of labor, and demand a rigid enforcement of the existing eight-hour law on Government work, and ask that a penalty clause be added to the said law.

6. RESOLVED, That we regard the maintenance of a large standing army of mercenaries, known as the Pinkerton system, as a menace to our liberties, and we demand its abolition. . . .

7. RESOLVED, That we commend to the favorable consideration of the people and the reform press the legislative system known as the initiative and referendum.

8. RESOLVED, That we favor a constitutional provision limiting the office of President and Vice-President to one

term, and providing for the election of Senators of the United States by a direct vote of the people.

9. RESOLVED, That we oppose any subsidy or national aid to any private corporation for any purpose.

❀ ❀ ❀

In the election of 1892, Populist Presidential candidate James B. Weaver won 22 electoral votes with 8.5 percent of the popular vote. The Populists also elected about a dozen congressmen, including a majority of the Kansas delegation. With good reason, Populist leaders like Donnelly, Mary Ellen Lease, "Sockless Jerry" Simpson, and the urban reformer, Henry Demarest Lloyd, believed the future belonged to them. They tirelessly crisscrossed the country visiting local organizations and rallying enthusiasm.

A serious economic depression strengthened the Populist appeal to farmers. In fact, in one sense, it strengthened it too much. Within the Democratic party, midwestern and some southern politicians adopted the evangelical style of Populism and embraced a single plank of the Populist platform, the call for increasing the amount of currency in circulation through the free and unlimited coinage of silver. At the Democratic party's convention in 1896, Free Silver forces nominated an orator hero from Nebraska, William Jennings Bryan, to run for President. The Democrats calculated that the Populists would nominate Bryan too. This, they believed, would ensure his victory.

Some Populists, like Georgia's Thomas E. Watson, begged the party not to "fuse" with the Democrats. They pointed out that Bryan opposed virtually every other plank of the Omaha Platform. But midwestern Populists smelled victory, even if for just one of their principles. The party named Bryan its candidate. When he went down to defeat before a well-organized Republican campaign that painted the Populist-Democrats as dangerous radicals, the Populists died. By 1900, the Populist party was a dry husk, less important than the Prohibitionists.

The principal reason for the collapse of the Populists was the return of economic prosperity during the final four years of the nineteenth century. Just as important, despite frequent appeals to industrial workers in the party platforms, and the support of important social critics like Henry Demarest Lloyd, the Populists never won many urban votes. Populism was a "Hayseed's Revolt" in a nation that was increasingly urban and industrial.

In time, ironically, the Omaha Platform became, next to the

Republican party platform of 1860, the best-enacted comprehensive program for reform in the history of political platforms. The progressive movement of the early twentieth century and the New Dealers of the 1930s enacted into law the Australian ballot, the initiative, the referendum, and the recall. Also, the popular election of United States Senators, graduated income tax, the eight-hour day, and immigration restriction became law. During World War I, the federal government even took control of the nation's railroads, but they were never federally owned.

4

The Supreme Court
❖ ❖ ❖

Plessy v. Ferguson
1896

*I*n the southern states, the Populist agitation was complicated by a "Negro question" that dated back to the days following the Civil War: What place were the freedmen, as the former slaves were called, to occupy in American society? Were they to enjoy the full rights of citizenship, civil equality with whites, as the Thirteenth Amendment implied they were, or some other lesser station?

In the immediate wake of the war, southern state governments enacted a series of "Black Codes" that defined a clearly inferior role for the freedmen. These laws placed stringent restrictions upon where blacks could reside and what kinds of work they could perform. Blacks were denied most of the rights of citizenship—the vote, the right to serve on juries, and so on. It appeared to blacks and many northern Republicans that the old slavocracy was trying to reinstitute slavery under a different name.

Partly as a reaction to the Black Codes, the Radical Republicans won an overwhelming victory in the congressional elections of 1866. Many of the Radicals were former abolitionists who were determined to destroy the political power of the former slaveowners and to create a Republican party in the South based on a black electorate. They dissolved the Black-Code governments and pushed through the Fourteenth Amendment, which explicitly forbade states to deny the rights of citizenship on account of race, color, creed, or country of origin; and the Fifteenth, guaranteeing all

PLESSY V. FERGUSON   From Supreme Court, 163, 537 (1896).

citizens the right to vote (See Appendix). But Republican commitment to black civil equality was unsteady, and the southern white Democrats were determined not to share power with blacks. By 1877, every southern state had been "redeemed" for white supremacy.

The conditions under which southern blacks lived varied widely from place to place. In a few places blacks retained the right to vote. Elsewhere, intimidated by terrorism, or simply out of the necessity to choose between a modicum of economic security as tenants and the exercise of their constitutional rights, blacks withdrew from political life. In still other parts of the South, black voters used their ballots as their exploitative but paternalistic landlords dictated in return for protection against frustrated, lower-class, white "cracker" mobs.

Some Populists, like Thomas E. Watson of Georgia, attempted to form an alliance of poor white and black farmers based on social class. More common, however, was the solution to the "Negro problem" offered by the populistic South Carolina Democrat, "Pitchfork Ben" Tillman. He combined a call for radical agrarian reform with emotional and often vicious demands that blacks be excluded from politics and banished to behind a strictly drawn color line in everyday social intercourse.

Tillman's brand of demagoguery triumphed over Watson's and, in time, even Watson was converted. All over the South during the 1890s, lynch law, directed primarily against blacks, accounted for more deaths than state executioners. Legislatures vied with one another to segregate public facilities. The "Jim Crow" laws fastened "White" and "Colored" placards over drinking fountains, in parks, on the doors of toilet facilities, above tax collection desks in courthouses, even on the Bibles used to swear in witnesses at trials.

One of the early Jim Crow laws was Louisiana's ordinance of 1890 requiring railroads to "provide equal but separate accommodations for the white and colored races." Louisiana's railroads disliked the law because it meant they must provide two sets of facilities rather than one. They joined with a group of New Orleans blacks in a test case to challenge its constitutionality under the Thirteenth and Fourteenth Amendments. Homer Adolph Plessy, white to all appearances but "colored" under Louisiana's legal definition of race, was selected to board a train in June 1892. He took a seat in the "Whites Only" section, and was asked by a conductor privy to the arrangement to move to the "colored" compartment. Plessy refused, was arrested, and took his case through the lower courts to the Supreme Court. Judge John H. Ferguson was a district judge who had ruled against Plessy and for the Jim Crow law. Seven Supreme Court Justices upheld Ferguson's decision. Justice John Marshall Harlan was alone in dissent.

❋ This case turns upon the constitutionality of an act of the general assembly of the state of Louisiana, passed in 1890, providing for separate railway carriages for the white and colored races. . . .

The constitutionality of this act is attacked upon the ground that it conflicts both with the 13th Amendment of the Constitution, abolishing slavery, and the 14th Amendment, which prohibits certain restrictive legislation on the part of the states.

1. That it does not conflict with the 13th Amendment, which abolished slavery and involuntary servitude, except as a punishment for crime, is too clear for argument. . . . Indeed, we do not understand that the 13th Amendment is strenuously relied upon by the plaintiff. . . .

The object of the [14th] amendment was undoubtedly to enforce the absolute equality of the two races before the law, but in the nature of things it could not have been intended to abolish distinctions based upon color, or to enforce social, as distinguished from political, equality, or a commingling of the two races upon terms unsatisfactory to either. Laws permitting, and even requiring their separation in places where they are liable to be brought into contact do not necessarily imply the inferiority of either race to the other, and have been generally, if not universally, recognized as within the competency of the state legislatures in the exercise of their police power. . . .

We consider the underlying fallacy of the plaintiff's argument to consist in the assumption that the enforced separation of the two races stamps the colored race with a badge of inferiority. If this be so, it is not by reason of anything found in the act, but solely because the colored race chooses to put that construction upon it. . . .

The argument also assumes that social prejudice may be overcome by legislation, and that equal rights cannot be secured to the Negro except by an enforced commingling of the two races. We cannot accept this proposition. If the two races are to meet on terms of social equality, it must be the result of natural affinities, a mutual appreciation of each other's merits and a voluntary consent of individuals. . . . Legislation is powerless to eradicate racial instincts or to abolish distinctions based upon physical differences, and the attempt to do so can only result in accentuating the difficulties of the present situation. If the civil and political right of both races be equal, one cannot be inferior (552) to the other civilly or politically. If one race be inferior to the other socially, the Constitution of the United States cannot put them upon the same plane.

Justice Harlan, dissenting. . . . In respect of civil rights, common to all citizens, the Constitution of the United States does not, I think, permit any public authority to know the race of those entitled to be protected in the enjoyment of such rights. . . . I deny that any legislative body or judicial tribunal may have regard to the race of citizens when the civil rights of those citizens are involved. Indeed such legislation as that here in question is inconsistent, not only with that equality of rights which pertains to citizenship, national and state, but with the personal liberty enjoyed by every one within the United States. . . .

The destiny of the two races in this country are indissolubly linked together, and the interests of both require that the common government of all shall not permit the seeds of race hate to be planted under the sanction of law. What can more certainly arouse race hate, what more certainly create and perpetuate a feeling of distrust between these races, than state enactments which in fact proceed on the ground that colored citizens are so inferior and degraded that they cannot be allowed to sit in public coaches occupied by white citizens? That, as all will admit, is the real meaning of such legislation as was enacted in Louisiana. . . .

We boast of the freedom enjoyed by our people above all other peoples. But it is difficult to reconcile that boast with a state of the law which, practically, puts the brand of servitude and degradation upon a large class of our fellow citizens, our equals before the law. The thin disguise of "equal" accommodations for passengers in railroad coaches will not mislead anyone, or atone for the wrong this day done. . . .

I am of opinion that the statute of Louisiana is inconsistent with the personal liberty of citizens, white and black, in that state, and hostile to both the spirit and letter of the Constitution of the United States. If laws of like character should be enacted in the several states of the Union, the effect would be in the highest degree mischievous. . . .

I am constrained to withhold my assent from the opinion and judgment of the majority.

❂ ❂ ❂

The *Plessy* decision merely accelerated what was underway in the former slave states. Like the *Wabash* decision in the area of business regulation, *Plessy* reflected the significant drift in American attitudes since the Civil War. A goodly portion of the American people had come to feel at home with racial discrimination as with the unfettering of big business. After the social tumult in industry and agriculture accompanying the economic depression of the 1890s and a generation-long period of chronic "race problems," the national mood was ripe for the stabilization of race relations at almost any price. Thus was the Supreme Court able to sidestep Harlan's argument that the Constitution must be color-blind and to rule that state, local, or federal law could institutionalize the racist sentiments of a dominant group.

During the reform era that followed in 1900, a few progressives like journalist Ray Stannard Baker decried "the color line." But most progressives, northern and southern, shrugged off discrimination against blacks. By 1910, when the National Association for the Advancement of Colored People was founded to combat racial discrimination in the law, Jim Crow was the rule in all fifteen of the former slave states and on the books in states such as Kansas and Oklahoma which bordered on the old South. When southern-born-and-bred Woodrow Wilson became President in 1913, he sanctioned racial segregation in the federal government. Not until the late 1940s would institutionalized racism receive a serious blow.

5

Eugene V. Debs
❖ ❖ ❖

Outlook for Socialism in the United States
1900

*D*uring the first half of the
nineteenth century, the United States was the center of world socialism.
Before about 1850, most socialist theorists, envisioning a future in which
the means of production were owned collectively for the public good
rather than privately for individual profit, urged their followers to
establish small, self-contained new communities in which their principles
reigned. By their example of living in peace, security, comfort, and
brotherhood in the midst of the strife, anxiety, hardship, and competition
of the larger society, these communities thought they would convert others
to the truth, not unlike John Winthrop's "city upon a hill."

Because the United States was itself "new," with abounding cheap
and unsettled land for the taking, European visionaries planted their
idealistic communities here. Americans too founded separatist microcosms
of what they considered more just societies. Some were stridently secular.
Some, like the Shaker communities, were religiously oriented. Although
their socialism was never complete and their "socialistic" period brief,
the early Mormons rejected the individualism and competitiveness of

OUTLOOK FOR SOCIALISM IN THE UNITED STATES   From Eugene V. Debs, "Outlook
for Socialism in the United States," *International Socialist Review* (September 1900).

American capitalistic society. Nowhere else in the world were social experiments so common.

Then, in 1848, two young German revolutionaries, Karl Marx and Friedrich Engels, published *The Communist Manifesto*. In this exhortatory pamphlet, and in Marx's massive *Capital*, published between 1867 and 1894, "utopian" socialism was ridiculed. Marx even adopted the word *communist* to distinguish himself from the utopian socialists. The Marxists said that only by transforming the entire society could people usher in the final stage of historical evolution in which property was not a means of exploitation, but of human fulfillment for all.

Marxist socialism was brought to the United States by immigrants, particularly Germans, who formed socialist clubs, labor unions, and political parties. During the 1890s, many middle-class Americans arrived at similar socialist conclusions through their belief that the injustices created by industrial capitalism were unchristian. Others rejected capitalism after reading the works of Edward Bellamy, who held that the American promise of liberty, democracy, and justice could only be fulfilled by the abolition of private property.

Eugene V. Debs was not middle-class—he was a railroad brakeman— and he was never much of a Marxist. The teutonic ponderousness of Marx's writings and the rigorous intellectualism of the "scientific" Marxist explanation of history were not calculated to affect such an essentially simple man. Debs also claimed not to be a Christian. But, in coming to socialism because he was appalled and sorrowed by the poverty and injustice suffered by so many and because he was infuriated by the aggressiveness with which every attempt of the workers to improve their lot was suppressed, his radicalism established a very moralistic tone.

Debs claimed that he became a socialist when, in 1894, the Attorney-General joined the railroad interests in crushing the American Railway Union which Debs headed. In jail for defying an injunction, Debs was visited by Victor Berger of Milwaukee who recognized him as the passionate, consummately American leader the movement needed to rid socialism of its foreign associations and attract native-born Americans who were oriented more to action than ideology.

In fact, Debs did not become a socialist right away. In 1896, he supported the Populist and therefore the Democratic party candidate for President, William Jennings Bryan. As late as 1898, he was urging discontents to move west and found a separatist utopian colony. By 1900, however, he was the presidential candidate for the newly organized Socialist Party of America. Those who heard his volatile, evangelical, spread-eagle speeches were electrified. Debs was instantly vaulted into the position of socialism's American spokesman. Although he claimed that "ink pots have never been inviting to me," he wrote the following article for the *International Socialist Review* of September 1900. It expresses the moral spirit of his socialism and his buoyant American optimism for the future.

❀ The sun of the passing century is setting upon scenes of extraordinary activity in almost every part of our capitalistic old planet. Wars and rumors of wars are of universal prevalence. . . . and through all the flame and furore of the fray can be heard the savage snarlings of the Christian "dogs of war" as they fiercely glare about them, and with jealous fury threaten to fly at one another's throats to settle the question of supremacy and the spoil and plunder of conquest. . . .

Cheerless indeed would be the contemplation of such sanguinary scenes were the light of Socialism not breaking upon mankind. . . . From out of the midnight of superstition, ignorance and slavery the disenthralling, emancipating sun is rising. I am not gifted with prophetic vision, and yet I see the shadows vanishing. I behold near and far prostrate men lifting their bowed forms from the dust. I see thrones in the grasp of decay; despots relaxing their hold upon scepters, and shackles falling, not only from the limbs, but from the souls of men.

It is therefore with pleasure that I respond to the invitation of the editor of the *International Socialist Review* to present my views upon the "Outlook for Socialism in the United States." Socialists generally will agree that the past year has been marked with a propaganda of unprecedented activity and that the sentiment of the American people in respect to Socialism has undergone a most remarkable change. It would be difficult to imagine a more ignorant, bitter and unreasoning prejudice than that of the American people against Socialism during the early years of its introduction. . . .

Socialism was cunningly associated with "anarchy and bloodshed," and denounced as a "foul foreign importation" to pollute the fair, free soil of America, and every outrage to which the early agitators were subjected won the plaudits of the people. But they persevered in their task; they could not be silenced or suppressed. Slowly they increased in number and gradually the movement began to take root and spread over the country. . . .

The subject has passed entirely beyond the domain of sneer and ridicule and now commands serious treatment. Of course, Socialism is violently denounced by the capitalist press and by all the brood of subsidized contributors to magazine literature, but this only confirms the view that the advance of Socialism is very properly recognized by the capitalist class as the one cloud upon the horizon which portends an end to the system in which they have waxed fat, insolent and despotic through the exploitation of their countless wage-working slaves.

In school and college and church, in clubs and public halls everywhere, Socialism is the central theme of discussion, and its advocates, inspired by its noble principles, are to be found here, there and in all places ready to give or accept challenge to battle. In the cities the corner meetings are popular and effective. But rarely is such a gathering now molested by the "authorities," and then only where they have just been inaugurated. They are too numerously attended by serious, intelligent and self-reliant men and women to invite interference. . . .

On the whole, the situation could scarcely be more favorable and the final returns will more than justify our sanguine expectations. . . . The campaign this year will be unusually spectacular. The Republican Party "points with pride" to the "prosperity" of the country, the beneficent results of the "gold standard" and the "war record" of the administration. The Democratic Party declares that "imperialism" is the "paramount" issue, and that the country is certain to go to the "demnition bow-wows"[1] if Democratic office-holders are not elected instead of the Republicans. The Democratic slogan is "The Republic vs. the Empire," accompanied in a very minor key by 16 to 1 and "direct legislation where practical." . . . [2]

Needless is it for me to say to the thinking workingman that he has no choice between these two capitalist parties, that they are both pledged to the same system and that whether the one or the other succeeds, he will still remain the wage-working slave he is today.

What but meaningless phrases are "imperialism," "expansion," "free silver," "gold standard," etc., to the wage-worker? The large capitalists represented by Mr. McKinley and the small capitalists represented by Mr. Bryan are interested in these "issues," but they do not concern the working class.

What the workingmen of the country are profoundly interested in is the private ownership of the means of production and distribution, the enslaving and degrading wage-system in which they toil for a pittance at the pleasure of their masters and are bludgeoned, jailed or shot when they protest—this is the central, controlling, vital issue of the hour, and neither of the old party platforms has a word or even a hint about it. . . .

Whether the means of production—that is to say, the land, mines, factories, machinery, etc.—are owned by a few large Repub-

---

[1]"Demnition" = damnation; "bow-wows" = "the dogs." The country would go to damnation, to the dogs.

[2]"16 to 1" refers to the already obsolete call for the free coinage of silver, the paramount issue of the election of 1896 to which Bryan still appealed in 1900.

lican capitalists, who organize a trust, or whether they be owned by a lot of small Democratic capitalists, who are opposed to the trust, is all the same to the working class. Let the capitalists, large and small, fight this out among themselves.

The working class must get rid of the whole brood of masters and exploiters, and put themselves in possession and control of the means of production, that they may have steady employment without consulting a capitalist employer, large or small, and that they may get the wealth their labor produces, all of it, and enjoy with their families the fruits of their industry in comfortable and happy homes, abundant and wholesome food, proper clothing and all other things necessary to "life, liberty and the pursuit of happiness." It is therefore a question not of "reform," the mask of fraud, but of revolution. The capitalist system must be overthrown, class-rule abolished and wage-slavery supplanted by coöperative industry.

We hear it frequently urged that the Democratic Party is the "poor man's party," "the friend of labor." There is but one way to relieve poverty and to free labor, and that is by making common property of the tools of labor. . . .

The differences between the Republican and Democratic parties involve no issue, no principle in which the working class has any interest, and whether the spoils be distributed by Hanna and Platt, or by Croker and Tammany Hall is all the same to it. . . .[3]

For a time the Populist Party had a mission, but it is practically ended. The Democratic Party has "fused" it out of existence. The "middle-of-the-road" element will be sorely disappointed when the votes are counted, and they will probably never figure in another national campaign. Not many of them will go back to the old parties. Many of them have already come to Socialism, and the rest are sure to follow.

There is no longer any room for a Populist Party, and progressive Populists realize it, and hence the "strongholds" of Populism are becoming the "hot-beds" of Socialism.

It is simply a question of capitalism or Socialism, of despotism or democracy, and they who are not wholly with us are wholly against us. . . . Oh, that all the working class could and would use their eyes and see; their ears and hear; their brains and think. How soon this earth could be transformed and by the alchemy of social order made to blossom with beauty and joy.

---

[3]Mark Hanna, President McKinley's patron and promoter, was a Senator from Ohio. He was the most powerful man in the Republican party and was widely thought to be McKinley's boss. Thomas C. Platt was the Republican boss of New York State. Richard Croker was the head of Tammany Hall (George Washington Plunkitt's superior).

✿ ✿ ✿

Debs polled fewer than 100,000 votes in 1900. Four years later, however, with the party out of its infancy, he won more than 400,000. It was still a pittance compared to President Theodore Roosevelt's total of 7.6 million votes, but it heartened the candidate and other leading socialists.

In 1908 worsening conditions among working people and the conclusion of many reform-minded Americans that socialism was the answer for the country's ills led the party to charter a campaign train, the "Red Special," so that Debs could barnstorm around the country like the major party candidates did. His failure to increase the socialist vote by much was discouraging. But when the new President, William Howard Taft, abandoned the reforms of his predecessor, the party began to grow.

Beginning with the midterm election of 1910, the party put mayors into office in several large cities, including Milwaukee, sent Victor Berger to the House of Representatives, and, altogether, elected more than a thousand local and state officials. Once again, in 1912, Debs was the party's presidential candidate, winning 900,000 votes. Debs was particularly gratified, he said, because with two major party candidates running on reform platforms, his supporters were surely all committed to the socialist transformation of society and not mere reform.

Actually, 1912 was the high-water mark of the Socialist party. In part because of a return to reform in the federal government, in part because of factional squabbling within the party, most of the gains of 1910–1912 were lost beginning in 1913. In 1916, a far less exciting Socialist presidential candidate won fewer than 600,000 votes. But the old warrior had not exited the stage.

Militantly opposed to American participation in World War I, Debs offered himself as a martyr to his cause by publicly counselling resistance to conscription, a federal offense. He was arrested, tried, and imprisoned. He made his fifth and final "race" for the presidency from Atlanta penitentiary in 1920. Supported by many people who were not socialists but who admired his lifelong compassion, selflessness, idealism, and integrity, he won more than 900,000 votes. Never again would an avowedly anti-capitalist American command such support.

6

Lincoln Steffens

❖ ❖ ❖

The Shame of the Cities
1904

*B*y the end of the nineteenth century,
the "penny paper" had put the daily news within the grasp of virtually
every American. In 1900 there were almost 2000 dailies in the United
States. But until about 1890, weekly or monthly magazines which were
devoted to the leisurely discussion of important subjects circulated largely
among only the upper and upper-middle classes. There were exceptions,
of course. There were professional and occupational journals such as
magazines for farmers. Also, there were racy, suggestive, and abundantly
illustrated "scandal sheets" like the *Police Gazette*, with descriptions of
athletic events, murders, and sex scandals that today seem the epitome of
delicacy.

Because of their impropriety, the scandal sheets themselves rarely
reached large numbers of individual subscribers. Instead, they were
purchased by saloons, livery stables, and barbershops with an eye to
attracting customers. These institutions were totally masculine and
therefore suspect among the respectable middle classes.

Reputable periodicals such as *The Arena, Atlantic Monthly, Forum,
Harper's*, and *The Nation*—mixes of genteel poetry, stories, and elegant
essays—reached rather few homes because of their cost, twenty-five to fifty
cents an issue. Consequently, they reflected the patrician tastes, prejudices,
and limitations of their readers. Today they often strike readers as stodgy
and snobbish.

THE SHAME OF THE CITIES   From Lincoln Steffens, *The Shame of the Cities* (New York:
McClure, Phillips and Co., 1904), pp. 3–18.

Then, thanks to technological improvements in paper production and printing, a special mailing rate for magazines instituted by the Post Office in 1879, and the idea of making profit not from the price of a magazine, but from fees paid by advertisers, it became possible to slash the cost of a substantial-sized magazine to a dime and even a nickel. In order to exploit this opportunity for mass circulation, publishers like Cyrus McCormick, Frank A. Munsey, and Samuel S. McClure filled their magazines with illustrations and hired writers with lively styles to treat subjects with broad popular appeal to middle-class readers. Their journals grew like hollyhocks next to the stable in middle-class backyards— *Munsey's* from 40,000 subscribers in 1893 to 500,000 by 1895, *McClure's* from 8000 to 250,000 during the same two years.

It was the challenge of delivering writing that was popular but respectable that led the new publishers to the journalism of exposure. The same evils which had aroused isolated social critics for a generation— poverty, racial discrimination, concentrated economic power, unfair business practices, political corruption—flowed from the nimble pens of the "muckrakers" (so-called because the journalism of exposure meant a constant, industrious search for dirt) as an intoxicating brew. The great age of reform known as the Progressive Era, beginning uncertainly during the 1890s and convulsing the nation after 1900, owed much to the incessant delving of these men and women. Even Theodore Roosevelt, who gave the muckrakers their unattractive name, was moved to action by their writings.

One of the most influential muckraking works was a series of articles detailing corruption in municipal government which thirty-six-year-old Lincoln Steffens wrote for *McClure's* in 1902 and 1903. Steffens' popular essays were published in book form as *The Shame of the Cities* in 1904. The selection that follows is from his "Introduction and Some Conclusions."

❀ [My articles were written] with a purpose, . . . which was . . . to sound for the civic pride of an apparently shameless citizenship.

There must be such a thing, we reasoned. All our big boasting could not be empty vanity, nor our pious pretensions hollow sham. American achievements in science, art, and business mean sound abilities at bottom, and our hypocrisy a race sense of fundamental ethics. Even in government we have given proofs of potential greatness, and our political failures are not complete; they are simply ridiculous. But they are ours. Not alone the triumphs and the statesmen, the defeats and the grafters also represent us, and just as truly. Why not see it so and say it?

Because, I heard, the American people won't "stand for" it. You may blame the politicians, or, indeed, any one class, but not all classes, not the people. Or you may put it on the ignorant foreign immigrant, or any one nationality, but not on all nationalities, not on the American people. . . .

[One] such conceit of our egotism is that which deplores our politics and lauds our business. This is the wail of the typical American citizen. Now, the typical American citizen is the business man. The typical business man is a bad citizen; he is busy. If he is a "big business man" and very busy, he does not neglect, he is busy with politics, oh, very busy and very businesslike. I found him buying boodlers in St. Louis, defending grafters in Minneapolis, originating corruption in Pittsburg, sharing with bosses in Philadelphia, deploring reform in Chicago, and beating good government with corruption funds in New York. He is a self-righteous fraud, this big business man. He is the chief source of corruption, and it were a boon if he would neglect politics. But he is not the business man that neglects politics; that worthy is the good citizen, the typical business man. He too is busy, he is the one that has no use and therefore no time for politics. When his neglect has permitted bad government to go so far that he can be stirred to action, he is unhappy, and he looks around for a cure that shall be quick, so that he may hurry back to the shop. Naturally, too, when he talks politics, he talks shop. His patent remedy is quack; it is business.

"Give us a business man," he says ("like me," he means). "Let him introduce business methods into politics and government; then I shall be left alone to attend to my business."

There is hardly an office from United States Senator down to Alderman in any part of the country to which the business man has not been elected; yet politics remains corrupt, government pretty bad, and the selfish citizen has to hold himself in readiness like the old volunteer firemen to rush forth at any hour, in any weather, to prevent the fire; and he goes out sometimes and he puts out the fire (after the damage is done) and he goes back to the shop sighing for the business man in politics. The business man has failed in politics as he has in citizenship. Why?

Because politics is business. That's what's the matter with it. That's what's the matter with everything,—art, literature, religion, journalism, law, medicine,—they're all business, and all—as you see them. Make politics a sport, as they do in England, or a profession, as they do in Germany, and we'll have—well, something else than we have now,—if we want it, which is another question. But don't try to reform politics with the banker, the lawyer, and the dry-goods merchant, for these are business men. . . .

The commercial spirit is the spirit of profit, not patriotism; of credit, not honor; of individual gain, not national prosperity; of trade and dickering, not principle. "My business is sacred," says the business man in his heart. "Whatever prospers my business, is good; it must be. Whatever hinders it, is wrong; it must be. A bribe is bad, that is, it is a bad thing to take; but it is not so bad to give one, not if it is necessary to my business." . . .

But do the people want good government? Tammany says they don't. Are the people honest? Are the people better than Tammany? Are they better than the merchant and the politician? Isn't our corrupt government, after all, representative?

President Roosevelt has been sneered at for going about the country preaching, as a cure for our American evils, good conduct in the individual, simply honesty, courage, and efficiency. "Platitudes!" the sophisticated say. Platitudes? If my observations have been true, the literal adoption of Mr. Roosevelt's reform scheme would result in a revolution, more radical and terrible to existing institutions, from the Congress to the Church, from the bank to the ward organization, than socialism or even than anarchy. Why, that would change all of us—not alone our neighbors, not alone the grafters, but you and me.

No, the contemned methods of our despised politics are the master methods of our braggart business, and the corruption that shocks us in public affairs we practice ourselves in our private concerns. There is no essential difference between the pull that gets your wife into society or for your book a favorable review, and that which gets a heeler into office, a thief out of jail, and a rich man's son on the board of directors of a corporation; none between the corruption of a labor union, a bank, and a political machine; none between a dummy director of a trust and the caucus-bound member of a legislature; none between a labor boss, . . . a boss of banks, . . . a boss of railroads, and a political boss. . . . The boss is not a political, he is an American institution, the product of a freed people that have not the spirit to be free.

And it's all a moral weakness; a weakness right where we think we are strongest. Oh, we are good—on Sunday, and we are "fearfully patriotic" on the Fourth of July. But the bribe we pay to the janitor to prefer our interests to the landlord's, is the little brother of the bribe passed to the alderman to sell a city street, and the father of the air-brake stock assigned to the president of a railroad to have this life-saving invention adopted on his road. And as for graft, railroad passes, saloon and bawdy-house blackmail, and watered stock, all these belong to the same family. We are pathetically proud of our democratic institutions and our republican form of government, of our grand Constitution and our just laws. We are a free and sovereign people, we govern ourselves and the government is ours. But that is the point. We are responsible, not our leaders, since we follow them. We *let* them divert our loyalty from the United States to some "party"; we *let* them boss the party and turn our municipal democracies into autocracies and our republican nation into a plutocracy. We cheat our government and we let our leaders loot it, and we let them wheedle and bribe our sovereignty from us. True, they pass for us strict laws, but we are content to let them pass also bad laws, giving away public property in exchange; and our good, and often impossible, laws we allow to be used for oppression and blackmail. And what can we say? We break our own laws and rob our own government, the lady at the custom-house, the lyncher with his rope, and the captain of industry with his bribe and his rebate. The spirit of graft and of lawlessness is the American spirit. . . .

❖ ❖ ❖

In his ribald commentaries on big city politics and *The Shame of the Cities* (see "Machine Politics" in Part 1), George Washington Plunkitt's observation of reform governments was that "they were mornin' glories—looked lovely in the mornin' and withered up in a short time, while the regular machines went on flourishin' forever, like fine old oaks."

The painful truth of his wit was the bane of reformers. Writing his articles thirty years after the exposure and fall of the first of the notorious urban machines, New York's "Tweed Ring," Steffens discovered malfeasance just as bald and gross in St. Louis, Minneapolis, Pittsburgh, Philadelphia, and Chicago. In 1903, after Steffens' article on New York City was published in *McClure's Magazine*, but before it was collected in book form with the others, the reform government of Mayor Seth Low, which Steffens celebrated as his hope for the future of American cities, was decisively defeated at the polls by the Tammany machine Tweed had done so much to build.

Consequently, the tone of Steffens' introduction to the book was bitter, pessimistic, and torn between cynicism and muddleheadedness. On the one hand, he had moved significantly beyond the self-righteous class provincialism of genteel reformers like George William Curtis by heaping blame for the orgy of corruption on the businessmen in whom Liberal

Republicans and Mugwumps had vested their hopes. On the other hand, in seeing almost every aspect of American society as saturated by business values, and the people themselves therefore responsible, Steffens became not a political or social critic but a moralist who called for nothing less than a regeneration of human nature. His ideas, however, were only a chimera with which even the haughtiest of the Gilded Age reformers, those who found the trouble in southerners, Democrats, blacks, Irishmen, labor unions, professional politicos, two-bit farmers, hayseed demagogues, or any other specific group, would not distract themselves.

The dream of an elemental reorganization of the human spirit informed the rest of Steffens' life. Convinced that Theodore Roosevelt would lead the national regeneration when *The Shame of the Cities* was published in 1904, Steffens later became a supporter of Woodrow Wilson in 1916. He visited Soviet Russia in 1919 and returned to say "I have seen the future and it works." After Benito Mussolini came to power in Italy in 1922 (and fiercely persecuted Italy's Communists and democrats), Steffens invested his hopes in Mussolini's fascists. After the stock market crash of 1929, he again praised the Soviet system, by then being transformed into a totalitarian state by Joseph Stalin.

The progressives, whose fiery era Steffens and the other muckrakers helped to fuel, were not often as erratic as he. Theodore Roosevelt, whose soaring evangelical rhetoric inspired millions like Lincoln Steffens, was also a hard-headed realist who worked easily with big businessmen and professional pols. In the states, progressives like Robert M. LaFollette of Wisconsin and Hiram Johnson of California beat the corrupt old business-supported machines by adopting their methods of mobilizing and marshaling voters. Nevertheless, the dichotomous combination of concrete reform proposals to meet specific abuses and visions of moral perfection were to characterize the Progressive Era first to last.

PART 3

❀ ❀ ❀

Progressivism and World War

1898–1919

1

Albert J. Beveridge

❊ ❊ ❊

The March of the Flag
1898

*I*n April 1898 the United States declared war on Spain. It was an immensely popular war. Perhaps there has been no American war before or since into which the American people flung themselves with comparable zest. President William McKinley reversed his earlier opposition to war with Spain in order to catch up with the popular clamor. Secretary of State John Hay called the Spanish-American War "a splendid little war," in part because of its intoxicating effects on the nation. Theodore Roosevelt resigned from the Navy Department to fight in it. William Jennings Bryan, McKinley's Democratic opponent in the election of 1896, sought a commission in a front-line unit. In New York City, according to George Washington Plunkitt, a district leader of the Democratic machine offered to raise a Tammany regiment. In the small towns, according to William Allen White, "crowds gathered to hurrah for the soldiers and throw hats in the air."

The war was over within a few months. The Spanish navy and army were destroyed. The victorious Americans were in a position to dictate the terms of the peace treaty. That Cuba should be free of its Spanish suzerains, all agreed. The repression of the Cuban rebels was the ostensible reason the United States had gone to war; the nobility of the cause was a major factor in explaining the widespread enthusiasm for it. And, a rider on the declaration of war, the Teller Amendment, stated that the United

THE MARCH OF THE FLAG   Printed in the *Indianapolis Journal*, September 17, 1898. From Albert J. Beveridge, *The Meaning of the Times* (Indianapolis: Bobbs-Merrill, 1908) pp. 47–49, 56–57.

States renounced all claims to annexing Cuba: the island would be independent.

But what of other Spanish possessions under American control, specifically Puerto Rico and the Philippines? Anti-imperialists, a mixed bag from different generations and political persuasions, including old line Republican organization men like Thomas B. Reed of Maine, old line liberal reformers like Carl Schurz, and new leaders like William Jennings Bryan, argued against annexing any Spanish territory. In part their argument was based on democratic ideals. A nation born in a war against imperial control, they said, must surely never govern others without their consent. A note of racism sometimes crept into the anti-imperialist argument too: very few of the inhabitants of the Philippines were Caucasian; the United States did not want any more nonwhites within its boundaries. Commenting disdainfully on the proposal that the United States pay $20 million to Spain in return for annexing the Philippines, Speaker of the House Reed snorted, "Ten million Malays at two dollars a head."

But any argument based upon the perceived racial superiority of "American stock" necessarily stacked up on the imperialist side. As an ambitious young politician, Albert J. Beveridge used it in his campaign to win a Senate seat in Indiana. The incompetence of the Filipinos, the Puerto Ricans, *and the Cubans* to govern themselves justified an American takeover, he urged. Although he did not use the phrase, Beveridge believed it was the "white man's burden" to bring the blessings of "anglo-saxon" government to peoples less blessed in their ancestors. One of the most eloquent statements on behalf of American imperialism was "The March of the Flag," a speech Beveridge delivered in Indianapolis in September 1898.

It is a noble land that God has given us; a land that can feed and clothe the world; a land whose coastlines would inclose half the countries of Europe; a land set like a sentinel between the two imperial oceans of the globe, a greater England with a nobler destiny.

It is a mighty people that He has planted on this soil; a people sprung from the most masterful blood of history; a people perpetually revitalized by the virile, man-producing working folk of all the earth; a people imperial by virtue of their power, by right of their institutions, by authority of their Heaven-directed purposes—the propagandists and not the misers of liberty.

It is a glorious history our God has bestowed upon His chosen people; a history heroic with faith in our mission and our future; a history of statesmen who flung the boundaries of the Republic out into unexplored lands and savage wilderness; a history of soldiers who carried the flag across blazing deserts and through the ranks of hostile mountains, even to the gates of sunset; a history of a multiplying people who overran a continent in half a century; a history of prophets who saw the consequences of evils inherited from the past and of martyrs who died to save us from them; a history divinely logical, in the process of whose tremendous reasoning we find ourselves to-day.

Therefore, in this campaign, the question is larger than a party question. It is an American question. It is a world question. Shall the American people continue their march toward the commercial supremacy of the world? Shall free institutions broaden their blessed reign as the children of liberty wax in strength, until the empire of our principles is established over the hearts of all mankind?

Have we no mission to perform, no duty to discharge to our fellowman? Has God endowed us with gifts beyond our deserts and marked us as the people of His peculiar favor, merely to rot in our own selfishness, as men and nations must, who take cowardice for their companion and self for their deity—as China has, as India has, as Egypt has?

Shall we be as the man who had one talent and hid it, or as he who had ten talents and used them until they grew to riches? And shall we reap the reward that waits on our discharge of our high duty; shall we occupy new markets for what our farmers raise, our factories make, our merchants sell—aye, and, please God, new markets for what our ships shall carry?

Hawaii is ours,[1] Porto Rico is to be ours; at the prayer of her people Cuba finally will be ours; in the islands of the East, even to the gates of Asia, coaling stations are to be ours at the very least; the flag of a liberal government is to float over the Philippines, and may it be the banner that Taylor unfurled in Texas and Fremont carried to the coast.

The Opposition tells us that we ought not to govern a people without their consent. I answer, The rule of liberty that all just

---

[1]The Hawaiian Islands, long under the sway of a few powerful American families, were annexed to the United States in 1898.

government derives its authority from the consent of the governed, applies only to those who are capable of self-government. We govern the Indians without their consent, we govern our territories without their consent, we govern our children without their consent. How do they know that our government would be without their consent? Would not the people of the Philippines prefer the just, human, civilizing government of this Republic to the savage, bloody rule of pillage and extortion from which we have rescued them?

And, regardless of this formula of words made only for enlightened, self-governing people, do we owe no duty to the world? Shall we turn these peoples back to the reeking hands from which we have taken them? Shall we abandon them, with Germany, England, Japan, hungering for them? Shall we save them from those nations, to give them a self-rule of tragedy? . . . Then, like men and not like children, let us on to our tasks, our mission, and our destiny.

There are so many real things to be done—canals to be dug, railways to be laid, forests to be felled, cities to be builded, fields to be tilled, markets to be won, ships to be launched, peoples to be saved, civilization to be proclaimed and the flag of liberty flung to the eager air of every sea. Is this an hour to waste upon triflers with nature's laws? Is this a season to give our destiny over to word-mongers and prosperity-wreckers? No! It is an hour to remember our duty to our homes. It is a moment to realize the opportunities fate has opened to us. And so it is an hour for us to stand by the Government.

Wonderfully has God guided us. Yonder at Bunker Hill and Yorktown His providence was above us. At New Orleans and on ensanguined seas His hand sustained us. Abraham Lincoln was His minister and His was the altar of freedom the Nation's soldiers set up on a hundred battle-fields. His power directed Dewey in the East[2] and delivered the Spanish fleet into our hands, as He delivered the elder Armada into the hands of our English sires two centuries ago. The American people can not use a dishonest medium of exchange; it is ours to set the world its example of right and honor. We can not fly from our world duties; it is ours to execute the purpose of a fate that has driven us to be greater than

---

[2]As commander of the Asiatic Squadron in 1898, George Dewey surprised and devastated the Spanish fleet in Manila harbor at the outbreak of the Spanish-American War. Although the nation's ardor was soon to fade, he was a hero in September 1898. In 1900 he was mentioned as a possibility for the Democratic presidential nomination.

our small intentions. We can not retreat from any soil where Providence has unfurled our banner; it is ours to save that soil for liberty and civilization.

✥ ✥ ✥

By the time Beveridge delivered "The March of the Flag," President McKinley had already decided to ask Congress to annex the Philippines (and Puerto Rico). A long and acrimonious debate followed, but a Republican sweep in the congressional elections of 1898, and McKinley's own reelection in 1900, sealed the bargain: the United States had now, as Beveridge had insisted, taken its place with the European powers and Japan as an imperialist nation.

Beveridge was elevated to the Senate by the Indiana legislature he helped elect in 1898. There, he continued to defend imperialism while, in matters of domestic policy, he was a flaming progressive. Beveridge mobilized the same rhapsodic, bumptious, evangelical rhetoric of the "Flag" speech on behalf of Theodore Roosevelt's antitrust prosecutions, the Pure Food and Drug Act, child labor laws, and the rhetorical campaign against government by special interests. The Indiana legislature reelected him to the Senate in 1904, but he was ousted in favor of a more conservative candidate in 1910.

His reform impulses hardly dampened, Beveridge bolted the Republican party in 1912 and helped to organize the Progressive, or "Bull Moose," party which designated Theodore Roosevelt—in the evangelical language of which the progressives were fond—to "stand at Armageddon and do battle for the Lord."

Some progressives were anti-imperialist. They regretted the American acquisition of colonies. But the same impulse that called for perfecting American institutions at home, for making government more just and democratic, was also reflected in the foreign policy of progressive leaders like Albert J. Beveridge and Theodore Roosevelt. Their very impulse toward reform, such progressives believed, proved the right and duty of the American people to spread their institutions throughout the world.

2

Elizabeth Cady Stanton and Jane Addams
❖ ❖ ❖

Woman Suffrage
1892, 1910

Seventy years of organized effort
elapsed between the time pioneer feminists first claimed the right to vote
at Seneca Falls, New York, in 1848, and eventual victory in 1920 when the
Nineteenth Amendment was ratified during the last months of Woodrow
Wilson's presidency. But only after 1890 did the movement begin to
snowball. In that year the National American Woman Suffrage Association
was organized, and through its efforts over the next thirty years the
amendment was skillfully guided through Congress. In the same year
Wyoming became the first state to adopt woman suffrage and was soon
joined by three other western states.

By the turn of the century the suffrage movement had become a
prominent part of the general ferment of reform that characterized the
progressive period. Politicians, understandably reluctant to see new,
unknown quantities introduced into the political game, dragged their feet.
But by 1910 the snowball had become an avalanche, and most statesmen
had scattered for cover. Every year thereafter brought new states, and
every election year new political converts, into the suffragists' camp: the
Progressive Party in 1912, the Republicans in 1916, and the Democrats in
1918, when President Wilson personally appeared before the Senate to
plead for passage of the amendment before the fall elections.

WOMAN SUFFRAGE   From Elizabeth Cady Stanton, "The Solitude of Self," *The Woman's Column*, January, 1892, pp. 2–3; Jane Addams, "Why Women Should Vote," *Ladies' Home Journal*, XXVII (January 1910), 21–22.

Because the Nineteenth Amendment enfranchised fully half of the American people, almost all of them the close relatives of the other half, it would be foolish to expect to find unanimity of purpose among either its supporters or its opponents. Even active feminists tended to pursue at least two very different lines of argument, coalescing only in their common support for a woman's right to vote.

Elizabeth Cady Stanton was, by the 1890s, one of the grand old women of the movement. An upper middle-class New Yorker, high-spirited and humorous, married at twenty-four, the mother of seven, Mrs. Stanton had spent her lifetime kicking against the traces of a domesticity that she found personally oppressive as well as theoretically unjust. One of the sponsors of the Seneca Falls meeting, her activities had run the gamut of women's rights. She had adopted the wearing of pantaloons from a neighbor, Amelia Bloomer, and condemned corsets. She advocated equal pay for women, birth control, divorce virtually upon demand, and, of course, the franchise as a basic human right. In 1890 she was elected first president of the Suffrage Association. Two years later, nearing eighty and scarcely able any longer to hoist her corpulent frame onto the platforms she had frequented for half a century, she relinquished the post. Her valedictory was the remarkable and moving address reprinted, in part, below. While it recalled the Emersonian ideals of Mrs. Stanton's youth, it was clearly even more indebted to her own experience of a long life perceived with exceptional intelligence and candor.

For Mrs. Stanton and many other women, suffrage was only one aspect of the most intimate transformation in American social history. It was a transformation in which women sought to redirect their own and men's expectations of each other for the sake of the improved well-being of women. Their efforts took many forms—some, like suffrage, were aimed at changes in public behavior; others, like the work of the Anti-Saloon League or efforts to support women's education, concentrated on social behavior.

Much of it took place in the privacy of the marriage bed. During the nineteenth century in the United States the average number of births per woman declined from seven to three, at least partially freeing women from the risks of frequent parturition and the burden of life-long infant care. Since few nineteenth-century couples had access to birth-control devices, this decline in fertility required the cooperation of husbands, as did the increasingly common efforts of women to find some occupational freedom for themselves. Viewed in this light, the clamor for the vote was one aspect of changing family relationships which some found liberating, others threatening, and few middle-class Americans entirely escaped.

Other progressive feminists were less concerned with asserting the equality of the sexes than they were with serving the specific interests of women, the great majority of whom were still wholly occupied by domestic tasks and exposed by an industrial civilization to a variety of new hazards. They therefore worked for special protective legislation for women and came to view the vote as a means by which women's domestic interests and experience could be brought to bear upon the formulation of public policy.

Jane Addams, more than a generation younger than Mrs. Stanton, was the best-known woman among progressive reformers. Her writings and her settlement-house work in Chicago's West Side eventually won her a Nobel prize in 1931. She was hailed as the most admired woman in America, the Mother Theresa of her day. Her essay, written in 1910, described some of the distinctive contributions she believed women voters could make in their special capacity as women.

Elizabeth Cady Stanton
The Solitude of Self

❀ The point I wish plainly to bring before you on this occasion is the individuality of each human soul; our Protestant idea, the right of individual conscience and judgment; our republican idea, individual citizenship. In discussing the rights of woman, we are to consider, first, what belongs to her as an individual, in a world of her own, the arbiter of her own destiny, an imaginary Robinson Crusoe, with her woman, Friday, on a solitary island. Her rights under such circumstances are to use all her faculties for her own safety and happiness. . . .

The strongest reason why we ask for woman a voice in the government under which she lives; in the religion she is asked to believe; equality in social life, where she is the chief factor; a place in the trades and professions, where she may earn her bread, is because of her birthright to self-sovereignty; because as an individual, she must rely on herself. No matter how much women prefer to lean, to be protected and supported, nor how much men desire to have them do so, they must make the voyage of life alone, and for safety in an emergency, they must know something of the laws of navigation. To guide our own craft, we must be captain, pilot, engineer. . . . It matters not whether the solitary voyager is man or woman; nature, having endowed them equally, leaves them to their own skill and judgment in the hour of danger, and, if not equal to the occasion, alike they perish.

To appreciate the importance of fitting every human soul for

independent action, think for a moment of the immeasurable solitude of self. We come into the world alone, unlike all who have gone
before us, we leave it alone, under circumstances peculiar to ourselves. . . . In youth our most bitter disappointments, our brightest
hopes and ambitions, are known only to ourselves. Even our friendship and love we never fully share with another; there is something
of every passion, in every situation, we conceal. Even so in our
triumphs and our defeats. . . . Alike amid the greatest triumphs
and darkest tragedies of life, we walk alone. On the divine heights
of human attainment, eulogized and worshipped as a hero or saint,
we stand alone. In ignorance, poverty and vice, as a pauper or
criminal, alone we starve or steal; alone we suffer the sneers and
rebuffs of our fellows. . . . In hours like these we realize the awful
solitude of individual life, its pains, its penalties, its responsibilities. . . . Seeing, then, that life must ever be a march and a battle,
that each soldier must be equipped for his own protection, it is the
height of cruelty to rob the individual of a single natural right. . . .

Inasmuch, then, as woman shares equally the joys and sorrows
of time and eternity, is it not the height of presumption in man to
propose to represent her at the ballot box and the throne of grace,
to do her voting in the state, her praying in the church, and to
assume the position of high priest at the family altar? . . . Whatever
the theories may be of woman's dependence on man, in the supreme moments of her life, he cannot bear her burdens. Alone she
goes to the gates of death to give life to every man that is born into
the world; no one can share her fears, no one can mitigate her
pangs; and if her sorrow is greater than she can bear, alone she
passes beyond the gates into the vast unknown. . . .

When all artificial trammels are removed, and women are recognized as individuals, responsible for their own environments,
thoroughly educated for all positions in life they may be called to
fill; with all the resources in themselves that liberal thought and
broad culture can give; guided by their own conscience and judgment, trained to self-protection, by a healthy development of the
muscular system, and skill in the use of weapons and defense; and
stimulated to self-support by a knowledge of the business world and
the pleasure that pecuniary independence must ever give; when
women are trained in this way, they will in a measure be fitted for
those hours of solitude that come alike to all, whether prepared or
otherwise. As in our extremity we must depend on ourselves, the
dictates of wisdom point to complete individual development. . . .

Women are already the equals of men in the whole realm of
thought, in art, science, literature and government. . . . The poetry

and novels of the century are theirs, and they have touched the keynote of reform, in religion, politics and social life. They fill the editor's and professor's chair, plead at the bar of justice, walk the wards of the hospital, speak from the pulpit and the platform. Such is the type of womanhood that an enlightened public sentiment welcomes today, and such the triumph of the facts of life over the false theories of the past. . . .

Whatever may be said of man's protecting power in ordinary conditions, amid all the terrible disasters by land and sea, in the supreme moments of danger, alone woman must ever meet the horrors of the situation. . . . In that solemn solitude of self, that links us with the immeasurable and the eternal, each soul lives alone forever. . . . There is a solitude which each and every one of us has always carried with him, more inaccessible than the ice-cold mountains, more profound than the midnight sea; the solitude of self. Our inner being which we call ourself. . . . Such is individual life. Who, I ask you, can take, dare take on himself the rights, the duties, the responsibilities of another human soul?

Jane Addams
Why Women Should Vote

For many generations it has been believed that woman's place is within the walls of her own home, and it is indeed impossible to imagine the time when her duty there shall be ended or to forecast any social change which shall release her from that paramount obligation.

This paper is an attempt to show that many women today are failing to discharge their duties to their own households properly simply because they do not perceive that as society grows more complicated it is necessary that woman shall extend her sense of responsibility to many things outside of her own home. . . . One could illustrate in many ways. A woman's simplest duty, one would say, is to keep her house clean and wholesome and to feed her children properly. Yet if she lives in a tenement house, as so many of my neighbors do, she cannot fulfill these simple obligations by her own efforts because she is utterly dependent upon the city administration for the conditions which render decent living possible. Her basement will not be dry, her stairways will not be fireproof, her house will not be provided with sufficient windows to give light and air, nor will it be equipped with sanitary plumbing, unless the Public Works Department sends inspectors who constantly insist that these elementary decencies be provided. . . . In a crowded city quarter, . . . if the street is not cleaned by the city authorities no amount of private sweeping will keep the tenement free from grime; if the garbage is not properly collected . . . a tenement-house mother may see her children sicken and die of diseases from which she alone is powerless to shield them. . . . She cannot even secure untainted meat for her household, . . . unless the meat has been inspected by city officials. . . . In short, if woman would keep on with her old business of caring for her house and rearing her children she will have to have some conscience in regard to public affairs lying quite outside of her immediate household. The individual conscience and devotion are no longer effective. . . .

The duty of a woman toward the schools which her children attend is so obvious that it is not necessary to dwell upon it, . . . and yet women have never been members of a Board of Education in sufficient numbers to influence largely actual school curriculi. If they had been, kindergartens, domestic science courses, and school playgrounds would be far more numerous than they are. . . .

One industry after another is slipping from the household into the factory. Ever since steam power has been applied to the processes of weaving and spinning woman's traditional work has been carried on largely outside of the home. . . . If woman's sense of obligation had enlarged as the industrial conditions changed she might naturally and almost imperceptibly have inaugurated the movements for social amelioration in the line of factory legislation and shop sanitation. That she has not done so is doubtless due to the fact that her conscience is slow to recognize any obligation outside of her own family circle. . . . It would be interesting to know how far the consciousness that she had no vote and could not change matters operated in this direction. . . . If conscientious women were convinced that it was a civic duty to be informed in regard to these grave industrial affairs, and then to express the conclusions which they had reached by depositing a piece of paper in a ballot-box, one cannot imagine that they would shirk simply because the action ran counter to old traditions. . . .

In a complex community like the modern city all points of

view need to be represented;[1] the resultants of diverse experiences need to be pooled if the community would make for sane and balanced progress. If it would meet fairly each problem as it arises, . . . it must not ignore the judgments of its entire adult population. To turn the administration of our civic affairs wholly over to men may mean that the American city will continue to push forward in its commercial and industrial development, and continue to lag behind in those things which make a city healthful and beautiful. After all, woman's traditional function has been to make her dwelling-place both clean and fair. Is that dreariness in city life, that lack of domesticity which the humblest farm dwelling presents, due to a withdrawal of one of the naturally coöperating forces? If women have in any sense been responsible for the gentler side of life which softens and blurs some of its harsher conditions, may they not have a duty to perform in our American cities?

In closing, may I recapitulate that if woman would fulfill her traditional responsibility to her own children; if she would educate and protect from danger factory children who must find their recreation on the street; if she would bring the cultural forces to bear upon our materialistic civilization; and if she would do it all with the dignity and directness fitting one who carries on her immemorial duties, then she must bring herself to the use of the ballot—that latest implement for self-government. May we not fairly say that American women need this implement in order to preserve the home?

❊ ❊ ❊

An exaggerated faith in the effectiveness of the popular ballot to shape public policy was a common failing of the progressive period. It would be hard to demonstrate that woman suffrage very greatly altered the course of American history after 1920, for better or worse. Doubling the size of the electorate did not change its behavior, and until the 1950s many fewer women than men even bothered to exercise their franchise. Thus the Nineteenth Amendment simply made available, to women who cared to claim it, the traditional perquisite of the free citizen.

---

[1]Several American philosophers contributed to a school of thought called "Pragmatism" which influenced many progressives, including Miss Addams. Pragmatists taught that truth was not single but plural—arrived at not by correct reasoning, such as a single mind could manage, but by a cooperative process involving everybody's ideas. It was a democratic creed which demanded that all points of view be included in any definition of the common good.

Thus, too, Jane Addams' prescriptions seem dated, in a way that Elizabeth Stanton's do not. In 1923 Alice Paul, in the spirit of Mrs. Stanton, raised the banner of another constitutional amendment—the Equal Rights Amendment, the potential effects of which were far more sweeping and complex than those of the Nineteenth. Consequently, it failed to command among women the same unanimity of support. Jane Addams was one of many former suffragists who opposed it, as did many, probably most, women leaders until the 1970s because of the minimal gains it offered and the threats it posed to protective legislation for working women. Despite the undeniable justice of its basic principle, the failure of the ERA to win ratification during the 1970s, when Congress at last sent it out to the states, indicates the extent to which many among the two-thirds of American women who are still primarily housewives continue to feel anxiety about the meaning for them of the individual liberation being won by others of their sex.

3

Theodore Roosevelt
❖ ❖ ❖

The New Nationalism
1910

Albert J. Beveridge and other
expansion minded progressives enthusiastically supported President
Theodore Roosevelt. Not only did the popular "TR" pursue the active,
interventionist foreign policy a "world power" should; in his boisterous
high-voltage personality he provided the electrifying leadership for which
progressives yearned and pursued policies under which big business
groaned and sometimes buckled.

By 1908, however, with the reform impulse still waxing, TR was
nearing the end of two full terms, in effect, as chief executive. With
reluctance, he announced his retirement, contenting himself with that fact
that he was the first President since Andrew Jackson powerful and popular
enough to name his successor—William Howard Taft.

Taft was a loyal aide, an able administrator, and a jovial clubman with
a better than average legal mind. The trouble was that public reform was in
search of a messiah and he was neither a reformer nor a public figure. Taft
had served Roosevelt in good conscience, and as President, he sanctioned
far more antitrust proceedings than his predecessor had. But Taft's soul-
fellows were not progressives with burning consciences and flaming eyes,
men like Beveridge and Robert M. LaFollette of Wisconsin and William E.
Borah of Idaho. Instead, he associated with old-time party regulars who
were given to phlegmatic lolling in leather chairs and smoking fine cigars
with friends highly placed in business and finance.

THE NEW NATIONALISM   From Ernest Hamlin, ed., *The New Nationalism* (New York:
The Outlook Company, 1910), pp. 1–18.

By 1910 Taft was the target of progressive attacks in Washington and throughout the country. When Roosevelt returned from a long trip abroad, he kept his distance from the man he had put in the White House. At his home at Oyster Bay, Long Island, TR received one anti-Taft progressive Republican after another, each adding to the list of the President's sins against reform. On August 31, 1910, without once mentioning Taft by name or even clear allusion, Roosevelt nevertheless broke with him. At Osawatomie, Kansas, TR outlined a philosophy of government for the 20th century that he called "The New Nationalism."

Roosevelt had voiced the sentiments expressed in the Osawatomie speech for more than ten years. Indeed, the Liberal Republicans of the nineteenth century would not have taken exception to his call for a government that was uncorrupted by the demands of the special interests, the great corporate conglomerations of economic power. Where Roosevelt departed from them, from the Taft administration, from many of his own earlier policies, and from the progressivism of Louis Brandeis and Woodrow Wilson of the Democratic party, was in calling not for less government of all kinds but for a central government that would oversee and regulate national economic life in the public interest. Instead of calling for the break-up of massive corporations, Roosevelt acknowledged the inevitability and advantages of big, even oligopolistic, business combinations. The point was to make the most of these advantages by subordinating the corporations to the common good.

Historians disagree about the extent of Roosevelt's debt to journalist and political philosopher Herbert Croly. In 1909 Croly had published a book, *The Promise of American Life*, in which he had urged progressive reformers to abandon the old principle of trust-busting. Instead, he promoted "Jeffersonian ends," the interests of democracy and the welfare of the people (as opposed to special interests), by using "Hamiltonian means," a large, powerful, activist government. Whether or not TR "stole" ideas from Croly—there is no mention of the writer in the Osawatomie speech—there is no doubt that Croly's philosophy suited TR's temperament very well.

❀ Every special interest is entitled to justice—full, fair, and complete. . . . If there were any attempt by mob violence to plunder and work harm to the special interest, whatever it may be, that I most dislike, and the wealthy man, whomsoever he may be, for whom I have the greatest contempt, I would fight for him, and you would if you were worth your salt. He should have justice. For every special interest is entitled to justice, but not one is entitled to a vote in Congress, to a voice on the bench, or to representation in any public office. The Constitution guarantees protection to property, and we must make that promise good. But it does not give the right of suffrage to any corporation.

The true friend of property, the true conservative, is he who insists that property shall be the servant and not the master of the commonwealth; who insists that the creature of man's making shall be the servant and not the master of the man who made it. The citizens of the United States must effectively control the mighty commercial forces which they have themselves called into being.

There can be no effective control of corporations while their political activity remains. To put an end to it will be neither a short nor an easy task, but it can be done.

We must have complete and effective publicity of corporate affairs, so that the people may know beyond peradventure whether the corporations obey the law and whether their management entitles them to the confidence of the public. It is necessary that laws should be passed to prohibit the use of corporate funds directly or indirectly for political purposes; it is still more necessary that such laws should be thoroughly enforced. Corporate expenditures for political purposes, and especially such expenditures by public service corporations, have supplied one of the principal sources of corruption in our political affairs.

It has become entirely clear that we must have government supervison of the capitalization, not only of public service corporations, including, particularly, railways, but of all corporations doing an interstate business. I do not wish to see the nation forced into the ownership of the railways if it can possibly be avoided, and the only alternative is thoroughgoing and effective regulation, which shall be based on a full knowledge of all the facts. . . .

I believe that the officers, and, especially, the directors, of corporations should be held personally responsible when any corporation breaks the law.

Combinations in industry are the result of an imperative economic law which cannot be repealed by political legislation. The effort at prohibiting all combination has substantially failed. The way out lies, not in attempting to prevent such combinations, but in completely controlling them in the interest of the public welfare. For that purpose the Federal Bureau of Corporations[1] is an agency of first importance. Its powers, and, therefore, its efficiency, as well

---

[1]The Federal Bureau of Corporations was established during Roosevelt's presidency as a "watchdog" commission. It was merged into the Federal Trade Commission in 1914.

as that of the Interstate Commerce Commission,[2] should be largely increased. We have a right to expect from the Bureau of Corporations and from the Interstate Commerce Commission a very high grade of public service. We should be as sure of the proper conduct of the interstate railways and the proper management of interstate business as we are now sure of the conduct and management of the national banks, and we should have as effective supervision in one case as in the other. . . .

Nothing is more true than that excess of every kind is followed by reaction; a fact which should be pondered by reformer and reactionary alike. We are face to face with new conceptions of the relations of property to human welfare, chiefly because certain advocates of the rights of property as against the rights of men have been pushing their claims too far. The man who wrongly holds that every human right is secondary to his profit must now give way to the advocate of human welfare, who rightly maintains that every man holds his property subject to the general right of the community to regulate its use to whatever degree the public welfare may require it. . . .

I do not ask for overcentralization; but I do ask that we work in a spirit of broad and far-reaching nationalism when we work for what concerns our people as a whole. We are all Americans. Our common interests are as broad as the continent. I speak to you here in Kansas exactly as I would speak in New York or Georgia, for the most vital problems are those which affect us all alike. The national government belongs to the whole American people, and where the whole American people are interested, that interest can be guarded effectively only by the national government. The betterment which we seek must be accomplished, I believe, mainly through the national government.

The American people are right in demanding that New Nationalism, without which we cannot hope to deal with new problems. The New Nationalism puts the national need before sectional or personal advantage. It is impatient of the utter confusion that results from local legislatures attempting to treat national issues as local issues. It is still more impatient of the impotence which springs from overdivision of governmental powers, the impotence which makes it possible for local selfishness or for legal cunning, hired by wealthy special interests, to bring national activities to a deadlock.

---

[2]The Interstate Commerce Commission, established in 1887 to regulate interstate trade after the Wabash Case (see Part 1), continues in this role with considerably augmented powers today.

This New Nationalism regards the executive power as the steward of the public welfare. It demands of the judiciary that it shall be interested primarily in human welfare rather than in property, just as it demands that the representative body shall represent all the people rather than any one class or section of the people.

❖ ❖ ❖

Roosevelt's indirect criticism of the administration soon became a frontal assault as Republican progressives "convinced" the former President to battle Taft for the 1912 Republican nomination. Within the party, TR had no chance. As the incumbent, Taft controlled the patronage, including a large bloc of voting delegates from the southern states (which almost never elected Republicans to office). This, plus the support of the conservative old guard of the North and West, allowed him to walk away with the prize.

A meager prize it was. The reformers bolted the Republican party and, at Albany, formed the Progressive party, nominating TR for President with Hiram Johnson of California as his running mate. Recalling a statement Roosevelt had made as Republican vice-presidential nominee in 1900—"I'm as fit as a bull moose"—the Progressives had a mascot to contend with the Democratic donkey and the Republican elephant. Thus, to all appearances, they were a permanent major party. But for 1912, as both Roosevelt and Taft surely knew, the Republican split ensured the election of the Democratic candidate Woodrow Wilson, then governor of New Jersey.

Nevertheless, the "Bull Moosers" ran a campaign as spirited as that of Bryan's in 1896. Notwithstanding a gloss of middle-class propriety such as had been beyond Bryan, the Progressives were as excited—almost delirious—with their vision of a reordered 20th century America as had been the Populists and "hayseeds" of 1896. But the results were inevitable. Roosevelt outpolled Taft in the popular vote, apparently justifying Progressive dreams of their party's future, and buried him in the electoral college 88–8. But with only 42 percent of the popular vote, Woodrow Wilson became President. The immediate future of reform lay in his and the Democratic party's hands.

The Progressive party did not even last four years. They were "all dressed up" for TR in 1916, William Allen White wrote, but Roosevelt declined to run and left them "nowhere to go." Actually, many Bull Moosers joined Woodrow Wilson's administration, further strengthening the reform wing within the Democratic party. Others returned to the Republican standard, but only after some years had passed. Still others, like Hiram Johnson, returned right away but full of bitterness toward the reactionaries among their copartisans.

In 1920, Johnson scornfully turned down an invitation to bring

unity to the Republican party by running for vice-president on a ticket
led by the conservative party hack Warren G. Harding. He might have
followed the example his hero, Theodore Roosevelt, had set in 1900
when he agreed to be running mate with another conservative, William
McKinley. Like McKinley, Harding died in office. Instead of elevating
Hiram Johnson to the presidency, however, the event put Calvin Coolidge,
the epitome of the accommodating and unimaginative professional
politician, the antithesis of TR and Johnson, into the White House. Never
again would the impassioned and constructive reform spirit of 1912
inform the Grand Old Party. The most significant consequence for
the Republican party of the revolt of the Progressives and their New
Nationalism was to ensure that the Grand Old Party remained under
the control of its conservatives.

4

Louis D. Brandeis

❖ ❖ ❖

The Curse of Bigness
1913

"*P*eople of the same trade," Adam
Smith remarked, "seldom meet together, even for merriment and
diversion, but the conversation ends in a conspiracy against the public,
or in some contrivance to raise prices." The father of the free market thus
identified one of its principal contradictions. The competitor who delights
in gaining at the expense of his rivals also fears being driven to the wall by
them, and the same self-interest which encourages him to compete for
success also encourages him to combine against failure. The ubiquity
of trade associations, mergers, and other monopolistic devices in the
American economy by the end of the nineteenth century evidenced the
fact that in economics the profit motive not only encourages producers to
risk their necks, it also inspires among them the equally healthy desire to
save their skins.

There is another contradiction. If cutthroat competition injures the
producer, and restraints on competition afford him security, where does
the public interest lie? Simple price theory indicates that the public is
injured by monopolies which not only soak the public for the goods they
purchase, but, by leaving them less able to buy other things, also distort the
efficiency of the whole economy. (Economists call this allocative efficiency.)
On the other hand, big businesses, because of economies of scale, superior
technical resources, and better business organization, are often able to
produce more efficiently than a welter of small competitors (productive

THE CURSE OF BIGNESS   From Louis Brandeis, "Competition," *American Legal News*,
XLIV (January 1913), 5–14.

efficiency). Hence the public may benefit from an abundance of cheap goods despite a dearth of competition.

So finally what does competition mean? Does it mean a rabble of independent firms, even if they are all producing relatively inefficiently? Or does it mean the most efficient production possible in the market, even if only a few giant firms are able to accomplish it? Is competition a matter of structure or of conduct?

None of these are easy questions to answer because in each case both arguments are valid and every direction points to some real danger.

The nation's first antitrust legislation, the Sherman Act of 1890, proposed a simple standard, which thereby left everyone dissatisfied. Congress had in mind only the prohibition of practices which artificially increased prices. The Sherman Act was a consumer welfare measure both in intent and as the courts subsequently interpreted it. Therefore even monopolistic business combinations which could demonstrate superior productive efficiency (and most could) were largely beyond the reach of the act, a fact affirmed in the Supreme Court's "rule of reason" in 1911. It should have surprised no one, therefore, that of the approximately two hundred suits filed by the Justice Department under the Sherman Act before 1914, most concerned price-fixing agreements among *small* businessmen, some were filed against labor unions, and only a handful were entered against any of the giant "trusts."

Antitrust discontent peaked during the first dozen years of the twentieth century. Muckraking journalists paraded the dirt of the nation's boardrooms through the very streets. President Roosevelt responded with a few well-chosen, headline-grabbing prosecutions; his successor filed many more. Everybody agreed that something better than the Sherman Act was needed, but there was no agreement on what it should be.

Critics of the trusts proposed to re-arm the Sherman Act with harsher penalties, swifter enforcement, and an aim at higher targets. For every plea to tighten loopholes in the law, however, there were others, equally insistent, to relax some of them. Organized labor demanded complete exemption from antitrust prosecution even though higher wages necessarily meant higher consumer prices. Small businessmen, battered by the titans, clamored for recognition of their trade associations—always easy targets for antitrust prosecutors and another source of higher prices. Big businessmen, confident that the public benefited from their productive efficiency, were nonetheless fearful of popular hostility and perturbed by the uncertainties and delays of occasional antitrust litigation. Many of them advocated junking the Sherman Act altogether and replacing it with a regulatory agency to which businessmen could apply beforehand for advice and permission, thus circumventing the courts.

By 1912 this solution had attracted the influential support of several economists, leading intellectuals, and Theodore Roosevelt. To veteran opponents of the trusts, however, it seemed to threaten to equip monopoly with the government's stamp of approval. Meanwhile, as the journalist Ray Stannard Baker worried, "The unorganized public, where will it come in?

The professional man, . . . the farmer, the salaried government employee, and all the host of men who are not engaged in the actual production or delivery of necessary material things, how will they fare?"

Woodrow Wilson's legislative achievements have been equalled by only a few other American presidents. His deft control of Congress, and the public's enthusiasm for reform by 1912, enabled him to win legislation enacting much of the progressive program. Antitrust he wisely left until last, and if his approach to this question seemed sometimes vague and inconsistent, the fact only reflected the inherent difficulty of the problem. The President at least was no more bewildered than anybody else.

The Clayton Antitrust Act and the companion Federal Trade Commission which Congress produced in 1914 were, inevitably, compromises. The Clayton measure, for example, did not wholly exempt organized labor from antitrust prosecution, but it provided that labor unions and strikes were not *per se* restraints on trade, permitting Samuel Gompers to hail it as labor's "Magna Carta." Similarly the FTC gave big business the executive agency it requested, but Wilson avoided arming it with authority to issue prior advice. Instead it was to be mostly a "sunshine" commission, charged with clarifying, as occasion demanded, matters left deliberately vague in the statutes.

The most important feature of the 1914 legislation, however, was that it significantly broadened the goals of antitrust law in the United States, shifting them away from the Sherman Act's exclusive preoccupation with the standard of consumer welfare. If the Sherman Act can be called a consumers' measure, the Clayton Act may be called a producers' measure. While the Sherman Act implicitly endorsed any competitive behavior that had the effect of driving prices down, the Clayton Act proscribed certain competitive practices deemed "unfair" to producers (such as local price-cutting), and thus it sought to shield small businessmen in particular from the ravages of unchecked competition. The Sherman Act had attempted to enforce competitive behavior across the board, even if it promoted big business. The Clayton Act sought to preserve the competitive structure of the economy by restraining competitive conduct. For the consumer the Sherman law remained on the books. But the survival of the small businessman, even at some cost in productive efficiency, was advanced to equal importance as a goal of antitrust law under the Clayton Act.

"The little fellow" was especially dear to Wilson. "What this country needs above everything else," he said in the 1912 campaign, "is a body of laws which will look after the men who are on the make, rather than the men who are already made." Wilson found a sympathetic counselor in Louis Brandeis, a brilliant Boston attorney passionately devoted to the interests of the small businessmen he usually represented before the bar. Together, he and Wilson fashioned the antitrust aspects of the New Freedom. Wilson's critics were right when they labeled it a "Jeffersonian revival." Wilson and Brandeis hoped, by regulating competition, to preserve among the businessmen of the nation a sturdy, independent yeomanry.

❀ Practically all Americans agree there is a trust problem; but upon every matter relating to the problem there is the greatest diversity of opinion. . . .

Some men who believe in competition think we have adequate governmental machinery now to secure competition, and all that is necessary is to enforce the Sherman law as it stands. Other men who believe in competition think we lack governmental machinery necessary to secure and maintain it, and that appropriate machinery should be devised and adopted for regulating competition. Likewise, some men who believe that private monopoly should be permissible think that the public will be best served if we simply repeal the Sherman law and let business take care of itself. Other men who believe in private monopoly think that we should devise and introduce new governmental machinery by which monopoly would be regulated. . . .

In saying that the New Party[1] stands for monopoly I do not mean that it wants to introduce monopoly generally in private industry, but merely that it accepts private monopoly as permissible, and the trusts as in themselves unobjectionable, requiring only that they be "good." It is prepared to protect existing trusts from dismemberment, if only they will be "good" hereafter, thus leaving them in the possession of the huge profits obtained through violations of law. But once we treat monopoly as permissible, we have given away the whole case of competition, for monopoly is the path of least effort in business, and is sure to be pursued, if opened.

On the other hand those who stand for competition do not advocate what has been frequently described as "unrestricted" or "destructive" competition. They demand a regulated competition or, if one may adopt the phrase, competition which is "good."

Regulation is essential to the preservation of competition and to its best development just as regulation is necessary to the preservation and development of civil or political liberty. To preserve civil and political liberty to the many we have found it necessary to restrict the liberty of the few. Unlicensed liberty leads necessarily to despotism or oligarchy. Those who are stronger must to some extent be curbed. We curb the physically strong in order to protect those physically weaker. . . .

The right of competition must be similarly limited; for ex-

---

[1]Theodore Roosevelt's Progressive party, organized in 1912. (See "The New Nationalism" by Theodore Roosevelt.)

cesses of competition lead to monopoly just as excesses of liberty have led to despotism. It is another case where the extremes meet. What are those excesses of competition which should be prevented because they lead to monopoly? The answer to that question should be sought—not in theorizing, but in the abundant experiences of the last twenty-five years, during which the trusts have been developed. We have but to study the facts and ascertain:

"How did monopoly, wherever it obtained foothold, acquire its position?"

And we can, in the first place, give the comprehensive answer, which should relieve the doubts and fears of many: no monopoly in private industry in America has yet been attained by efficiency alone. No business has been so superior to its competitors in the processes of manufacture or of distribution as to enable it to control the market solely by reason of its superiority. There is nothing in our industrial history to indicate that there is any need whatever to limit the natural growth of a business in order to preserve competition. We may emphatically declare: "Give fair play to efficiency."

One has heard of late the phrases: "You can't make people compete by law." "Artificial competition is undesirable." These are truisms, but their implication is false. Believers in competition make no suggestion that traders be compelled to compete. They ask merely that no trader should be allowed to kill competition. Competition consists in trying to do things better than someone else; that is, making or selling a better article, or the same article at a lesser cost, or otherwise giving better service. It is not competition to resort to methods of the prize ring, and simply "knock the other man out." That is killing a competitor. . . .

Earnest argument is constantly made in support of monopoly by pointing to the wastefulness of competition. Undoubtedly competition involves some waste. What human activity does not? The wastes of democracy are among the greatest obvious wastes, but we have compensations in democracy which far outweigh that waste and make it more efficient than absolutism. So it is with competition. Incentive and development which are incident to the former system of business result in so much achievement that the accompanying waste is relatively insignificant. The margin between that which men naturally do and which they can do is so great that a system which urges men on to action, enterprise, and initiative is preferable in spite of the wastes that necessarily attend that process. I say, "necessarily" because there have been and are today wastes incidental to competition that are unnecessary. Those are the wastes which attend that competition which do not develop, but kill. Those wastes the law can and should eliminate. It may do so by regulating competition. . . .

But the efficiency of monopolies, even if established, would not justify their existence unless the community should reap benefit from the efficiency; experience teaches us that whenever trusts have developed efficiency, their fruits have been absorbed almost wholly by the trusts themselves. From such efficiency as they have developed the community has gained substantially nothing. . . .

Diagnosis shows monopoly to be an artificial, not a natural, product. Competition, therefore, may be preserved by preventing that course of conduct by which in the past monopolies have been established. If we had in the past undertaken by appropriate legal and administrative machinery to prevent our financiers and others from carrying out agreements to form monopolies; if we had seriously attempted to prevent those methods of destructive or unfair competition, as are manifest in "cut-throat competition"—discrimination against customers who will not deal exclusively with the combination; if we had made any persistent, intelligent effort to stop advantages gained by railroad discrimination, espionage, or the practice of establishing "fake independents," or to stop those who have secured control of essential raw material from denying business rivals access to it—few of the trusts, of which we now complain, would have come into existence, or would, at all events, have acquired power to control the market. We made no serious attempt to stop monopoly—certainly no intelligent attempt; partly because we lacked knowledge, partly because we lacked desire; for we had a sneaking feeling that perhaps, after all, a private monopoly might be a good thing, and we had no adequate governmental machinery to employ for this purpose. But in the past twenty-two years we have acquired much experience with trusts. We know their ways. We have learned what the defects in the existing machinery are; and if we will but remedy those defects by appropriate legal and administrative machinery—somewhat on the lines proposed in the La Follette–Stanley and Newlands bills[2]—and supplement the prohibition of monopoly by the regulation of competition, we shall be able, not only to preserve the competition we now enjoy, but grad-

[2]Brandeis had helped to draft the La Follette bill; Senator Newlands' bill was one of the first to propose an "Interstate Trade Commission." These were two of several measures introduced into the legislative hopper before 1914 from which the Clayton and FTC acts eventually emerged.

ually regain the free soil upon which private monopoly has encroached, and we may be assured that, despite all industrial changes, the day for industrial liberty has not yet passed.

❖ ❖ ❖

Popular antitrust sentiment disappeared in the United States after 1914 making it, in the words of one historian, "one of the faded passions of American reform." Not so the antitrust machinery enacted during the progressive period, which still employs batteries of legal specialists whose present institutional clout makes comic the five lawyers and four stenographers available to Theodore Roosevelt. In fact each decade since World War II has witnessed a larger number of antitrust prosecutions than were filed during the whole first fifty years of the Sherman Act.

Until the 1970s the small-business bias written into antitrust law by Wilson and Brandeis also persisted. It was strengthened by court decisions (Brandeis himself contributed to some of these after Wilson appointed him to the Supreme Court in 1916) and by subsequent legislation, including the Robinson-Patman Act of 1936 and the Celler-Kefauver Act of 1950. Robinson-Patman prosecutions, which were for many years the bread and butter of the FTC, provided a classic example of the conflict between consumer interests and the interests of small businessmen since they aimed to halt price cutting by large chain stores in order to protect independent (and expensive) small retailers.

Brandeis always swept aside such conflicts, sometimes denying (erroneously) that big business had any superior efficiency, at other times stubbornly insisting that the preservation of a "democracy of business" was worth the added cost. So contemptuous of consumer values himself that he refused to use either telephones or typewriters, Brandeis once flatly denied that the FTC had any responsibility to the consumer at all. Instead, he and Wilson hoped that its protection of small businessmen would permit them to give the monopolists a run for their money. They were wrong.

Business historians now teach us that antitrust law has had little effect on the structure of American business. Industries capable of economies of scale have consolidated anyway. Small-scale business persists only in other industries where such economies are not possible. Big businessmen and small businessmen do not ordinarily compete against each other at all. Wilson and Brandeis were all along flogging a dead horse.

Nor did they foresee another change in American society equally fatal to their program. In their day starting up in business was still the best way for individuals to rise in the world. Since World War II millions of Americans have discovered instead that education and employment by a

giant corporation or public agency offers a better opportunity for middle-
or lower-class mobility than the old system of entrepreneurship ever did.
As long ago as 1949 a survey of college seniors disclosed that most of them
wanted to work for somebody else–preferably a big company.

As the public's interest in small business has declined, its interest in
consumer issues has increased, with predictable consequences for antitrust
law. During the 1960s several well-publicized consumer-interest groups
appeared including Ralph Nader's "Raiders." In 1969 Nader wrote a
scathing attack on the FTC for having sacrificed the interests of
consumers to those of producers. In response the FTC changed course.
During the 1970s the Robinson-Patman type of prosecution virtually
disappeared, replaced by a host of consumer-safety edicts.

The consumerism of the 1970s has also played into the hands of
the "deregulators" of the 1980s. With the sympathetic ear of the Reagan
White House, free-trade advocates argue that the ultimate interest of
consumers is best served by business efficiency which regulation only
hinders. Several of them propose a return to the simple standard of the
Sherman Act. But if any part of the Brandeis legacy is still pertinent, it is
that the public interest includes more than only productive efficiency.
While antitrust law and regulation may have proved powerless to alter
the structure of American business, their historic impact upon business
conduct has been undeniable. Few consumers would welcome the
reappearance of the snake-oil salesmen who once freely roamed the
American marketplace. Because the public interest has never been easy
to identify does not mean that it does not exist, or that the free market
can find it unassisted.

5

Woodrow Wilson

❖ ❖ ❖

The League of Nations
1919

*A*t no time in our history (except, perhaps, just at the end of World War II) was the United States more honored in the world, more widely regarded as the champion of mankind's best hopes, than in December 1918 when President Woodrow Wilson arrived in Paris en route to the peace conference at Versailles which ended World War I. As the President's carriage rolled through the boulevards, great banners proclaimed "Welcome to Wilson," and "Honor to Wilson the Just," as tens of thousands of cheering Parisians voiced the extent to which the American president had become the focus of the hopes and fears of millions.

Fifteen months later "Wilson the Just" lay a broken man, the peace he had fashioned at Versailles repudiated by his own people. The failure of a distracted American democracy to recognize its responsibilities as the world's richest and most powerful nation constitutes one of history's most tragically bungled opportunities.

During the years at the turn of the century when the United States first emerged as a world power, there were sharp disagreements, even among those who thought of themselves as progressives, about America's global role. Some American progressives, especially in the Midwest, were isolationists: they reviled the rest of the world as hopelessly reactionary and disclaimed any responsibility for it. Denizens of the prairies, it mattered little to them if the ancient centers of western culture and Christianity went

THE LEAGUE OF NATIONS   From Woodrow Wilson, "Addresses Delivered on Western Tour," Ray Stannard Baker and William E. Dodd, eds., *The Public Papers of Woodrow Wilson: War and Peace* (New York: Harper, 1927), I, 590–645; II, 1–416.

smash, so long as they could thump their Bibles in ugly board churches
and the sun shone in Main Street. They opposed America's entry into
World War I, and they opposed the treaty which ended it.

A second group of progressives, of whom Theodore Roosevelt was
the foremost example, were imperialists who viewed international relations
as a Darwinian struggle for survival and advocated an America guided by
her own self-interest and armed to the teeth. William Howard Taft, who
knew Roosevelt well, said of him, "He loves war. He thinks it is essential to
develop the highest traits in manhood, and he believes in forcible rather
than peaceful methods." Roosevelt and close associates such as Henry
Cabot Lodge and Oliver Wendell Holmes were patricians, who sometimes
supported progressive antibusiness reforms, less out of sympathy for the
people who were oppressed than out of snobbish disdain for the money-
grubbers who oppressed them. Likewise, they exalted military valor as an
alternative to the vulgar materialism they found so offensive in Gilded-
Age America.

Roosevelt would have given his eye teeth to have been a wartime
President. It was America's good fortune that the role came instead to a
calmer and more thoughtful progressive, Woodrow Wilson, who early in
his presidency unveiled a third variant of the Progressives' response to the
world. Wilson deeply distrusted militarism. Besides being dangerous and
self-defeating in the long run, he recognized its reactionary character. In
his apology to Colombia for Roosevelt's shameless seizure of the Panama
Canal Zone in 1903, and in his refusal to intervene to arrest the course of
a great revolution in Mexico, despite enormous pressures from American
business interests, the Catholic church, and Republican critics, Wilson
evinced a moral sense and an awareness of the forces of history that few
of his enemies approached.

Then, during his second term, the world collapsed. The war which,
for a generation, everyone had feared, none had wanted, and all had
prepared for broke out in Eastern Europe. When it ended four years later,
the Europe Americans had always known had vanished. Germany lay
defeated. France and England, nominally the victors, were impoverished.
All of Central and Eastern Europe was in chaos, its archaic régimes—the
Kaiser's, the Tsar's, and the Hapsburg Emperor's—having collapsed
under the strain of the war. Already the *bolsheviki* had seized control in
Moscow and Petrograd.

Wilson's response to the European catastrophe was measured—a
search for ways in which the United States might best use its influence to
halt the carnage and secure a constructive peace. For nearly three years
he kept the United States neutral, while Roosevelt and other Republicans
spoiled for the fight. (Roosevelt, in his rage, called Wilson "yellow.") For
a long while he succeeded in forcing Germany to moderate its use of
submarine warfare. In 1915 and again in 1916 he seemed to be making
progress toward getting the belligerents to the negotiating table. Early in
1917 he called for a "peace without victory," convinced that only a peace
between equals, not one dictated by victors to the vanquished, could be
just and enduring. (This time Roosevelt called him a "tory" and a

"copperhead.") Only when German victory threatened to impose upon
Europe the least acceptable peace of all did Wilson reluctantly lead his
nation into the war. When the tide turned against the Germans in 1918, he
issued his Fourteen Points, a proposal offering a nonpunitive peace and a
settlement in Europe on the basis of national independence rather than
division of the spoils. Now it was the Allies, scenting victory, who balked.
Wilson opened negotiations with the Germans over their heads (and over
the protests of the outraged Roosevelt and General Pershing, both of
whom wished to annihilate the "Hun"). In November 1918, the Germans
accepted an armistice on the terms of the Fourteen Points, and peace came
at last to a weary Europe.

Wilson arrived at Versailles convinced that the old system of hostile
alliances which had dragged each of the nations of Europe willy-nilly into
the war was practically and morally bankrupt. Instead he proposed a
system of collective security—a League of Nations—with machinery for
collective defense and the negotiation of differences between nations short
of war. In Eastern Europe he insisted on independence for the multitude
of minor nationalities previously part of some stronger neighbor's empire.
Arranging all this was not easy. Wilson was virtually the only statesman
among the great powers at Versailles not pledged to serve some selfish
national interest. Nevertheless, he threw himself into the conference with
a characteristic sense of duty. It was said that Clemenceau of France fell
asleep when the discussion did not concern France's interests, and Lloyd-
George of Britain once interrupted to ask, "Is it Upper or Lower Silesia
that we are giving away?" But Wilson could be found until the small hours
of the morning in his suite on his hands and knees poring over the maps
he had spread upon the floor. Five exhausting months later he had his
treaty, including the League of Nations, and once back in Washington he
presented it to the Senate. The League, he told the Senators, was the only
hope for mankind. "Shall we or any other free people hesitate to accept this
great duty? Dare we reject it and break the heart of the world?"

When the Senate failed to act, Wilson determined to appeal directly
to the American people, just as he had appealed to the hopes of the people
of Europe over the heads of their governments. In September he set out on
a nationwide speaking tour. Driving himself beyond endurance, he spoke
forty times in three weeks. Each speech was different, as the President sat
up nights aboard his train banging out notes to himself on his portable
typewriter. The following selections are taken from several of them.

❧ I have not come here to make a speech in the ordinary
sense of that term. I have come upon a very sober errand indeed. I
have come to report to you upon the work which the representatives

of the United States attempted to do at the conference of peace on the other side of the sea, because, my fellow citizens, I realize that my colleagues and I in the task we attempted over there were your servants. We went there upon a distinct errand, which it was our duty to perform in the spirit which you had displayed in the prosecution of the war and in conserving the purposes and objects of that war. . . . It is very important, my fellow citizens, that we should not forget what this war meant. I am amazed at the indications that we are forgetting what we went through. . . . I venture to think that there are thousands of mothers and fathers and wives and sisters and sweethearts in this country who are never going to forget. Thousands of our gallant youth lie buried in France, and buried for what? For the redemption of America? America was not directly attacked. For the salvation of America? America was not immediately in danger. No; for the salvation of mankind. It is the noblest errand that troops ever went on. . . . I feel that there is a certain sense in which I am rendering my account to the soldiers and sailors whose Commander in Chief I have been, for I sent them across the sea believing that their errand was not only to defeat Germany, but also to redeem the world from the danger to which Germany had exposed it, to make the world a place in which arbitration, discussion, the processes of peace, the processes of justice should supplant the brutal processes of war. I came back from the other side proud that I was bringing with me a document which contained a great constructive plan to accomplish that very thing. . . .

If I were to state what seems to me the central idea of this treaty, it would be this: It is almost a discovery in international conventions that nations do not consist of their governments but consist of their people. That is a rudimentary idea. It seems to us in America to go without saying, but, my fellow citizens, it was never the leading idea in any other international congress that I ever heard of. . . . They were always thinking of national policy, of national advantage, of the rivalries of trade, of the advantages of territorial conquest. There is nothing of that in this treaty. . . . The treaty begins with the Covenant of the League of Nations, which is intended to operate as a partnership, a permanent partnership, of the great and free self-governing peoples of the world to stand sponsor for the right and for civilization. . . . This is the first treaty ever framed by such an international convention, whose object was not to serve and defend governments but to serve and defend peoples. This is the first people's treaty in the history of international dealings. Every member of that great convention of peace was poignantly aware that at last the people of the world were awake, that at last the people of the world were aware of what wrong had been wrought by irresponsible and autocratic governments, that at last all the peoples of the world had seen the vision of liberty, had seen the majesty of justice, had seen the doors thrown open to the aspirations of men and women and the fortunes of children everywhere, and they did not dare assume that they were the masters of the fortunes of any people, but knew that in every settlement they must act as the servants not only of their own people but of the people who were waiting to be liberated, the people who could not win their own liberty, the people who had suffered for centuries together the intolerable wrongs of misgovernment. . . .

The heart and center of this treaty is that it sets at liberty people all over Europe and in Asia who had hitherto been enslaved by powers which were not their rightful sovereigns and masters. . . . We in America have stood from the day of our birth for the emancipation of people throughout the world who were living unwillingly under governments which were not of their own choice. The thing which we have held more sacred than any other is that all just government rests upon the consent of the governed, and all over the world that principle has been disregarded, that principle has been flouted by the strong, and only the weak have suffered. The heart and center of this treaty is the principle . . . that every great territory in the world belongs to the people who are living on it, and that it is not the privilege of any authority anywhere . . . to impose upon those peoples any government which they accept unwillingly and not of their own choice. . . . The characteristic of this treaty is that it gives liberty to peoples who never could have won it for themselves. By giving that liberty, it limits the ambitions and defeats the hopes of all the imperialistic governments in the world. Governments which had theretofore been considered to desire dominion, here in this document forswore dominion. . . . It is astonishing that this great document did not come as a shock upon the world. If the world had not already been rent by the great struggle which preceded this settlement, men would have stood at amaze at such a document as this; but there is a subtle consciousness throughout the world now that this is an end of governing people who do not desire the government that is over them. . . .

But the thing does not end there, because the treaty includes the Covenant of the League of Nations, and what does that say? That says that it is the privilege of any member state to call attention to anything, anywhere, that is likely to disturb the peace of the world or the good understanding between nations upon which the peace of the world depends, and every people in the world that has not got what it thinks it ought to have is thereby given a world forum in which to bring the thing to the bar of mankind. An incomparable thing, a thing that never was dreamed of before! . . . There never before has been provided a world forum in which the legitimate grievances of peoples entitled to consideration can be brought to the common judgment of mankind. . . . That compulsion is the most tremendous moral compulsion that could be devised by organized mankind. . . .

I hear some gentlemen, who are themselves incapable of altruistic purposes, say: "Ah, but that is altruistic. It is not our business to take care of the weak nations of the world." No, but it is our business to prevent war, and if we do not take care of the weak nations of the world, there will be war. . . . The peace of the world is everybody's business. Yet this is the first document that ever recognized that principle. We now have the attitude of the Irishman, you know, who went into one of those antique institutions known as a saloon. It was rather a large place, and he saw two men fighting over in the corner. He went up to the bartender and he said, "Is this a private fight, or can everybody get in?" Now, in the true Irish spirit, we are abolishing private fights, and we are making it the law of mankind that it is everybody's business and everybody can get in. The consequence is that there will be no attempt at private fights. . . .

My fellow citizens, imagine what would have happened if there had been a league of nations in 1914. . . . Every foreign office was telegraphing to its representative at Berlin, begging that there might be an international conference to see if a settlement could not be effected, and Germany did not dare sit down in conference. It is the common judgment of every statesman I met on the other side of the water that if this thing had been delayed and discussed, not six months, but six days, it never could have happened. . . .

War is a process of heat. Exposure is a process of cooling; and what is proposed in this is that every hot thing shall be spread out in the cooling air of the opinion of the world and after it is thoroughly cooled off, then let the nations concerned determine whether they are going to fight about it or not. . . .

If there had been nine days of discussion, Germany would not have gone to war. If there had been nine days upon which to bring to bear the opinion of the world, the judgment of mankind, upon the purposes of those Governments, they never would have dared to execute those purposes. So that what is important for us to remember is that when we sent those boys in khaki across the sea we promised them, we promised the world, that we would not conclude this conflict with a mere treaty of peace. We entered into solemn engagements with all the nations with whom we associated ourselves that we would bring about such a kind of settlement and such a concert of the purpose of nations that wars like this could not occur again. If this war has to be fought over again, then all our high ideals and purposes have been disappointed. . . .

This is the Covenant of the League of Nations that you hear objected to, the only possible guarantee against war. . . . You say, "Is it an absolute guarantee?" No; there is no absolute guarantee against human passion; but even if it were only 10 per cent of a guarantee, would not you rather have 10 per cent guarantee against war than none? If it only creates a presumption that there will not be war, would you not rather have that presumption than live under the certainty that there will be war? . . . The difficulties cannot be overcome unless we try to overcome them. I believe much can be done. Probably it will be impossible to stop all wars, but it certainly will be possible to stop some wars, and thus diminish their number. . . . This is the best treaty that can possibly be got, and, in my judgment, it is a mighty good treaty, for it has justice, the attempt at justice at any rate, at the heart of it. . . .

I have sought . . . to understand the point of view of the men who have been opposing the treaty and the Covenant of the League of Nations. . . . I have heard gentlemen say, "America can take care of herself." . . . They believe that the United States is so strong, so financially strong, so industrially strong, if necessary so physically strong, that it can impose its will upon the world if it is necessary. . . .

Very well, then, if we must stand apart and be the hostile rivals of the rest of the world, then we must do something else. We must be physically ready for anything that comes. We must have a great standing army. We must see to it that every man in America is trained to arms. We must see to it that there are munitions and guns enough for an army that means a mobilized nation; that they are not only laid up in store, but that they are kept up to date; that they are ready to use tomorrow; that we are a nation in arms; because you cannot be unfriendly to everybody without being ready that everybody shall be unfriendly to you. . . . What is much more serious than that, we have got to have the sort of organization that can handle arms of that sort. We may say what we please of the German Government that has been destroyed, my fellow citizens, but it was the only sort of government that could handle an armed nation. You cannot handle an armed nation by vote. You cannot handle an armed nation if it is democratic, because democracies do not go to war that way. You have got to have a concentrated, militaristic organization of government to run a nation of that sort. You have got to think of the President of the United States, not as the chief counsellor of the Nation, elected for a little while, but as the man meant constantly and every day to be the Commander in Chief. . . . And you cannot do that under free debate. . . . Plans must be kept secret. Knowledge must be accumulated by a system which we have condemned, because we have called it a spying system. The more polite call it a system of intelligence. You cannot watch other nations with your unassisted eye. You have got to watch them by secret agencies planted everywhere. . . .

And you know what the effect of a military government is upon social questions. You know how impossible it is to effect social reform if everybody must be under orders from the Government. You know how impossible it is, in short, to have a free nation, if it is a military nation and under military order. You may say, "You have been on the other side of the water and got bad dreams." I have got no dreams at all. I am telling you the things, the evidence of which I have seen with awakened eyes and not with sleeping eyes, and I know that this country, if it wishes to stand alone, must stand alone as part of a world in arms. . . .

But if you did nobody would recognize America in those strange and altered circumstances. All the world would stand at amaze and say, "Has America forgotten everything that she ever professed?" The picture is one that every American repudiates; and I challenge any man who has that purpose at the back of his thought to avow it. If he comes and tells you that America must stand alone and take care of herself, ask him how it is going to be done, and he will not dare tell you, because you would show him the door and say, "We do not know any such American." . . .

I want you to realize, my fellow countrymen, that those Americans who are opposing this plan of the League of Nations offer no substitute. They offer nothing that they pretend will accomplish the same object. On the contrary, they are apparently willing to go back to that old and evil order which prevailed before this war began and which furnished a ready and fertile soil for those seeds of envy which sprung up like dragon's teeth out of the bloody soil of Europe. They are ready to go back to that old and ugly plan of armed nations, of alliances, of watchful jealousies, of rabid antagonisms, of purposes concealed. . . .

Everywhere we go, the train when it stops is surrounded with little children, and I look at them almost with tears in my eyes, because I feel my mission is to save them. These glad youngsters with flags in their hands—I pray God that they may never have to carry that flag upon the battlefield! . . . I have felt that this errand that I am going about upon was to save them the infinite sorrows through which the world has just passed, and that if by any evil counsel or unhappy mischance this great enterprise for which we fought should fail, then women with boys at their breasts ought now to weep, because when those lads come to maturity the great battle will have to be fought over again. . . . The next time will come; it will come while this generation is living, and the children that crowd about our car as we move from station to station will be sacrificed upon the altar of that war. It will be the last war. Humanity will never suffer another, if humanity survives. . . .

I beg, my fellow citizens, that you will carry this question home with you, not in little pieces, not with this, that, and the other detail at the front in your mind, but as a great picture including the whole of the Nation and the whole of humanity, and know that now is the golden hour when America can at last prove that all she has promised in the day of her birth was no dream but a thing which she saw in its concrete reality, the rights of men, the prosperity of nations, the majesty of justice, and the sacredness of peace. . . .

✿ ✿ ✿

On September 25 at Pueblo, Colorado, the 63-year-old President collapsed, and the remainder of the tour was cancelled. A week later he suffered a crippling stroke which left his mind and judgment impaired. The fate of the treaty now rested wholly in the hands of the Senate, controlled by the Republican opposition and, in particular, by Theodore Roosevelt's lifelong friend and closest associate, Henry Cabot Lodge, Chairman of the Senate Foreign Relations Committee. Lodge put together a coalition of cynically reactionary nationalists like himself, and vacant-eyed liberal perfectionists from the Midwest. Between them they killed the treaty. Having routed the reactionaries of Europe, Wilson was powerless to prevent their triumph at home. America would not be a party to the League, virtually assuring its futility.

The three-way debate over the conduct of American foreign policy, begun during the early years of this century, continues in the United States. "Realists" still find no security except in the pursuit of national self-interest supported by unlimited military power. Their numbers and institutionalized influence have swelled infinitely since Theodore Roosevelt's day. On the other hand, their most vocally idealistic opponents, like the midwestern isolationists, often condemn virtually any American involvement overseas, as though the richest nation in the world could somehow be a hermit. And above all there persists the indifference of the American electorate, by any standard the least curious about the world of any people who have ever exercised world power.

The *via media* charted by Wilson has fared less well. Subsequent events proved that Wilson was no idle visionary, but a student of the world profoundly aware of the forces transforming it in the twentieth century. The success of his League depended upon the firm support of Britain, France, and above all the United States. Had these great democracies used their power wisely in support of international comity after 1919, Hitler might have been contained, German re-armament prevented, and the map of Europe been very different from its present terrible divisions.

As it was, it was all left to do over again in the 1940s under vastly more difficult circumstances. Franklin Roosevelt, who always thought of himself as a Wilsonian in foreign affairs, tried to learn from Wilson's mistakes so as to avoid his failures. The United Nations, inspired by Wilson's League, has been one salutary result.

A far less happy result of the rise of Hitler and World War II has been the lost independence of the smaller nations of Eastern Europe which Wilson tried to protect. Wilson never had, in his own country, even many streets named for him. But after 1919 the principal railway station in Prague was the *Wilsonavá nádražny*. Hitler changed its name, then Stalin. In 1968, however, the old name appeared again, briefly, as the Czechs tried vainly to reassert their independence. They, at least, insofar as they are able, still honor the memory of a great and good American.

6

Andrew J. Volstead

❁ ❁ ❁

The Volstead Act
1919

*P*rogressivism was a powerful force in
the making of twentieth-century America. But there was never a unitary,
or even particularly coherent, progressive program to which all or nearly
all progressives adhered. There wasn't even a progressive "personality" to
make easier our attempts to empathize with that remarkable generation of
Americans.

The progressives were as diverse a lot as the personnel of any mass
movement must necessarily be. Some were Republicans, some Democrats,
some keen supporters of the Socialist party. Some progressives believed
that the more democracy that could be infused into American public life,
the healthier American society would be. Others ennobled the role of the
expert, whether technologist or professional city administrator, whose
greater power by definition meant a muting of the *vox populi*. Some looked
forward, some yearned back to mythical arcadias. Some fought against
racial discrimination, others expanded the realm of Jim Crow segregation.
Some supported woman suffrage, others ridiculed the very idea (albeit
more quietly as the 1910s progressed). Some progressives gladly welcomed
"Mr. Wilson's War" as right internationally and an opportunity for reform
at home. Other progressives opposed it at the risk of their careers and
reputations. Some progressives were tolerant, broad-minded, good-
humored, and thoroughly appealing human beings. Others were
dreadfully grim and humorless bluenoses who pulled off the greatest,

THE VOLSTEAD ACT   From *U.S. Statutes at Large*, XXXXI, 305 ff.

most ludicrous adventure in our national history by legislating morality through the regimentation of individual behavior.

Until the progressive era, prohibitionism was a movement of evangelical Protestant moralists who were able to enact statewide ordinances at various times but were never able to command more than a handful of votes in a national election. But their contention that denying alcoholic beverages to the masses would, at one swoop, cure such social evils as the political power of the saloon, tumult among the working class, radicalism and trade unionism, wife-beating and desertion, impoverishment of children, unpleasant behavior on the streets, frightening the horses, and any of a dozen other social problems, inevitably appealed to some progressives.

The spread of woman suffrage helped the cause of prohibition. (The Women's Christian Temperance Union was the nation's largest women's organization at the turn of the century.) World War I, with the opportunities the crisis provided for economic, social, and military mobilization, provided another boost for the cause. The Lever Act of 1917 barred the sale of grain to distilleries on the grounds that basic food resources were too precious in a time of national emergency to be squandered on a product of so little merit as whiskey. The desirability of a sober work force and soldiery won converts. Anti-German hysteria allowed prohibitionists to extend the mantle of villainy over brewers as well as distillers: most American breweries were operated by Germans who had proudly emblazoned their teutonic names on their bottles.

On December 18, 1917, Congress sent the Eighteenth Amendment to the Constitution to the states (see Appendix). On January 16, 1919, it was ratified and took effect one year later. In October 1919 Congress enacted the Volstead Act, named for Minnesota Congressman Andrew J. Volstead, who had supported progressive acts regulating railroads and business. In its excruciatingly detailed definitions of how the "Noble Experiment" was to work, the Volstead Act reflected progressive belief in social engineering as much as the bluenose's love of canons and litanies.

Sec 1. The word "liquor" or the phrase "intoxicating liquor" shall be construed to include alcohol, brandy, whisky, rum, gin, beer, ale, porter, and wine, and in addition thereto any spirituous, vinous, malt, or fermented liquor, liquids, and compounds, whether medicated, proprietary, patented, or not, and by whatever name called, containing one-half of 1 per centum or more of alcohol by volume which are fit for use for beverage purposes. . . .

SEC 3. No person shall on or after the date when the Eighteenth Amendment to the Constitution of the United States goes into effect, manufacture, sell, barter, transport, import, export, deliver, furnish or possess any intoxicating liquor except as authorized in this act, and all the provisions of this act shall be liberally construed to the end that the use of intoxicating liquor as a beverage may be prevented.

Liquor for non-beverage purposes and wine for sacramental purposes may be manufactured, purchased, sold, bartered, transported, imported, exported, delivered, furnished, and possessed, but only as herein provided, and the Commissioner[1] may, upon application, issue permits therefore. . . .

SEC. 4. The articles enumerated in this section shall not, after having been manufactured and prepared for the market, be subject to the provisions of this act if they correspond with the following descriptions and limitations, namely:

(a) Denatured alcohol[2] or denatured rum produced and used as provided by laws and regulations now or hereafter in force.

(b) Medicinal preparations manufactured in accordance with formulas prescribed by the United States Pharmacopoeia, National Formulary, or the American Institute of Homeopathy that are unfit for use for beverage purposes.

(c) Patented, patent, and proprietary medicines that are unfit for use for beverage purposes.

(d) Toilet, medicinal, and antiseptic preparations and solutions that are unfit for use for beverage purposes.

(e) Flavoring extracts and syrups that are unfit for use as a beverage, or for intoxicating beverage purposes.

(f) Vinegar and preserved sweet cider. . . .

Any person who shall knowingly sell any of the articles mentioned in Paragraphs a, b, c, and d of this section for beverage purposes, or any extract or syrup for intoxicating beverage purposes, or who shall sell any of the same under circumstances from which the seller might reasonably deduce the intention of the purchaser to use them for such purposes, or shall sell any beverage containing one-half of 1 per centum or more of alcohol by volume in which any extract, syrup, or other article is used as an ingredient,

---

[1]The Commissioner of Internal Revenue was authorized to enforce the Volstead Act.

[2]Denatured alcohol was alcohol otherwise drinkable that was rendered unfit for drinking by the addition of a toxic substance. During Prohibition, it was the cause of numerous poisonings.

shall be subject to the penalties provided in Section 29 of this Title[3]. . . .

SEC. 5. . . . Nothing in this title shall be held to apply to the manufacture, sale, transportation, importation, possession, or distribution of wine for sacramental purposes, or like religious rites. . . . No person to whom a permit may be issued to manufacture, transport, import, or sell wines for sacramental purposes or like religious rites shall sell, barter, exchange, or furnish any such to any person not a rabbi, minister of the gospel, priest, or an officer duly authorized for the purpose by any church or congregation, nor to any such except upon an application duly subscribed by him, which application, authenticated as regulations may prescribe, shall be filed and preserved by the seller. The head of any conference or diocese or other ecclesiastical jurisdiction may designate any rabbi, minister, or priest to supervise the manufacture of wine to be used for the purposes and rites in this section mentioned, and the person so designated may, in the discretion of the Commissioner, be granted a permit to supervise such manufacture.

SEC. 7. No one but a physician holding a permit to prescribe liquor shall issue any prescription for liquor. And no physician shall prescribe liquor unless after careful physical examination of the person for whose use such prescription is sought, or if such examination is found impracticable, then upon the best information obtainable, he in good faith believes that the use of such liquor as a medicine by such person is necessary and will afford relief to him from some known ailment. Not more than a pint of spirituous liquor to be taken internally shall be prescribed for use by the same person within any period of ten days and no prescription shall be filled more than once. Any pharmacist filing a prescription shall at the time indorse upon it over his own signature the word "canceled," together with the date when the liquor was delivered, and then make the same a part of the record that he is required to keep as herein provided.

Every physician who issues a prescription for liquor shall keep a record, alphabetically arranged in a book prescribed by the Commissioner, which shall show the date of issue, amount prescribed, to

---

[3]Section 29 provided various penalties for violation of the Volstead Act. For example, people convicted of manufacturing liquor were to be fined not more than $1000 and imprisoned for no more than six months for a first offense. For subsequent offenses they were fined not less than $200 nor more than $2000 and imprisoned for one month to five years.

whom issued, the purpose or ailment for which it is to be used and directions for use, stating the amount and frequency of the dose.

Sec. 8. The Commissioner shall cause to be printed blanks for the prescriptions herein required, and he shall furnish the same, free of cost, to physicians holding permits to prescribe. The prescription blanks shall be printed in book form and shall be numbered consecutively from one to one hundred, and each book shall be given a number, and the stubs in each book shall carry the same numbers as and be copies of the prescriptions. The books containing such stubs shall be returned to the Commissioner when the prescription blanks have been used, or sooner if directed by the Commissioner. All unused, mutilated, or defaced blanks shall be returned with the book. No physician shall prescribe and no pharmacist shall fill any prescription for liquor except on blanks so provided, except in cases of emergency, in which event a record and report shall be made and kept as in other cases. . . .

Sec. 17. It shall be unlawful to advertise anywhere, or by any means or method, liquor, or the manufacture, sale, keeping for sale, or furnishing of the same, or where, how, from whom, or at what price the same may be obtained. No one shall permit any sign or billboard containing such advertisement to remain upon one's premises. . . .

Sec. 18. It shall be unlawful to advertise, manufacture, sell, or possess for sale any utensil, contrivance, machine, preparation, compound, tablet, substance, formula, direction, or recipe advertised, designed or intended for use in the unlawful manufacture of intoxicating liquor.

Sec. 19. No person shall solicit or receive, nor knowingly permit his employé to solicit or receive, from any person any order for liquor or give any information of how liquor may be obtained in violation of this act. . . .

Sec. 21. Any room, house, building, boat, vehicle, structure, or place where intoxicating liquor is manufactured, sold, kept, or bartered in violation of this title, and all intoxicating liquor and property kept and used in maintaining the same, is hereby declared to be a common nuisance, and any person who maintains such a common nuisance shall be guilty of a misdemeanor and upon conviction thereof shall be fined not more than $1,000, or be imprisoned for not more than one year, or both. If a person has knowledge or reason to believe that his room, house, building, boat, vehicle, structure, or place is occupied or used for the manufacture or sale of liquor contrary to the provision of this title, and suffers the same to be so occupied or used, such room, house, building, boat, vehicle, structure, or place shall be subject to a lien for and may be sold to pay all fines and costs assessed against the person guilty of such nuisance for such violation, and any such lien may be enforced by action in any court having jurisdiction. . . .

SEC. 23. That any person who shall, with intent to effect a sale of liquor, by himself, his employé, servant, or agent, for himself or any person, company, or corporation, keep or carry around on his person, or in a vehicle, or other conveyance whatever, or leave in a place for another to secure, any liquor, or who shall travel to solicit, or solicit, or take, or accept orders for the sale, shipment, or delivery of liquor in violation of this title is guilty of a nuisance and may be restrained by injunction, temporary and permanent, from doing or continuing to do any of said acts or things. . . .

SEC. 26. When the Commissioner, his assistants, inspectors, or any officer of the law shall discover any person in the act of transporting in violation of the law, intoxicating liquors in any wagon, buggy, automobile, water or air craft, or other vehicle, it shall be his duty to seize any and all intoxicating liquors found therein being transported contrary to law. Whenever intoxicating liquors transported or possessed illegally shall be seized by an officer he shall take possession of the vehicle and team or automobile, boat, air or water craft, or any other conveyance, and shall arrest any person in charge thereof. . . .

❂ ❂ ❂

There is no missing the irony that prohibition fell upon the land in the same year that the more admirable variety of progressivism, personified in the haunting, haunted figure of a dying Woodrow Wilson, who vetoed the Volstead Act, exited stage rear. The final accomplishment of the progressives was to stand as a mockery to the perils, as Max Weber put it, of seeing politics and the powers of government as media for the salvation of souls. "Moonshining," illegal distillation of liquor, formerly a minor vexation to collectors of federal taxes, became a major industry. (One of the first stills seized under the Volstead Act was found on

Volstead's Minnesota farm.) "Speakeasies," illegal bars, sprang up where saloons were closed. In New York City, it was estimated, 32,000 speakeasies replaced 15,000 licensed saloons.

Because officials in "wet" areas (most big cities and urban, industrial states) refused to enforce the Volstead Act, and Congress would not appropriate nearly enough money for effective federal enforcement, open defiance of an important law was wider spread than at any other time in American history. Organized crime, earlier a matter of small gangs of thugs with scarcely more than neighborhoods for a province and theft and petty graft for a commerce, became a significant factor in American life. It was said that the Al Capone organization in Chicago, dabbling in all vices but largely dependent upon supplying illegal liquor and beer, raked in as much as $125 million a year. To mock the progressive prohibitionists further, syndicates like Capone's typically allied with and reinvigorated reactionary political machines more corrupt than Tammany had been since the days of Tweed.

By the end of the decade, most old progressives and their heirs had had enough. On the national level, Herbert Hoover and Republican party conservatives were stuck with defending the disaster while the Democrats, always excluding representatives of the Bible Belt, called for repeal. As something of an emergency measure, the Volstead Act was amended early in 1933 to allow for the sale of 3.2 percent beer and wine. By the end of 1933, the Twenty-first Amendment to the Constitution—with an air of mortification to it—tersely repealed the Eighteenth.

PART 4

Depression, New Deal, and War
1922–1944

1

Herbert C. Hoover

❖ ❖ ❖

American Individualism

1922

*T*here were many kinds of
progressives, but progressivism was mostly a middle-class movement,
an effort to find a middle way between the extremes of plutocracy and
socialism. Even the minority of progressives who advocated public
ownership recoiled from the Marxist program of class conflict. Unwilling
to believe that capital was so obdurate, modern technology so niggardly,
or industrial workers so brutalized that society must degenerate into a dog
fight, most progressives hoped to moderate class conflict by timely reform
and were confident that the problems of industrial society would yield to
good will, common sense, and economic abundance in which all could
share. No one has ever denounced American businessmen in terms so acid
as those employed by the progressive writer Thorstein Veblen—he called
them thugs and hoodlums straight out of the dark ages—but even Veblen
believed that the business predator would soon be a thing of the past,
elbowed aside by a quiet army of technical experts, efficient administrators,
engineers. If progressives had a watchword, it was not *competition* or *conflict*,
but *cooperation*.

Herbert Hoover was acclaimed the "Engineer of the Century" by
his colleagues in the American Institute of Mining Engineers. His degree

AMERICAN INDIVIDUALISM From Herbert Hoover, *American Individualism* (New
York: Doubleday, 1922), pp. 4–72.

in geology outfitted him in his youth to cash in on the world's last great mining frontier, as remote regions in Africa, Australia, and the Far East were opened to American and European capital. By 1914 the young mining engineer, with offices in New York and London and investments in places ranging from Burma to the Antipodes, was several times a millionaire. A man who "has not made a million dollars by the time he is forty . . . is not worth much," he commented modestly.

Hoover was in many respects Veblen's technocrat personified. Efficiency was his mania. He played medicine ball each morning because it gave him three times the exercise of tennis, six times that of golf. He could down a five-course dinner in eleven minutes flat, regretted that he had a middle name for all the time he wasted signing it, hated shaking hands, and amused himself at picnics by constructing dams across any handy stream. He had no humor and even less tact, but he had high ideals and fine abilities which, like many progressives, he ached to place in the service of mankind.

His opportunity came in 1914 when the European war broke out while he was in London. He and his wife organized an American Relief Committee to assist thousands of frightened and stranded American tourists who poured into the city during the early weeks of the war. After learning that the civilian population of German-occupied, British-blockaded Belgium faced starvation, he organized a private Commission for the Relief of Belgium which raised a billion dollars and delivered five million tons of food by the end of the war. The American ambassador described Hoover to President Wilson: "He's a simple, modest, energetic man who began his career in California and will end it in Heaven." Wilson made Hoover head of the wartime Food Administration, and after the war director of the American Relief Administration which shipped five billion dollars worth of American food to Europe, including Soviet Russia. By 1920 the self-effacing master organizer who had helped avert chaos and famine in Europe was a hero to many of the independent progressives who had rallied behind Theodore Roosevelt in 1912 and Woodrow Wilson in 1916.

Although he was not elected President until 1928, Hoover was the most able and effective American public figure of the 1920s. The affably incompetent Warren Harding, calling him "the smartest geek I know," appointed him to the Cabinet as Secretary of Commerce. He served President Coolidge, who disliked him thoroughly, in the same capacity. (Coolidge, who spent much of his presidency in his pajamas, was as annoyed by his secretary's boundless energy as Hoover was appalled by his chief's unshakable torpor.) A giant among pygmies, meddling in everyone's department in addition to his own, from 1921 until the Wall Street crash, Hoover was the master technician of the "New Era."

New Era economics meant vigorous government intervention in the economy to promote cooperation and deflect antagonism. It presupposed a basic community of interest between employers, labor, and consumers, all of whom would benefit from increased prosperity. The role of government was not ordinarily coercive. Instead, following a pattern established in the late-nineteenth century by many of the first government regulatory commissions, it recognized that the most effective regulation was that which worked through business incentives rather than against them, promoting the interest of the public and of the businesses concerned at the same time. The role of government was to supply business information and technical advice, to initiate voluntary reforms, and to provide a forum for the negotiation of disputes. It was an approach to public regulation which many of the best-informed progressives had always advocated. For Hoover, the most useful technique was the government-sponsored conference—he convened thousands of them—in which he skillfully guided participants toward the conclusions he and his experts had already worked out. The results were considerable. For example, one of his great triumphs was the negotiated end of the brutal twelve-hour day in the steel industry.

In 1922 the new Secretary of Commerce published a brief creed for "a new economic system." *Laissez-faire*, he said, had been "dead in America for generations." Economic problems could not be solved by the unorganized actions of individual businessmen; they required "national guidance and a national plan." The vitality and freedom of "American individualism," he insisted, had to be voluntarily harnessed in a cooperative effort to promote the public good.

❀ Five or six great social philosophies are at struggle in the world for ascendency. There is the Individualism of America. There is the Individualism of the more democratic states of Europe with its careful reservations of castes and classes. There are Communism, Socialism, Syndicalism, Capitalism. . . . All these thoughts are in ferment today in every country in the world. . . . Some of these ideas are perhaps more adapted to one race than another. Some are false, some are true. What we are interested in is their challenge to the physical and spiritual forces of America. . . .

For myself, let me say at the very outset that my faith in the essential truth, strength, and vitality of the developing creed by which we have hitherto lived in this country of ours has been confirmed and deepened by the searching experiences of seven years of service in the backwash and misery of war. . . . And from it all I emerge an individualist—an unashamed individualist. But let me say also that I am an American individualist. For America has been steadily developing the ideals that constitute progressive individualism. . . .

In our individualism we have long since abandoned the laissez faire of the 18th Century—the notion that it is "every man for himself and the devil take the hindmost." We abandoned that when we adopted the ideal of equality of opportunity—the fair chance of Abraham Lincoln. We have confirmed its abandonment in terms of legislation, of social and economic justice,—in part, because we have learned that it is the hindmost who throws the bricks at our social edifice, in part because we have learned that the foremost are not always the best nor the hindmost the worst—and in part because we have learned that social injustice is the destruction of justice itself. We have learned that the impulse to production can only be maintained at a high pitch if there is a fair division of the product. We have also learned that fair division can only be obtained by certain restrictions on the strong and the dominant. We have indeed gone even further in the 20th Century with the embracement of the necessity of a greater and broader sense of service and responsibility to others as a part of individualism. . . .

It is not capitalism, or socialism, or syndicalism, nor a cross breed of them. . . . The social force in which I am interested is far higher and far more precious a thing than all these. It springs from something infinitely more enduring; it springs from the one source of human progress—that each individual shall be given the chance and stimulation for development of the best with which he has been endowed in heart and mind; it is the sole source of progress; it is American individualism. . . .

On the philosophic side we can agree at once that intelligence, character, courage, and the divine spark of the human soul are alone the property of individuals. These do not lie in agreements, in organizations, in institutions, in masses, or in groups. They abide alone in the individual mind and heart.

Production both of mind and hand rests upon impulses in each individual. These impulses are made of the varied forces of original instincts, motives, and acquired desires. Many of these are destructive and must be restrained through moral leadership and authority of the law and be eliminated finally by education. All are modified by a vast fund of experience and a vast plant and equipment of civilization which we pass on with increments to each succeeding generation. . . .

The problem of the world is to restrain the destructive instincts while strengthening and enlarging those of altruistic character and constructive impulse—for thus we build for the future.

From the instincts of kindness, pity, fealty to family and race; the love of liberty; the mystical yearnings for spiritual things; the desire for fuller expression of the creative faculties; the impulses of service to community and nation, are moulded the ideals of our people. And the most potent force in society is its ideals. . . .

If we examine the impulses that carry us forward, none is so potent for progress as the yearning for individual self-expression, the desire for creation of something. Perhaps the greatest human happiness flows from personal achievement. Here lies the great urge of the constructive instinct of mankind. But it can only thrive in a society where the individual has liberty and stimulation to achievement. Nor does the community progress except through its participation in these multitudes of achievements. . . .

The vast multiplication of voluntary organizations for altruistic purposes are themselves proof of the ferment of spirituality, service, and mutual responsibility. These associations for advancement of public welfare, improvement, morals, charity, public opinion, health, the clubs and societies for recreation and intellectual advancement, represent something moving at a far greater depth than "joining." They represent the widespread aspiration for mutual advancement, self-expression, and neighborly helpfulness. . . .

That high and increasing standards of living and comfort should be the first of considerations in public mind and in government needs no apology. We have long since realized that the basis of an advancing civilization must be a high and growing standard of living for all the people, not for a single class. . . . The economic development of the past fifty years has lifted the general standard of comfort far beyond the dreams of our forefathers. The only road to further advance in the standard of living is by greater invention, greater elimination of waste, greater production, . . . for by increasing their ratio to our numbers and dividing them justly we each will have more of them. . . .

To all practical souls there is little use in quarreling over the share of each of us until we have something to divide. . . . While there should be no minimizing of a certain fringe of injustices in sharing the results of production or in the wasteful use made by some of their share, yet there is vastly wider field for gains to all of us through cheapening the costs of production, . . . than will ever come to us even if we can think out a method of abstract justice in sharing which did not stifle production of the total product. . . .

Today business organization is moving strongly toward coöperation. There are in the coöperative great hopes that we can even gain in individuality, equality of opportunity, and an enlarged field for initiative, and at the same time reduce many of the great wastes of overreckless competition in production and distribution. . . . Indeed this phase of development of our individualism promises to become the dominant note of its 20th Century expansion. But it will thrive only in so far as it can construct leadership and a sense of service, and so long as it preserves the initiative and safeguards the individuality of its members. . . .

Our Government's greatest troubles and failures are in the economic field. . . . The entrance of the Government began strongly three decades ago, when our industrial organization began to move powerfully in the direction of consolidation of enterprise. We found in the course of this development that equality of opportunity and its corollary, individual initiative, was being throttled. . . . To curb the forces in business which would destroy equality of opportunity and yet to maintain the initiative and creative faculties of our people are the twin objects we must attain. . . . When we come to the practical problems of government in relation to these economic questions the test lies in two directions: Does this act safeguard an equality of opportunity? Does it maintain the initiative of our people? . . . Humanity has a long road to perfection, but we of America can make sure progress if we will preserve our individualism, if we will preserve and stimulate the initiative of our people, if we will build up our insistence and safeguards to equality of opportunity, if we will glorify service as a part of our national character. Progress will march if we hold an abiding faith in the intelligence, the initiative, the character, the courage, and the divine touch in the individual. We can safeguard these ends if we give to each individual that opportunity for which the spirit of America stands. We can make a social system as perfect as our generation merits and one that will be received in gratitude by our children.

❁ ❁ ❁

Hoover was President for only eight months before the stockmarket crash plunged the nation into the gravest economic crisis in its history, a disaster all the techniques of the New Era were helpless to avert. We can see in retrospect that voluntary cooperation worked well enough in good times (as it still does), but even in the heyday of the 1920s Hoover's repeated efforts had failed to make headway in chronically depressed industries—agriculture, coal, textiles. In contracting industries, cooperation dissolved into a bitter struggle for decreasing benefits. By 1930 the struggle had spread to the whole economy.

No one was more depressed than the President. Tight-lipped, grim-faced, he privately railed against the selfishness of businessmen whom he could no longer persuade to behave better. He was not inactive in the crisis; he introduced many measures to stimulate recovery on which the New Deal of his successor needed only to elaborate. But for all his remarkable administrative abilities, Hoover was wholly without political skills. Congress to him was *terra incognita*. He could not make a speech. Although he was a superb cabinet secretary, the technocrat made a miserable President.

Hoover lived until 1964, rather sadly devoting the last thirty years of his life to self-exculpation. His bitter animosity toward the New Deal, his close identification with the right-wing of the Republican Party, caused most Americans to forget that he had once been one of the best and brightest among American progressives. Unable to admit, apparently even to himself, that he had ever been less than wholly right, Hoover saw in the welfare state—which the New Deal helped to introduce—a force working to crush American individualism and to destroy the spirit of voluntary public service which he cherished.

The claim is hard to credit. A decade after his death, in a typical year, Americans voluntarily gave $20 billion to private charities—all but a small fraction of it from individuals. American churches, which have always depended on voluntary support, are as well off as they have ever been. More than a third of the money spent on education and almost two-thirds of that spent on health care still comes from private sources. Even more impressively, census figures for 1974 revealed that 37 million Americans—one out of every four adults—volunteered their time to some public effort. Eighteen million of them gave time to their churches; nine million of them volunteered to lead youth groups or youth athletic teams; six million worked in the schools, another six million in the hospitals, five million contributed time to civic and cultural efforts, including environmental protection; three million volunteered in social welfare programs for infants and the aged; and tens of thousands of Americans held unpaid posts on local school boards, public commissions, and city councils. Hoover might have been chagrined to learn that Americans employed by public agencies were almost half again as likely to volunteer time as those employed by private companies! Public service has always been a privilege of the comfortable middle class. To the extent that the welfare state has assisted Americans to make their way into that class, it has augmented, not diminished, the opportunity to volunteer.

2

Franklin Delano Roosevelt

❁ ❁ ❁

First Inaugural Address
1933

*A*fter the congressional elections
of 1930, there was little doubt which political party would carry the
presidency in 1932. In a convulsive reaction to the Great Depression that
descended on the nation within a mere twelve months after the crash of
the stock market, the voters of 1930 elected a Democratic majority to the
House of Representatives for the first time in a decade. In the Senate,
the Republicans lost eight of their fifty-six seats to the Democrats.

In the depths of economic catastrophe, Herbert Hoover's vision of
what had made his country great as well as his reputation as a humanitarian
died and rotted. Despite his repeated assurances that prosperity was just
around the corner, the depression worsened through 1931 and 1932. Each
week, a hundred thousand more people lost work; by 1932, a quarter of the
work force was unemployed. For those who held on to their jobs, average
weekly earnings fell from $25 to $17. Farmers were hit even harder.
Growers of corn burned their crop for fuel because it was cheaper than
coal or cordwood. By 1933 one farmer in four would be forced off the
land. In 1932 banks folded at the rate of seven each day, wiping out $3.2
billion in savings accounts.

No administration could survive such a disaster. Still worse, Hoover
was devoid of a public personality. He was at his best working in chambers
or meeting over a desk. In bad times the natural reserve that had once
signaled dignity now looked like arrogance, indifference, paralysis, and

FIRST INAUGURAL ADDRESS   From Franklin D. Roosevelt, *The Public Papers and Addresses, 1933* (New York: Random House, 1937), pp. 11–16.

gloom. Hoover also avoided public appearances for another good reason. During one motorcade through Detroit, unemployed workers lined the streets and stared silently as he drove by. Back in the Executive Mansion, intimates described the experience of talking to the President as so gloomy it was like sitting in a "bath of ink."

Contrasted sharply with this dreary spectre was the public personality of Hoover's Democratic opponent in 1932, Governor Franklin Delano Roosevelt of New York. "FDR" had very little in common with Hoover. The incumbent was a self-made man who struggled to earn an education, a fortune, and prominence and was, like many Horatio Alger types, a good deal of a prig. Roosevelt was born into an aristocratic New York family with more pride in ancestry than money. But he had enough of the latter to educate him in exclusive prep schools and Harvard University, and to shelter him from the world of toil.

Hoover had a vision of what the American state and society had been and should be. Roosevelt, while active in politics since before he was thirty, never thought deeply about statecraft. To FDR, government was rather a game, a series of challenges to be met with cheerful sporting grit, analyzed, and, one by one, played. Walter Lippman disdained FDR's lack of depth when he described him as "a pleasant man who, without any important qualifications for the office, would very much like to be President."

But the pleasantness and the affable confidence Roosevelt exuded were quite enough for voters when the alternative was Herbert Hoover. Without knowing much at all about Roosevelt's policies—like every front-runner, he refused to be pinned down during the campaign—the voters gave him 57.4 percent of the ballots and a 472 to 59 electoral vote landslide.

Between election day and inauguration day, FDR virtually disappeared from public view. Only now that he was to be President did he think about formulating a policy to contend with the depression, to prepare the "New Deal" that he had promised the American people. Day after day he met with prominent intellectuals and scholars—soon dubbed his "Brain Trust"—and set them to work preparing bills for Congress to act upon. The first draft of his inaugural address was prepared by the head of the Brain Trust, Columbia University Professor Raymond Moley, but its eloquence signals the considerable touch of the man who delivered it, one of our two or three best orator-presidents.

❖ This is a day of national consecration.

I am certain that my fellow Americans expect that on my induction into the Presidency I will address them with a candor and a decision which the present situation of our Nation impels. This is pre-eminently the time to speak the truth, the whole truth, frankly and boldly. Nor need we shrink from honestly facing conditions in our country today. This great Nation will endure as it has endured, will revive and will prosper. So, first of all, let me assert my firm belief that the only thing we have to fear is fear itself—nameless, unreasoning, unjustified terror which paralyzes needed efforts to convert retreat into advance. In every dark hour of our national life a leadership of frankness and vigor has met with that understanding and support of the people themselves which is essential to victory. I am convinced that you will again give that support to leadership in these critical days.

In such a spirit on my part and on yours we face our common difficulties. They concern, thank God, only material things. Values have shrunken to fantastic levels; taxes have risen; our ability to pay has fallen; government of all kinds is faced by serious curtailment of income; the means of exchange are frozen in the currents of trade; the withered leaves of industrial enterprise lie on every side; farmers find no markets for their produce; the savings of many years in thousands of families are gone.

More important, a host of unemployed citizens face the grim problem of existence, and an equally great number toil with little return. Only a foolish optimist can deny the dark realities of the moment.

Yet our distress comes from no failure of substance. We are stricken by no plague of locusts. Compared with the perils which our forefathers conquered because they believed and were not afraid, we have still much to be thankful for. Nature still offers her bounty and human efforts have multiplied it. Plenty is at our doorstep, but a generous use of it languishes in the very sight of the supply. Primarily this is because rulers of the exchange of mankind's goods have failed through their own stubbornness and their own incompetence, have admitted their failure, and have abdicated. Practices of the unscrupulous money changers stand indicted in the court of public opinion, rejected by the hearts and minds of men. . . .

The money changers have fled from their high seats in the temple of our civilization. We may now restore that temple to the ancient truths. The measure of the restoration lies in the extent to which we apply social values more noble than mere monetary profit. . . .

Restoration calls, however, not for changes in ethics alone. This Nation asks for action now.

Our greatest primary task is to put people to work. This is no unsolvable problem if we face it wisely and courageously. It can be accomplished in part by direct recruiting by the Government itself, treating the task as we would treat the emergency of a war, but at the same time, through this employment, accomplishing greatly needed projects to stimulate and reorganize the use of our natural resources.

Hand in hand with this we must frankly recognize the over-balance of population in our industrial centers and, by engaging on a national scale in a redistribution, endeavor to provide a better use of the land for those best fitted for the land. The task can be helped by definite efforts to raise the values of agricultural products and with this the power to purchase the output of our cities. It can be helped by preventing realistically the tragedy of the growing loss through foreclosure of our small homes and our farms. . . .

Finally, in our progress toward a resumption of work we require two safeguards against a return of the evils of the old order: there must be a strict supervision of all banking and credits and investments, so that there will be an end to speculation with other people's money; and there must be provision for an adequate but sound currency.

These are the lines of attack. I shall presently urge upon a new Congress, in special session, detailed measures for their fulfillment, and I shall seek the immediate assistance of the several States. . . .

Action in this image and to this end is feasible under the form of government which we have inherited from our ancestors. Our Constitution is so simple and practical that it is possible always to meet extraordinary needs by changes in emphasis and arrangement without loss of essential form. That is why our constitutional system has proved itself the most superbly enduring political mechanism the modern world has produced. It has met every stress of vast expansion of territory, of foreign wars, of bitter internal strife, of world relations.

It is to be hoped that the normal balance of Executive and legislative authority may be wholly adequate to meet the unprecedented task before us. But it may be that an unprecedented demand and need for undelayed action may call for temporary departure from that normal balance of public procedure.

I am prepared under my constitutional duty to recommend the measures that a stricken Nation in the midst of a stricken world may require. These measures, or such other measures as the Congress may build out of its experience and wisdom, I shall seek, within my constitutional authority, to bring to speedy adoption.

But in the event that the Congress shall fail to take one of these two courses, and in the event that the national emergency is still critical, I shall not evade the clear course of duty that will then confront me. I shall ask the Congress for the one remaining instrument to meet the crisis—broad Executive power to wage a war against the emergency, as great as the power that would be given to me if we were in fact invaded by a foreign foe. . . .

We do not distrust the future of essential democracy. The people of the United States have not failed. In their need they have registered a mandate that they want direct, vigorous action. They have asked for discipline and direction under leadership. They have made me the present instrument of their wishes. In the spirit of the gift I take it.

In this dedication of a Nation we humbly ask the blessing of God. May He protect each and every one of us. May He guide me in the days to come.

❁ ❁ ❁

Roosevelt's unveiled threat to seek emergency dictatorial powers if Congress rejected his legislative program proved gloriously unnecessary. His party held a 193 vote edge in the House and a 25 vote margin in the Senate. For a "Hundred Days," the bills prepared by the Brain Trust sailed through Congress. Several long and complex acts were approved by voice vote before anyone had a chance to read them through.

Only a few New Deal programs were prefigured in Roosevelt's speech. These included programs to get the unemployed to work immediately, tighter regulation of banking and the stock exchanges, and the noninterventionist "Good Neighbor" policy in Latin America that actually had its beginnings under Hoover. Roosevelt's unrealistic suggestion that people living in crowded cities should be encouraged to return to the soil was, of course, a pleasant sentiment soon forgotten.

Otherwise, the speech is a buoyant proclamation of confidence in the basic American institutions in an era of increasing totalitarianism. Indeed, many historians have suggested Roosevelt "saved" these foundations. True or not, his first inaugural speech reflected the same aura of confidence, optimism, and natural leadership that had emanated from FDR during the campaign. His impact on the American people was so great that there would be three more such addresses. In 1936, 1940, and 1944, the electorate returned him to the White House. No other President has been reelected more than once.

3

George Norris, Fiorello LaGuardia, Robert F. Wagner

✿ ✿ ✿

Depression Era Labor Legislation

1932, 1935

*F*ew congressional enactments of the 1930s represented so clean a break with earlier government policies than legislation dealing with labor unions. Before 1933, government policy toward unions of workers may fairly be defined as militant enmity at worst and selective toleration at best. With occasional exception, the powers of local government—most notably those of law enforcement—were intervened in labor disputes against striking workers. When striker violence did not serve as a pretext for the mobilization of police forces for the purpose of breaking up picket lines and harassing strikers and their supporters, employers dispatched their attorneys to the bar where accommodating judges issued injunctions against activities *that might lead to* a violation of the law or civil contracts. When union leaders refused to comply with such court orders, and compliance usually meant capitulation, the powers of city, county, or state could be marshaled to enforce them. One of the employers' most valuable tools for fighting unions was the "Yellow Dog Contract." As a condition of employment, all job applicants were required to agree not to join a union or to participate in strikes. When

DEPRESSION ERA LABOR LEGISLATION   From *U.S. Statutes at Large*, XLVII, 70–72; XLIX, 449–50.

any individual violated the terms of the contract, the employer had legal justification for an injunction.

The Clayton Act of 1914, part of Woodrow Wilson's New Freedom, had attempted to limit the use of injunctions in labor disputes but proved ineffective. (The Clayton Act did not, for example, bar injunctions in case of violations of Yellow Dog Contracts.) Only in 1932, with the business community and its President in disgrace, and the tide of reform welling in the country, were Senator George Norris of Nebraska and Congressman Fiorello LaGuardia of New York able to steer their anti-injunction act through Congress.

Despite the facts that both Norris and LaGuardia were progressive Republicans and that Hoover signed the bill readily, all but a few national labor leaders supported Franklin D. Roosevelt in the election of 1932. Partly in reward for this support, the National Recovery Act of June 1933 provided in Section 7(a) that all companies sharing in the benefits of this comprehensive program for economic planning were *required* to bargain collectively with any agency democratically selected by their employees.

If it represented a positive governmental protection of labor unions, Section 7(a) did not provide for specific machinery and procedures by which employers might be forced to recognize and deal with workers' unions. In any case, the National Recovery Act was declared unconstitutional in 1935. But even before the Supreme Court's decision was final, Senator Robert F. Wagner of New York rewrote and elaborated on Section 7(a) in the National Labor Relations Act, which easily passed Congress and won President Roosevelt's signature.

Norris-LaGuardia Anti-Injunction Bill
March 20, 1932

❇ *Be it enacted*, That no court of the United States, as herein defined, shall have jurisdiction to issue any restraining order or temporary or permanent injunction in a case involving or growing out of a labor dispute, except in a strict conformity with the provisions of this Act; nor shall any such restraining order or temporary or permanent injunction be issued contrary to the public policy declared in this Act.

SECTION 2. In the interpretation of this Act and in determining the jurisdiction and authority of the courts of the United States, as such jurisdiction and authority are herein defined and limited, the public policy of the United States is hereby declared as follows:

Whereas, under prevailing economic conditions, . . . the individual unorganized worker is commonly helpless to exercise actual liberty of contract and to protect his freedom of labor, and thereby to obtain acceptable terms and conditions of employment, wherefore, though he should be free to decline to associate with his fellows, it is necessary that he should have full freedom of association, self-organization, and designation of representatives of his own choosing, to negotiate the terms and conditions of his employment, and that he shall be free from the interference, restraint, or coercion of employers of labor, or their agents, in the activities for the purpose of collective bargaining or other mutual aid or protection; therefore, the following definitions of, and limitations upon, the jurisdiction and authority of the courts of the United States are hereby enacted. . . .

SECTION 4. No court of the United States shall have jurisdiction to issue any restraining order or temporary or permanent injunction in any case involving or growing out of any labor dispute to prohibit any person or persons participating or interested in such dispute (as these terms are herein defined) from doing, whether singly or in concert, any of the following acts:

(a) Ceasing or refusing to perform any work or to remain in any relation of employment;

(b) Becoming or remaining a member of any labor organization or of any employer organization, regardless of any such undertaking or promise as is described in section 3 of this Act;

(c) Paying or giving to, or withholding from any person participating or interested in such labor dispute, any strike or employment benefits or insurance, or other moneys or things of value;

(d) By all lawful means aiding any person participating or interested in any labor dispute who is being proceeded against in, or is prosecuting, any action or suit in any court in the United States or of any State;

(e) Giving publicity to the existence of, or the facts involved in, any labor dispute whether by advertising, speaking, patrolling, or by any other method not involving fraud or violence;

(f) Assembling peaceably to act or to organize to act in promotion of their interests in a labor dispute;

(g) Advising or notifying any persons of any intentions to do any of the acts heretofore specified;

(h) Agreeing with other persons to do or not to do any of the acts heretofore specified; and

(i) Advising, urging, or otherwise causing or inducing without fraud or violence the acts heretofore specified, regardless of any such undertaking or promise as is described in section 3 of this Act.

National Labor Relations Act
July 5, 1935

SECTION 1. The denial by employers of the right of employees to organize and the refusal of employers to accept the procedure of collective bargaining lead to strikes and other forms of industrial strife or unrest, which have the intent or the necessary effect of burdening or obstructing commerce. . . . The inequality of bargaining power between employees who do not possess full freedom of association or actual liberty of contract, and employers who are organized in the corporate or other forms of ownership association substantially burdens and affects the flow of commerce, and tends to aggravate recurrent business depressions, by depressing wage rates and the purchasing power of wage earners in industry and by preventing the stabilization of competitive wage rates and working conditions within and between industries.

Experience has proved that protection by law of the right of employees to organize and bargain collectively safeguards commerce from injury, impairment, or interruption, and promotes the flow of commerce by removing certain recognized sources of industrial strife and unrest, by encouraging practices fundamental to the friendly adjustment of industrial disputes arising out of differences as to wages, hours, or other working conditions, and by restoring equality of bargaining power between employers and employees.

It is hereby declared to be the policy of the United States to eliminate the causes of certain substantial obstructions to the free flow of commerce . . . by encouraging the practice and procedure of collective bargaining and by protecting the exercise by workers of full freedom of association, self-organization, and designation of representatives of their own choosing, for the purpose of negotiating the terms and conditions of their employment or other mutual aid or protection. . . .

SECTION 7. Employees shall have the right to self-organization, to form, join, or assist labor organizations, to bargain collectively through representatives of their own choosing, and to engage in concerted activities, for the purpose of collective bargaining or other mutual aid or protection.

SECTION 8. It shall be an unfair labor practice for an employer—
(1) To interfere with, restrain, or coerce employees in the exercise of the rights guaranteed in section 7. . . .
(3) By discrimination in regard to hire or tenure of employment or any term or condition of employment to encourage or discourage membership in any labor organization. . . .
(4) To discharge or otherwise discriminate against an employee because he has filed charges or given testimony under this Act.
(5) To refuse to bargain collectively with the representatives of his employees, subject to the provisions of section 9.

🔹 🔹 🔹

The Wagner Act was organized labor's Magna Carta. The National Labor Relations Board it created enforced the rights of unions to organize and bargain for employees of all companies involved in interstate commerce. In 1936, virtually every important labor leader, including the lifelong Republican head of the United Mineworkers, John L. Lewis, and socialists such as David Dubinsky of the International Ladies Garment Workers Union, endorsed FDR's reelection. Union membership, about 3 million in 1933, rose to 10.5 million in 1941 and more than 15 million after World War II.

Politically, New Deal labor legislation wedded organized labor to the Democratic party. With the exception of a few crafts unions and the United Brotherhood of Teamsters, which found some shelter from Democratic anticorruption investigations with the Republicans, organized labor has been a more dependable component of the Democratic party political alliance than any other except, among ethnic groups, black people.

4

Henry A. Wallace

❊ ❊ ❊

The Ever-Normal Granary
1938

*F*armers, someone has said, are
people whose assets are in land and whose liabilities are in money. Farming
in the United States has always been commercial and therefore prey to all
the usual disorders of the marketplace. As early as the seventeenth century
mobs of planters roamed the Chesapeake burning their neighbors' crops
to forestall ruin by low tobacco prices. Confronted by the fact that the free
market cannot adjust supply to demand without terrible carnage, most
American businessmen in the nineteenth century took cover behind
producers' associations and mergers which permitted them to control
production and prices with greater safety (see Johnson Newlon Camden,
"The Standard Oil Company," in Part 1). American farmers faced the same
problems as these other businessmen, but they were much less able to do
anything about them.

Adjusting supply to demand in farming is especially difficult. A
manufacturer knows that by shaving a little off the price of his surplus
goods he can usually get people to buy more of them. The farmer knows
that people will eat only so much, even if he is giving food away. In the
language of economics, the demand for foodstuffs is extremely *inelastic*,
so that even a little supply in excess of demand will send farm prices into a
nosedive. Unable to influence his market, the farmer is even more helpless

THE EVER-NORMAL GRANARY   From Henry A. Wallace, *Report of the Secretary of Ag-riculture, 1938* (Washington, D.C., 1938), pp. 11–33.

to regulate his production. If the market is glutted with foodstuffs, the
farmer is pitched onto a production treadmill which he can accelerate but
not slow down. The land, farm buildings, and equipment in which he has
invested his capital may not earn a profit, but he cannot cart them to the
city to be sold for other uses. Rather than suffer their total loss, the farmer
must typically accept the smaller loss of producing crops which no one
wants for sale at prices less than his cost to produce them. When he lays his
plans each year, even in good times, the farmer has no way to guess the
behavior of millions of his counterparts around the world whose efforts
will affect his own prices, nor can he foretell the effects of weather which
in a typical year in the United States may cause his harvest to be 40 percent
smaller or 20 percent greater than average. He must also try to outguess
the insects and rodents which still consume a third of the food grown even
on pesticide-drenched American farms. Under these circumstances every
seedtime on the farm is a shot in the dark.

Farm families experience other special hardships. The American
farmstead, with rowcrops stretching from dwelling to horizon, is a lonely,
often not very pretty place. From income lags behind that enjoyed by
nonfarm families, and while the necessities of life are cheaper in the
countryside, the amenities are almost always dearer. Before World War II
few American farms had electricity; therefore water was usually pumped
from wells by hand, indoor plumbing was out of the question, and the
outdoor privy an inescapable part of rural living. "How are you going to
keep them down on the farm," Groucho Marx asked, "after they've seen the
farm?" Beginning in the nineteenth century the exodus of the most eager
and alert farm youth to the cities threatened to leave the management of
the nation's principal industry in the hands of its poorest and least
competent citizens.

By the 1870s American agriculture was in trouble. Between 1870 and
1900 geographic expansion brought more new land under the plow in
three decades than had been farmed during the whole of the nation's
past—an area equal to that of Western Europe. Farm production shot
far ahead of any equivalent growth in population causing farm prices to
plummet. Crops that had sold for $1 in 1867 brought only 30¢ in 1896.
Good times returned briefly between 1900 and World War I as the closing
of the frontier and the war emergency temporarily permitted demand to
catch up with supply. When the war ended, however, agriculture fell again
into its chronic slump, aggravated by the slowed rate of population growth
characteristic of twentiety-century industrial societies. Between 1880
and 1920 farms operated by tenants in the United States increased from
25 percent to 38 percent of the total number. The sharecropping
system introduced in the South after the Civil War for the freedmen was
spreading to include increasing numbers of hardpressed white farmers in
an expanding American peasantry.

The Great Depression of the 1930s did not cause the farm crisis in
the United States. The American farmer had been on the ropes for the
better part of half a century before the Depression delivered its knockout
blow. Nonetheless the effects were dreadful. Net farm income in the

United States fell 70 percent between 1929 and 1932. Then drought completed the havoc together with great winds which carried the parched topsoil of the nation's wheatlands thousands of miles to the sea, darkening the skies over Washington where New Deal legislators pondered the country's farm problem. The Depression gave them the opportunity to introduce some fundamental agricultural reforms which had been advocated by the nation's farm leaders for decades.

Henry A. Wallace, Franklin Roosevelt's Secretary of Agriculture, came from a long line of such leaders. His grandfather had been editor of a progressive Iowa farm journal, and his father had been Secretary of Agriculture during the 1920s, when his proposals had made little headway against the opposition of Secretary of Commerce Hoover. The younger Wallace was a strangely ramshackle idealist, a dreamer who could nonetheless, when it came to his family's preoccupation of agriculture, be hard as nails. Early New Deal farm measures were framed to cope with the immediate emergency, but by 1938 the elements of a permanent solution to the farm problem were in place.

The Agricultural Adjustment Act of 1938, as revised in the 1940s, is still the basic farm law of the United States, all subsequent farm bills being amendments to this permanent legislation. Thus for half a century since 1938 the federal government has intervened in the farm economy to provide farmers with a system of price supports and production controls covering most basic farm commodities. The Department of Agriculture has become, after the Pentagon and the Post Office, the largest federal agency, administering more regulatory laws and programs than any other. The principal price support mechanism has been the Commodity Credit Corporation which makes production loans to farmers on their crops. A farmer may then sell the crop and repay the loan, or, if the market price falls below the amount loaned, transfer ownership of the crop to the CCC. Thus CCC loans introduce a floor below which the commercial price of commodities cannot fall, and the public winds up owning any farm surpluses. Other provisions have offered even higher but more limited price supports as direct subsidies to farmers, usually for keeping part of their land out of production as market conditions warrant.

In his report for 1938 Secretary Wallace explained the purposes of the new legislation. Throughout the report he emphasized, not the crisis of the Depression, but the long-range "adjustment" of agricultural prices and supply.

❀ American agriculture grew up to supply the world market as well as the home market. When its production for export cannot be sold, or can be sold only at a very low price, crops produced for the domestic market drop in price too. It is then impossible, without special remedial measures, to prevent ruinous disparities between farm and nonfarm incomes. . . .

These conditions necessitate governmental action. There is no way for the farmers individually to deal effectively with the partial loss of the export market, the rapid approach of stationary populations, and the increasing rural congestion in many areas that results from industrial depression and unemployment. Nor is there any individual remedy for the fact that technology increases farm production per agricultural worker, while other forces contract the market. Some people believe agriculture should decommercialize itself and become more self-sufficient. That would be a backward step. Moreover, the resulting reduced purchasing power of farmers would force some urban people into subsistence farming. Agriculture needs to get back on a business footing, and well-conceived national programs must help it to do so.

There is no escaping the necessity to adjust the farm output through measures that will not drive farmers from their farms. There is no escaping the further necessity of finding new outlets or of providing marketing controls to deal with surpluses when they accumulate unavoidably. Also, we must arrest the increase of tenancy and increase the equities of owner operators. Left uncontrolled, the prevailing trends will tremendously increase these evils. With farm youth backed up on farms and with the urban unemployed flocking to the country in periods of depression, land hunger is likely to produce absentee landlordism. These problems constitute an obvious national responsibility. . . .

We are now in the middle of the first year's operation of a new Agricultural Adjustment Act. It is timely to glance at what the act contains, to indicate the origins and application of its more important principles, and to notice some of the difficulties involved. The act is a coordinating and integrating measure based on our experience during the period 1933–1937, first with the Agricultural Adjustment Act of 1933 and then with the Soil Conservation and Domestic Allotment Act of 1936.[1] It represents the main stream of our developing agricultural policy. It embodies principles hammered out in nearly two decades of Nation-wide discussion on the

---

[1]The Agricultural Adjustment Act of 1933 was the pioneer New Deal farm measure, responding to the Depression crisis with drastic crop reduction programs. Its method of financing was found unconstitutional by the Supreme Court in 1936, but it was replaced by the Soil Conservation and Domestic Allotment Act. The latter measure, enacted in the wake of the Dust Bowl, shifted emphasis to soil conservation as a means of regulating production.

farms, in the cities, and in Congress. Indeed, to a considerable extent it includes principles unwittingly championed as substitute proposals. In short, the Agriculture Adjustment Act of 1938, and the programs in operation under it, are the Nation's well-matured answer to the challenge of an undisputed need for profound agricultural readjustments. . . .

In its developed form, therefore, the adjustment policy becomes the ever-normal granary. This term is a good short description of the whole process. As the words imply, it covers far more than the concept of the first emergency period, when the predominant purpose was adjustment to the fact of a smaller world market. It promotes jointly the interest of producer and consumer through means that protect both parties—namely, the reciprocal action of acreage adjustment and crop storage. In the ever-normal granary program there is room, as occasion requires, for expansion of the farm output. It rejects the notion that farm welfare always requires acreage reduction and looks instead to the production of different crops in the proper amounts and proportions. Moreover, it looks toward the stabilization of supplies through the conservation of soil and soil productivity. It does not waste land following seasons of overproduction but devotes it through conservational activities to the uses of the future. . . .

The machinery of the ever-normal granary provides for commodity loans under certain specified conditions of supply and price, and these loans involve certain hazards. The best protection against these hazards is a clear grasp of the purposes the loans should fulfill.

Obviously, since the ever-normal granary exists to carry surpluses from fat to lean years, the commodity loans should finance the storage and measurably stabilize the price of the stored commodities from one season to the next.

In terms of prices for commodities stored, the result should be a higher price level than would otherwise prevail in the big-crop years and a lower price level than would otherwise prevail in the short-crop years. In other words, the true function of the ever-normal-granary type of loan is to counteract fluctuations in market supplies and prices. It is not its function to maintain an average price level above that warranted by basic demand and supply factors. . . .

In a democracy such as ours economic legislation must promote certain noneconomic ends. Besides encouraging the production of wealth, it must maintain the freedom of the individual and of the community. The object cannot be exclusively material.

Man needs both bread and freedom; it is a calamity when he

must barter one for the other, and the result may be the breakdown of civilization. To promote abundance, both material and spiritual, at the same time and by the same means is not easy. Increased production calls for economic and social organization, with increasing interdependence and cooperation among different economic groups. How can we achieve this and at the same time preserve freedom and democracy?

This is a complex and delicate task, which depends for its accomplishment on a blend of physical and economic science with social justice. . . .

In the Agricultural Adjustment Act of 1938 we have an important instrument for promoting the twofold objective. On the economic side the law expresses the unity of interest among different groups in agriculture and safeguards the consumer through provisions for the maintenance of a continuous and stable supply of agricultural commodities at fair prices. On the social side it applies the principle of democracy. It is a new charter of economic and political freedom for both producer and consumer. Abundance and democracy are the twin foundations. . . .

Acknowledging that the Agricultural Adjustment Act truly promotes abundance and not scarcity, we come now to its methods. Are they compatible with our democracy? They introduce governmental planning into matters formerly not subject to governmental guidance, and place the power of the Government behind the necessary action programs. Opponents call this regimentation; they say it is not consistent with our traditions and principles. Manifestly, however, this begs the question, because it assumes that the scope of democracy has long since been established once for all. It sets up mere custom as the arbiter. In a constantly changing and evolving economic and social environment, the basic political principle must be capable of change and development likewise, or it will die and give place to something with life in it. . . .

Every American has his own definition of democracy, and the definitions vary widely. There is a mistaken view that it means freedom for every man to do just as he likes with his property, regardless of how his actions may affect the general welfare. In countless instances the courts have said he may not. Every democratic right has its limitations, even the right of free speech, which may not be blasphemous, seditious, or defamatory. Another obviously mistaken view is that democracy enjoins public agencies from doing anything that might conceivably be left to private initiative, and frowns on public enterprises like mail distribution, education, forestry, water-works, irrigation, drainage, crop reporting, and road building. Democracy is not just laissez faire; it includes the protection and the constructive advancement of public as well as of private interests. In proof we may note the progress of democracy in this and other countries side by side with a great extension of public works and services. We cannot define democracy in negative terms, and make of it a mere system of prohibitions. It is a positive doctrine that authorizes positive programs with regard to any issue of pressing national concern. Not to admit that is to condemn democracy to impotence. . . .

In times like these economic planning is the savior rather than the destroyer of democracy. It substitutes order for chaos, and appeasement for disaffection. In this way it averts dictatorship, which indeed cannot arise until orderly government has broken down and the masses are in revolt. Ancient and modern history testify to that. With unemployment unrelieved, and with agriculture in ruins, we should be in real danger of dictatorship. There would be bread riots in the cities and mortgage strikes in the country; it would be impossible to maintain order without the use of force. From that point to dictatorship the descent would be swift. Instead, we have domestic peace, increasing economic justice, and firm reliance on government by discussion. . . .

What the democracy produced it can manage, without going outside itself for the means, and without stultifying its own nature. That is not a mere assertion; it is an inference from the strong probability that progress and freedom are interdependent. . . . It is a fair assumption.

❊ ❊ ❊

Federal farm subsidies set the stage for a remarkable turnaround in American agriculture. During the four decades since World War II the farm economy has been reshaped so profoundly that the event constitutes a second agricultural revolution. Federal efforts to stabilize farm income and output stimulated massive long-term capital investment in agriculture which transformed a large, sick industry into the world's most efficient. The mule and the plowhorse became a thing of the past as tractors by the millions were added to the few hundred thousand in use in the 1930s. Chemical fertilizers, unknown before 1940, dramatically increased the productivity of the land, while new seed strains, often the result of USDA research, multiplied the productivity of crops. Overall the growth of productivity in farming has been three times as great as that of the nonfarm economy since World War II.

The statistics are breathtaking. In 1940 it took one farmer to feed every 12 Americans, and farmers were still one-quarter of the labor force, down only a little from the 30 percent employed in farming at the beginning of the century. By 1980 a single farmer could feed 61 persons, and farmers constituted 3.7 percent of the labor force! In the 1930s there were nearly 7 million American farms, most of them inefficient, marginal operations locked into a deadly cycle of rural poverty. In 1982 there were 2.4 million farms, most of them highly efficient, family-run businesses with capital resources large enough to take advantage of the best production techniques. (Only 7 percent of American farmland is presently owned by corporations.) During the postwar years farm income has been maintained at acceptably high levels, and American consumers still enjoy food prices which take a smaller share of their income than anywhere else in the industrialized world.

The wonderful efficiency of American agriculture since the war has brought other benefits, including our greatest competitive advantage in world trade. In 1940 only 6 percent of American farm production was exported. In 1981, a record year, 33 percent of the crop was sold overseas, earning precious credits against America's present trade deficits. Indeed the 3 percent of Americans engaged in farming produce a fifth of all American exports. As it was in the nineteenth century, the United States has again become the breadbasket of the world.

Government-owned stockpiles of surplus grains—Henry Wallace's "ever-normal granary"—have also permitted the United States to assume its responsibility as the world's leading food producer to relieve food crises around the world. Wallace himself was pleased to note that shortly after its inception the program made possible massive shipments of food to Europe under the Lend Lease program. After the war American surpluses assisted the economic recovery of Europe, where British housewives still had to queue up to purchase rationed food as late as 1950. In 1954 Public Law 480, later revised as the Food for Peace program, made American food available to the underdeveloped world, including large-scale aid to India in the 1960s and the present efforts to relieve famine in Africa.

From time to time critics have worried about the size and cost of American stockpiles; in 1963 they reached a record 1 billion bushels of wheat. But over the years the amounts stored have usually been less than America's fair share of the reserves recommended by the United Nations Food and Agricultural Organization as protection against a world shortage. In fact during the world food crisis of 1972–76, even the immense surpluses accumulated during the 1960s were wholly exhausted.

If Thomas Jefferson could have toured rural America in the 1930s, he would have encountered scenes mostly familiar to him. Thirty years later he would have been utterly dumbfounded. The transformation of American agriculture since 1938 stands as a model of what can be accomplished by a combination of private business and constructive public planning and support.

5

Franklin Delano Roosevelt
❧ ❧ ❧

The Four Freedoms
1941

"*I*t's a terrible thing to look over your shoulder when you are trying to lead—and to find no one there." By 1937, President Roosevelt was accustomed to leading. He had not been uniformly successful in enacting his program of domestic reform, nor, as a recession within the Great Depression in 1937 indicated, had four years of the New Deal restored the nation's economy to the pink of health. But never was the President so rebuked by American public opinion as when, in October of 1937, he told a Chicago audience that in order to halt the march of aggressor nations in the world, nations he likened to a physical disease, it was the moral obligation and in our national interest to join with other democratic countries in "quarantining" them. That is, the United States should enforce economic sanctions against nations that threatened world peace and lead an international campaign to isolate them morally.

Roosevelt did not name the "aggressor nations" who were "creating a state of international anarchy" in the world, but there was no doubt that he meant militaristic Japan, Fascist Italy, and Nazi Germany, which were, by the late 1930s, rearming massively and unambivalent in their designs on weaker neighbors.

FDR was a disciple of Woodrow Wilson. In the collapse of democratic governments in Europe and the bald aggressiveness of the antidemocratic states, he saw the direst predictions of his mentor coming true. (See Woodrow Wilson, "The League of Nations," in Part 3.) In failing to join

THE FOUR FREEDOMS From Annual Message to Congress, January 6, 1941, *Congressional Record*, 77th Congress, 1st Session, LXXXVII, Part I, 45–47.

the League of Nations in 1919, and thus cooperating with other countries in maintaining international security, the United States had contributed to the conditions in which the dictatorial, supernationalistic governments in Japan, Italy, and Germany had thrived. The message of his "Quarantine Speech" was: It was time to rectify that error.

In 1937, however, a majority of Americans drew quite another lesson from the history of World War I and its aftermath. Led and encouraged by "isolationists," legatees of the fight against the League, public opinion had come to the conclusion that American participation in World War I had been a horrendous blunder from the start. Influential historians and the Senate's Nye Committee had produced evidence that munitions makers and Wall Street had realized immense profits from the war and therefore favored it. These undeniable facts were popularly interpreted to mean that the banks, big business, and the "merchants of death" had positively conspired to involve the United States in the war. This mentality was a by-product of the antibusiness spirit of the 1930s that FDR did not welcome.

Nor was the movement to maintain American neutrality in the event of another conflagration a flurry on the political fringe. Between 1935 and 1939, Congress passed a series of Neutrality Acts designed to avert the involvement of American financiers in overseas wars and attacks on American shipping, such as the isolationists believed had led to intervention in World War I. In 1940, after general war had broken out in Europe, the America First Committee was formed to launch a well-financed and militant campaign to keep the United States out by arguing variously that Germany posed no threat to the United States, the war was England's fault, and the cause of Britain was already doomed. America First enjoyed the support of many distinguished individuals including historian Charles Beard, Senators Arthur Vandenberg and Robert M. LaFollette, Jr., and popular hero Charles Lindbergh.

By January 1941, however, when Roosevelt delivered his annual message to Congress, public opinion was shifting rapidly to support President Roosevelt's position that England was not lost and that Germany and Japan did indeed threaten American security. FDR exploited this opportunity to take the Wilsonian high road in his call for active intervention—short of war—in the international struggle.

❀ Armed defense of democratic existence is now being gallantly waged in four continents. If that defense fails, all the population and all the resources of Europe, Asia, Africa and Australasia will be dominated by the conquerors. The total of those populations and their resources . . . greatly exceeds the sum total of the popu-

lation and the resources of the whole of the Western Hemisphere—
many times over.

In times like these it is immature—and incidentally untrue—
for anybody to brag that an unprepared America, single-handed,
and with one hand tied behind its back, can hold off the whole
world.

No realistic American can expect from a dictator's peace international generosity, or return of true independence, or world dis-
armament, or freedom of expression, or freedom of religion—or
even good business. . . .

The need of the moment is that our actions and our policy
should be devoted primarily—almost exclusively—to meeting this
foreign peril. For all our domestic problems are now a part of the
great emergency.

Just as our national policy in internal affairs has been based
upon a decent respect for the rights and the dignity of all our fellow-
men within our gates, so our national policy in foreign affairs has
been based on a decent respect for the rights and dignity of all
nations, large and small. And the justice of morality must and will
win in the end.

Our national policy is this:

First, by an impressive expression of the public will and without regard to partisanship, we are committed to all-inclusive national defense.

Second, by an impressive expression of the public will and
without regard to partisanship, we are committed to full support of
all those resolute peoples, everywhere, who are resisting aggression
and are thereby keeping war away from our hemisphere. By this
support, we express our determination that the democratic cause
shall prevail, and we strengthen the defense and security of our
own nation.

Third, by an impressive expression of the public will and without regard to partisanship, we are commited to the proposition that
principles of morality and considerations for our own security will
never permit us to acquiesce in a peace dictated by aggressors and
sponsored by appeasers. We know that enduring peace cannot be
bought at the cost of other people's freedom. . . .

I also ask this Congress for authority and for funds sufficient
to manufacture additional munitions and war supplies of many
kinds, to be turned over to those nations which are now in actual
war with aggressor nations.

Our most useful and immediate role is to act as an arsenal for
them as well as for ourselves. They do not need man power. They
do need billions of dollars' worth of the weapons of defense. . . .

Let us say to the democracies, "We Americans are vitally concerned in your defense of freedom. We are putting forth our energies, our resources, and our organizing powers to give you the strength to regain and maintain a free world. We shall send you, in ever-increasing numbers, ships, planes, tanks, guns. This is our purpose and our pledge." . . .

There is nothing mysterious about the foundations of a healthy and strong democracy. The basic things expected by our people of their political and economic systems are simple. They are:

Equality of opportunity for youth and for others.

Jobs for those who can work.

Security for those who need it.

The ending of special privilege for the few.

The preservation of civil liberties for all.

The enjoyment of the fruits of scientific progress in a wider and constantly rising standard of living.

These are the simple and basic things that must never be lost sight of in the turmoil and unbelievable complexity of our modern world. The inner and abiding strength of our economic and political systems is dependent upon the degree to which they fulfill these expectations. . . .

In the future days, which we seek to make secure, we look forward to a world founded upon four essential human freedoms.

The first is freedom of speech and expression everywhere in the world.

The second is freedom of every person to worship God in his own way everywhere in the world.

The third is freedom from want, which, translated into world terms, means economic understandings which will secure to every nation a healthy peacetime life for its inhabitants everywhere in the world.

The fourth is freedom from fear—which, translated into world terms, means a world-wide reduction of armaments to such a point and in such a thorough fashion that no nation will be in a position to commit an act of physical aggression against any neighbor—anywhere in the world.

That is no vision of a distant millennium. It is a definite basis for a kind of world attainable in our own time and generation. That kind of world is the very antithesis of the so-called new order of tyranny which the dictators seek to create with the crash of a bomb.

To that new order we oppose the greater conception—the moral order. A good society is able to face schemes of world domination and foreign revolutions alike without fear.

Since the beginning of our American history we have been

engaged in change—in a perpetual peaceful revolution—a revolution which goes on steadily, quietly adjusting itself to changing conditions—without the concentration camp or the quicklime in the ditch. The world order which we seek is the cooperation of free countries, working together in a friendly, civilized society.

❀ ❀ ❀

Three weeks after the "Four Freedoms" speech, presidential aides met with British diplomats in Washington to agree on strategic principles should the United States be drawn into a declared war. In March, as German submarines devastated British shipping in the North Atlantic, Roosevelt extended "the sea frontier" of the United States to 26 degrees west longitude in order to allow the British to concentrate their naval resources around the home islands. In the same month, Congress adopted the Lend Lease Act which enabled nearly prostrate Britain to purchase American armaments. In April, the United States, in an agreement with the exile government of Denmark, pledged to defend Greenland in return for the right to construct military bases there. By the time Hitler invaded the Soviet Union in June and thus relieved the pressure on Britain, the United States was in effect fighting the Nazis.

The actual declaration of war came, of course, in December, when Japan—not Germany—attacked the American naval base at Pearl Harbor in the Territory of Hawaii. As Roosevelt had agreed earlier in January 1941, American materiel and men were concentrated on defeating Germany first. Not only did Germany pose a threat to humanity itself (the war with Japan was rather an imperial struggle), Germany was also the more powerful enemy, capable, if neglected, of establishing an impregnable "Fortress Europe." The prosecution of the war was carried out in good faith and compliance with the principles enunciated in both the Four Freedoms speech and the Atlantic Charter, jointly proclaimed by FDR and British Prime Minister Winston Churchill in August 1941.

The Atlantic Charter was Woodrow Wilson and the Four Freedoms written anew: The allies sought no territorial gains; any changes in the map of the world would accord with "the freely expressed wishes of the people concerned"; trade would be free and based on international economic cooperation; and—here Roosevelt made sure not to lead and find no one behind him—vague reference was made to some "wider and permanent system of general security."

What World War I had not taught, World War II did. By steps throughout the war, the *United Nations* were transformed from a military alliance into a permanent agency for the purposes of maintaining collective security and avoiding international wars. On April 25, 1945, fifty countries opened a series of meetings in San Francisco that formally constituted the UN. FDR did not attend the ceremony: He had died two weeks earlier.

6

David E. Lilienthal

❖ ❖ ❖

The Tennessee Valley Authority

1944

*T*he Tennessee River rises in the
Appalachians near Knoxville and winds its way for 652 miles through
several southeastern states. In one place or another it flows towards every
point of the compass, finally draining into the Ohio River at Paducah,
Kentucky. The strategic importance of the Tennessee's tortuous route
through Appalachia was indicated, during the Civil War, by the high
priority President Lincoln gave to the capture of Fort Henry, at the
river's mouth.

In the 20th century, the Tennessee Valley came to hold comparable
significance in the minds of progressive reformers. In "The New
Nationalism" (Part 3), Theodore Roosevelt had proclaimed that
"conservation means development as much as it does protection." He was
thinking of resources such as the Tennessee, the rapid descent of which
provided dozens of opportunities to build dams and generate electrical
power. The forest and mineral resources of the Tennessee Valley,
particularly in phosphates, were considerable. And yet, the banks the
river washed were home to some of the poorest and most ignorant people
in the United States. Indeed, the Tennessee was partly responsible for the

THE TENNESSEE VALLEY AUTHORITY   From David E. Lilienthal, *TVA—Democracy on
the March* (New York: 1944), pp. 5–6, 218–22.

retardation of Appalachia. Almost annually the river savagely flooded, making life in its wake scarcely better than a struggle for survival. There was little hope of securing the better, more prosperous way of life America was supposed to mean.

The idea of developing the Tennessee Valley also appealed to progressives because nature had created in it an integrated, interdependent region of some 40,000 square miles. It was apparent that piecemeal reclamation and dam projects, such as local and state governments had dabbled in, would not be productive so long as the river ran wild elsewhere along its length. But private investors were uninterested because the magnitude of regional development meant (as with the construction of the transcontinental railroad during the 1860s) there would be no returns on investment for a considerable period of time. The Tennessee Valley was a perfect region in which the progressives could demonstrate the necessity of government planning, economic development, and social engineering on a large scale.

In 1917, as the United States mobilized for war, President Wilson persuaded Congress to construct a dam and nitrates factory at Muscle Shoals, Alabama. It was envisaged that the facility would produce munitions and, after the war, fertilizers. However, beginning with the election of 1918, conservative Republicans regained control of, first, Congress, and then the presidency. Presidents Harding and Coolidge both tried to sell off Muscle Shoals (once to Henry Ford) at bargain rates. They were stymied by a makeshift alliance in Congress between old-time Republican progressives and Democratic congressmen and senators from the states through which the Tennessee flowed.

The leader of this alliance was Senator George Norris of Nebraska, a former Bull Mooser whose near obsession was the development of the Tennessee Valley for social purposes. Even during the 1920s, he managed to push two "TVA" (Tennessee Valley Authority) bills through Congress. In both cases, Republican Presidents vetoed the bills. Only with the election of Franklin D. Roosevelt was the old progressive spirit revived and the project given new appeal by the urgency of creating jobs for the unemployed. Simply in constructing the massive complex, the TVA would employ at least 15,000 people over a decade. During FDR's "Hundred Days," the Tennessee Valley Authority was created.

The director of the project was David E. Lilienthal of Chicago, a progressive who had devoted his career to investigating electrical utilities in Illinois and Wisconsin. He had exposed the exorbitance of the rates they charged and espoused just such regional planning as the TVA put into practice. In 1944, after eleven years directing the construction of some 30 dams, which brought the first electrical power to 40,000 square miles of Appalachia and provided jobs for 25,000 people on the TVA payroll, as well as many thousands more in plants made possible by the TVA, Lilienthal published *TVA—Democracy on the March*. In it he explained his and the progressive's vision of an experiment that was much more than a construction project.

❇ The spirit in which the task is undertaken; its purpose, whether for the welfare of the many or the few; the methods chosen—these will determine whether men will live in freedom and peace, whether their resources will be speedily exhausted or will be sustained, nourished, made solid beneath their feet not only for themselves but for the generations to come.

The physical achievements that science and technology now make possible may bring no benefits, may indeed be evil, unless they have a moral purpose, unless they are conceived and carried out for the benefit of the people themselves. Without such a purpose, advances in technology may be disastrous to the human spirit; the industralization of a raw material area may bring to the average man only a new kind of slavery and the destruction of democratic institutions.

But such a moral purpose alone is not enough to insure that resource development will be a blessing and not a curse. Out of TVA experience in this valley I am persuaded that to make such a purpose effective two other principles are essential. First, that resource development must be governed by the unity of nature herself. Second, that the people must participate actively in that development.

The physical job is going to be done; of that I think we can be sure. But if, in the doing, the unity of nature's resources is disregarded, the price will be paid in exhausted land, butchered forests, polluted streams, and industrial ugliness. And, if the people are denied an active part in this great task, then they may be poor or they may be prosperous but they will not be free. . . .

We have a choice. There is the important fact. Men are not powerless; they have it in their hands to use the machine to augment the dignity of human existence. True, they may have so long denied themselves the use of that power to decide, which is theirs, may so long have meekly accepted the dictation of bosses of one stripe or another or the ministrations of benevolent nursemaids, that the muscles of democratic choice have atrophied. But that strength is always latent; history has shown how quickly it revives. How we shall use physical betterment—that decision is ours to make. We are not carried irresistibly by forces beyond our control, whether they are given some mystic term or described as the "laws of economics." We are not inert objects on a wave of the future.

Except for saints and great ascetics, I suppose most people would agree that poverty and physical wretchedness are evils, in and of themselves. But because extreme poverty is an evil it does not follow that a comfortable or a high material standard of living is good. A Tennessee Valley farm wife who now has an electric pump that brings water into her kitchen may or may not be more generous of spirit, less selfish, than when she was forced to carry her water from the spring day after day. A once destitute sharecropper who now has an interesting factory job at good wages and lives in a comfortable house in town may or may not be more tolerant, more rational, more thoughtful of others, more active in community concerns. We all know that some of the least admirable men are found among those who have come up from poverty to a "high standard of living."

Whether happiness or unhappiness, freedom or slavery, in short whether good or evil results from an improved environment depends largely upon how the change has been brought about, upon the methods by which the physical results have been reached, and in what spirit and for what purpose the fruits of that change are used. . . .

Democracy is a literal impossibility without faith that on balance the good in man far outweighs the evil. Every effort to cherish the overtones of human imagination in music, painting, or poetry rests upon that same faith, makes that same assumption. And so it is with what we have been seeking to do in this valley. To call it "materialistic" answers nothing. The rock upon which all these efforts rest is a faith in human beings. . . .

The technical results in the Tennessee Valley, the achievements of many kinds of experts, are of course matters of no little importance. But, speaking as an administrator and a citizen, unless these technical products strengthen the conviction that machines and science can be used by men for their greater individual and spiritual growth, then so far as I am concerned the physical accomplishments and the material benefits would be of dubious value indeed.

There are few who fail to see that modern applied science and the machine are threats to the development of the individual personality, the very purpose of democratic institutions. It is for this reason that the experience of the last ten years in the valley of the Tennessee is heartening. In this one valley (in some ways the world in microcosm) it has been demonstrated that. . . . when the use of technology has a moral purpose and when its methods are thoroughly democratic, far from forcing the surrender of individual freedom and the things of the spirit to the machine, the machine can be made to promote those very ends.

❊ ❊ ❊

In 1944 Lilienthal left the TVA in order to become head of the Atomic Energy Commission. It was an appropriate change of job because the electrical power produced by TVA dams made possible the construction of many factories devoted to nuclear power in the Tennessee Valley. Today, about half of the electricity produced by the TVA is consumed by defense plants.

Between 1946 and 1950, when Lilienthal was head of the AEC, progressivism in the form of New Deal liberalism was once again on the defensive. Lilienthal himself was attacked as a dangerous radical because of his opposition to the development of the hydrogen bomb and his emphasis on international cooperation in the use of nuclear power for peaceful purposes. In 1953, when Dwight D. Eisenhower was inaugurated President, conservative Republicans within his administration suggested selling off the whole of TVA. The uproar from the people of the Valley, who clearly preferred public to private administration, and from liberals generally, who saw TVA as a shining example of the superiority of government planning and administration, quickly put an end to the idea. However, when the Eisenhower administration announced the intention of allowing a private corporation, Dixon-Yates, to construct a new dam *within* the TVA region, only a revelation of corrupt collusion between government officials and Dixon-Yates executives prevented it.

TVA remains the most splendid material achievement of the New Deal, but it is difficult to imagine Norris and Lilienthal pleased by the loss of the ideals with which, they believed, the dams and factories, floodgates and dynamos were part and parcel.

PART 5

❖ ❖ ❖

Our Times
1946–

1

George F. Kennan
❖ ❖ ❖

Containment Policy
1946

*N*azi Germany was defeated by
British pluck, Russian blood, and American industrial might. In standing
alone against Hitler's juggernaut between June 1940 and June 1941, Great
Britain confounded all military reason and confident German plans,
contributing to Hitler's ultimately fatal decision to invade the Soviet Union
in mid-1941. The decision was fatal because the immensity of the Eurasian
land mass, the severity of the Russian winter, and the desperate
determination of the Soviet people and leadership to resist to the end—
they were fighting literally for survival—proved too much even for the
German *Wehrmacht*. Through three years the Soviets slogged it out with
the invaders in a war of sickening savagery on both sides. The cost was
26 million Soviet citizens dead, about half of them civilians. As a point
of comparison, 407,000 Americans died in both the Pacific and European
theaters of the war. The contribution of the United States in defeating
Germany was in the materiel the great and untouched American industrial
complex churned out for the allies.

The alliance was an uneasy one. Soviet Premier Joseph Stalin had a
suspicious nature and a long memory. It gnawed on him that the United
States had landed troops in Russia in 1918 to help sabotage the Bolshevik
revolution, and that the United States had not recognized the Soviet Union
until 1933. Despite a cordial personal relationship with President Franklin

CONTAINMENT POLICY   From *Foreign Relations of the United States*, 1946, VI, 696–
709.

D. Roosevelt, he was aware that many high-ranking American policymakers and generals were fanatically anti-Communist: more than one had suggested that the Nazis and Soviets be allowed to fight on and on without interference, destroying one another. Although there were incontrovertible military reasons for delaying the opening of a second front in Europe until 1944, and both Roosevelt and Allied Supreme Commander Dwight D. Eisenhower shaped strategy in part to reassure the Soviets of their good intentions (delaying the Anglo-American advance, for example, so that the long-suffering Russians could occupy much of Germany), Stalin suspected that exhausting Russian power had been part of the western plan. His suspicions showed in his reticent and cagey dealings with the western allies both before and after the surrender.

In a "Long Telegram" dispatched to Washington in February 1946, the charge d'affaires at the American embassy in Moscow, George F. Kennan, explained that diplomatic problems with the Soviet Union were due to the Soviet belief that the western capitalist nations were determined to destroy Russia. This was due only accidentally to their official Marxist ideology, Kennan said. Marxism was just "a fig leaf of their moral and intellectual respectability," covering up the fact that the Russian Communists, like the Tsars before them, were determined to expand Russian hegemony as far into Europe as they could. The reason for this expansion was to assert Russia's status as a great nation (a sore point with a country traditionally disdained in the West as semi-civilized), and to ensure Russian security. Historically, Russia had been attacked by western aggressors: Sweden under Charles XII, Napoleonic France, and twice in the twentieth century—devastatingly—by Germany. After a brilliant historical analysis of the Russian diplomatic psychology, Kennan predicted the pattern of Soviet actions in the postwar world and suggested what the United States should do to counter them.

On official plane we must look for following [in Soviet policy].[1]

(A) Internal policy devoted to increasing in every way strength and prestige of Soviet state's intensive military-industrialization;

---

[1]The omission of definite and indefinite articles (the, a, an) in this document, and the generally abrupt quality of the prose, reflects the fact that, while later rewritten, Kennan's essay was originally a telegram.

maximum development of armed forces; great displays to impress outsiders; continued secretiveness about internal matters, designed to conceal weaknesses and to keep opponents in dark.

(B) Wherever it is considered timely and promising, efforts will be made to advance official limits of Soviet power. For the moment, these efforts are restricted to certain neighboring points conceived of here as being of immediate strategic necessity. . . .

(C) Russians will participate officially in international organizations where they see opportunity of extending Soviet power or of inhibiting or diluting power of others. Moscow sees in UNO[2] not the mechanism for a permanent and stable world society founded on mutual interest and aims of all nations, but an arena in which aims just mentioned can be favorably pursued. . . .

(D) Toward colonial areas and backward or dependent peoples, Soviet policy, even on official plane, will be directed toward weakening of power and influence and contacts of advanced western nations, on theory that in so far as this policy is successful, there will be created a vacuum which will favor communist-Soviet penetration. . . .

(E) Russians will strive energetically to develop Soviet representation in, and official ties with, countries in which they sense strong possibilities of opposition to western centers of power. . . .

(F) In international economic matters, Soviet policy will really be dominated by pursuit of autarchy[3] for Soviet Union and Soviet-dominated adjacent areas taken together. . . .

(G) With respect to cultural collaboration, lip service will likewise be rendered to desirability of deepening cultural contacts between peoples, but this will not in practice be interpreted in any way which could weaken security position of Soviet peoples. Actual manifestations of Soviet policy in this respect will be restricted to arid channels of closely shepherded official visits and functions, with super-abundance of vodka and speeches and dearth of permanent effects.

(H) Beyond this, Soviet official relations will take what might be called "correct" course with individual foreign governments, with great stress being laid on prestige of Soviet Union and its representatives and with punctilious attention to protocol, as distinct from good manners. . . .

In summary, we have here a political force committed fanati-

---

[2]In its first years, the United Nations was known as the United Nations Organization.

[3]Autarchy: economic self-sufficiency.

cally to the belief that with US there can be no permanent modus vivendi. . . . This is admittedly not a pleasant picture. Problem of how to cope with this force is undoubtedly greatest task our diplomacy has ever faced and probably greatest it will ever have to face. It should be point of departure from which our political general staff work at present juncture should proceed. It should be approached with same thoroughness and care as solution of major strategic problem in war, and if necessary, with no smaller outlay in planning effort. I cannot attempt to suggest all answers here. But I would like to record my conviction that problem is within our power to solve—and that without recourse to any general military conflict. And in support of this conviction there are certain observations of a more encouraging nature I should like to make:

(One) Soviet power, unlike that of Hitlerite Germany, is neither schematic nor adventuristic. It does not work by fixed plans. It does not take unnecessary risks. Impervious to logic of reason, and it is highly sensitive to logic of force. For this reason it can easily withdraw—and usually does—when strong resistance is encountered at any point. Thus, if the adversary has sufficient force and makes clear his readiness to use it, he rarely has to do so. If situations are properly handled there need be no prestige engaging showdowns.

(Two) Gauged against western world as a whole, Soviets are still by far the weaker force. Thus, their success will really depend on degree of cohesion, firmness and vigor which western world can muster. And this is factor which it is within our power to influence.

(Three) Success of Soviet system, as form of internal power, is not yet finally proven. It has yet to be demonstrated that it can survive supreme test of successive transfer of power from one individual or group to another. Lenin's death was first such transfer, and its effects wracked Soviet state for 15 years after. Stalin's death or retirement will be second. But even this will not be final test. Soviet internal system will now be subjected, by virtue of recent territorial expansions, to series of additional strains which once proved severe tax on Tsardom. We here are convinced that never since termination of civil war have mass of Russian people been emotionally farther removed from doctrines of communist party than they are today. In Russia, party has now become a great and— for the moment—highly successful apparatus of dictatorial administration, but it has ceased to be a source of emotional inspiration. Thus, internal soundness and permanence of movement need not yet be regarded as assured.

(Four) All Soviet propaganda beyond Soviet security sphere is basically negative and destructive. It should therefore be relatively easy to combat it by any intelligent and really constructive program.

For these reasons I think we may approach calmly and with good heart problem of how to deal with Russia. As to how this approach should be made, I only wish to advance, by way of conclusion, following comments:

(One) Our first step must be to apprehend, and recognize for what it is, the nature of the movement with which we are dealing. We must study it with same courage, detachment, objectivity, and same determination not to be emotionally provoked or unseated by it, with which doctor studies unruly and unreasonable individual.

(Two) We must see that our public is educated to realities of Russian situation. I cannot over-emphasize importance of this. Press cannot do this alone. It must be done mainly by government, which is necessarily more experienced and better informed on practical problems involved. . . . I am convinced that there would be far less hysterical anti-Sovietism in our country today if realities of this situation were better understood by our people. There is nothing as dangerous or as terrifying as the unknown. It may also be argued that to reveal more information on our difficulties with Russia would reflect unfavorably on Russian American relations. I feel that if there is any real risk here involved, it is one which we should have courage to face, and sooner the better. But I cannot see what we would be risking. Our stake in this country, even coming on heels of tremendous demonstrations of our friendship for Russian people, is remarkably small. We have here no investments to guard, no actual trade to lose, virtually no citizens to protect, few cultural contacts to preserve. Our only stake lies in what we hope rather than what we have; and I am convinced we have better chance of realizing those hopes if our public is enlightened and if our dealings with Russians are placed entirely on realistic and matter of fact basis.

(Three) Much depends on health and vigor of our own society. World communism is like malignant parasite which feeds only on diseased tissue. This is point at which domestic and foreign policies meet. Every courageous and incisive measure to solve internal problems of our own society, to improve self-confidence, discipline, morale and community spirit of our own people, is a diplomatic victory over Moscow worth a thousand diplomatic notes and joint communiqués. If we cannot abandon fatalism and indifference in face of deficiencies of our own society, Moscow will profit—Moscow cannot help profiting by them in its foreign policies.

(Four) We must formulate and put forward for other nations

a much more positive and constructive picture of sort of world we would like to see than we have put forward in past. It is not enough to urge people to develop political processes similar to our own. Many foreign people, in Europe at least, are tired and frightened by experiences of past, and are less interested in abstract freedom than in security. They are seeking guidance rather than responsibilities. We should be better able than Russians to give them this. And unless we do, Russians certainly will.

(Five) Finally we must have courage and self-confidence to cling to our own methods and conceptions of human society. After all, the greatest danger that can befall us in coping with this problem of Soviet Communism, is that we shall allow ourselves to become like those with whom we are coping.

✿ ✿ ✿

Kennan had bluntly predicted the "Cold War" between the Soviet Union and the West at a time when advisors to President Harry S. Truman (who succeeded FDR in April 1945) were still debating the question of whether to strive to maintain the cooperative relations of wartime or to take a "hard line" with the Soviets. Ever since, historians have debated the question of whether Soviet actions in preventing democratic elections in the nations of Eastern Europe occupied by the Red Army, or American bellicosity, exacerbating Soviet anxieties, was the real cause of the superpower hostility that casts a pall over the world to this day.

After the "Long Telegram" was published anonymously in the quasi-official *Foreign Affairs* in July 1947, Kennan's prescription of "containment" became the foundation of American foreign policy. In the Truman Doctrine of 1947, the United States actively supported anti-Communist regimes in Turkey and Greece in armed struggles with strong communist movements, and in both cases the Soviet Union withdrew its active support of the Communists in those countries. In the Marshall Plan of 1948 (named for Secretary of State George C. Marshall), the United States pumped billions of dollars into the economies of the Western European nations, enabling those countries to overcome the devastation of war and the conditions of poverty and demoralization in which indigenous Communist movements flourished. In France and Italy, very popular Communist parties ceased their rapid postwar growth and froze at about 25 percent of the electorate. Once again, as Kennan had predicted, the Soviets withdrew all but token encouragement of the western Communist parties. Granted that we can never know what might have happened had another course been followed, containment was highly successful in Europe.

It was so successful that American policy makers (but not Kennan) failed to see that it did not apply to every frustration the United States encountered elsewhere in the world. When Chinese Communists led by Mao Tse-tung defeated Chinese Nationalists in 1949, it was interpreted as an example of Russian aggression, despite overwhelming evidence that the pro-American Nationalist regime had lost popular support, that American policy in China had been badly bungled, and that the Soviets were themselves not pleased with the idea of a reinvigorated China on their long common border. When North Korean troops invaded pro-American South Korea in 1950, that too was seen as Russian mischief despite the fact that the American-backed president of South Korea, Syngman Rhee, had been as provocative as the North Koreans.

After 1953, Secretary of State John Foster Dulles transformed the "intelligent and really constructive" program of containment into the "negative and destructive" policy of "rolling back Communism" that, in Kennan's eyes, did precisely what he warned against in the final sentence of the document reprinted above. Retiring from the diplomatic service (he returned briefly in 1961–63), Kennan became an eloquent and telling critic of American foreign policy toward the Soviet Union, in Asia, in Vietnam in the 1960s and 1970s (see McNamara and Fulbright, "The Vietnam Debate"), and most urgently in the nuclear arms race of the 1980s.

2

Harry S. Truman

✦ ✦ ✦

The Fair Deal

1949

*A*t a press conference early in the war, President Franklin Roosevelt announced that "Dr. New Deal" was retiring from the case, to be replaced by "Dr. Win-the-War." Domestic reform would have to be shelved for the duration, FDR said, since "the overwhelming first emphasis should be on winning the war."

This decision left much unfinished business on the liberal agenda. The Social Security system introduced by the New Deal was not only modest by European standards, it also failed to include almost a third of the work force. Unlike other western democracies the United States had no program of national health insurance. Only the smallest starts at slum clearance and public housing had been made. Severe poverty afflicted perhaps a fifth of American families. In the last year before the war nine million American workers were still unemployed. While the war gave everybody something to do, the eventual return of twelve million servicemen in need of jobs prompted many New Dealers to project major government programs to guarantee full employment in the postwar nation. Other New-Deal economists and sociologists, such as those working with the National Resources Planning Board, envisaged broad new roles for government in the planning and direction of economic development, including new regional authorities modeled on TVA. Black Americans too had taken new hope during the New Deal that the ancient injustices which they suffered could be righted. Although during the 1930s the Roosevelt

THE FAIR DEAL   From Harry S. Truman, Annual Message to the Congress on the State of the Union, January 5, 1949, *Public Papers of the Presidents of the United States: Harry S. Truman, 1949* (Washington: U.S. Government Printing Office, 1964), pp. 1–7.

administration had usually sacrificed the interests of southern blacks for southern white support of New Deal measures, the massive migration of blacks to northern cities before and during the war gave blacks more effective organization and new political leverage. Wait until after the Depression, FDR had told them; then, wait until after the war. As the war drew to a conclusion, black Americans justly believed that their turn had come.

In 1944, with Allied victory in sight, "Dr. New Deal" reappeared. In the President's annual message to Congress FDR propounded "a second Bill of Rights" which recognized that "necessitous men are not free men." He proposed to guarantee every American a job, adequate food and clothing, a decent home, medical care, and education. The "Economic Bill of Rights" projected a bold program for postwar America, but before the war had ended, FDR was dead.

His successor had none of the extraordinary personal qualities that had enabled Roosevelt to wheedle, cajole, charm, and bully a generation of reluctant Americans to accept new programs. Harry S. Truman was a very ordinary American, a successful politician of the county-courthouse variety. A simple man of unquestionable decency, who carried his boyhood sweetheart's picture with him in World War I and married her when he got home, Truman never schemed to win high office. Rather, he worked very hard at any job he was given and never forgot his friends. His qualities were appealing but not especially presidential.

Truman's rise to the White House was in fact symptomatic of the case that long before 1945 the New Deal had run out of political steam. As early as 1937 southern Democrats had begun to make common cause with northern Republicans to obstruct liberal legislation. After 1938 this conservative coalition commanded a majority in Congress which steadily increased during the war years. Republicans made striking gains in the elections of 1942, producing a Congress which harassed and liquidated many New Deal agencies including the National Resources Planning Board.

To manage this growing deadlock and make wartime government possible, FDR had come increasingly to rely on "border-state" politicians, a group of congressional moderates in the Democratic party who mediated between its liberal northern and conservative southern wings and between Congress and the administration. Senator Harry Truman from Missouri was one of the most reliable members of this group, and in 1944, when FDR ran for a fourth term, he bumped liberal Vice-President Henry Wallace from the ticket and installed the Missourian in his place. Thus Truman's accession to the presidency a few months later was no accident, but the product of Democratic stalemate.

Liberals like David Lilienthal were dismayed by the turn of events which had put "that Throttlebottom, Truman" in the White House, and at first the new President's course only increased their apprehensions. Dozens of liberal New Dealers, including Henry Wallace whom Truman fired in 1946, were replaced by undistinguished Missouri cronies. Truman angered labor when he clumsily intervened in a threatened railroad strike, and alarmed liberals by his "get-tough" policies toward the Soviet Union. Meanwhile Congress moved pell-mell to dismantle wartime controls over business with the result that prices and corporate profits skyrocketed. After a year and a half of the Truman administration, the public was so disenchanted that it sent Republican majorities to both houses of Congress in 1946 for the first time since the 1920s. Desperate liberals began to coalesce behind Henry Wallace, who formed a new Progressive party to run against Truman in 1948. Attacked by conservatives, reviled by liberals, ignored by Congress, the middle-of-the-road Missourian had hit rock bottom.

As the 1948 presidential election approached, Truman's political advisors urged him to move to the left if he wished to avoid almost certain defeat. With nothing further to lose, Truman revealed a liberalism which may have been more genuine than many of his critics supposed. He appointed a Civil Rights Committee which made vigorous recommendations in support of blacks. His veto of congressional legislation hostile to the unions brought labor to his side, while many liberals, including Eleanor Roosevelt, applauded the Marshall Plan which softened his cold-war foreign policies. During the 1948 campaign the plucky Missourian proved to be "a natural." On whistle-stop tours which criss-crossed the nation, he lambasted the "do-nothing" Republican Congress, while sympathetic crowds shouted, "Give 'em hell, Harry!" Recalling the gains which many of his listeners had made under the New-Deal legislation of the 1930s, Truman urged them to "vote for your own interests."

The result was the greatest election upset in our history. Voters not only returned Truman to the White House, they gave him Democratic majorities in both houses of Congress. When Congress met a few months later, Truman unveiled a legislative program to enact much of the Economic Bill of Rights envisaged by FDR. Truman called it the Fair Deal.

Mr. President, Mr. Speaker, Members of the Congress:
I am happy to report to this 81st Congress that the state of the Union is good. Our Nation is better able than ever before to meet the needs of the American people, and to give them their fair chance in the pursuit of happiness. This great Republic is foremost among the nations of the world in the search for peace.

During the last 16 years, our people have been creating a

society which offers new opportunities for every man to enjoy his share of the good things of life.

In this society, we are conservative about the values and principles which we cherish; but we are forward-looking in protecting those values and principles and in extending their benefits. We have rejected the discredited theory that the fortunes of the Nation should be in the hands of a privileged few. We have abandoned the "trickle-down" concept of national prosperity. Instead, we believe that our economic system should rest on a democratic foundation and that wealth should be created for the benefit of all.

The recent election shows that the people of the United States are in favor of this kind of society and want to go on improving it.

The American people have decided that poverty is just as wasteful and just as unnecessary as preventable disease. We have pledged our common resources to help one another in the hazards and struggles of individual life. We believe that no unfair prejudice or artificial distinction should bar any citizen of the United States of America from an education, or from good health, or from a job that he is capable of performing.

The attainment of this kind of society demands the best efforts of every citizen in every walk of life, and it imposes increasing responsibilities on the Government.

The Government must work with industry, labor, and the farmers in keeping our economy running at full speed. The Government must see that every American has a chance to obtain his fair share of our increasing abundance. These responsibilities go hand in hand. . . .

If we want to keep our economy running in high gear, we must be sure that every group has the incentive to make its full contribution to the national welfare. At present, the working men and women of the Nation are unfairly discriminated against by a statute that abridges their rights, curtails their constructive efforts, and hampers our system of free collective bargaining. That statute is the Labor-Management Relations Act of 1947, sometimes called the Taft-Hartley Act.[1]

That act should be repealed! . . .

The Department of Labor should be rebuilt and strengthened

---

[1] The Republican 80th Congress passed this act over Truman's veto in 1947. Introduced by Senator Robert A. Taft, the leader of Republican conservatives, it repealed some key provisions of the Wagner Act of 1935. (See Norris, LaGuardia, and Wagner, "Depression Era Labor Legislation," in Part 4.)

and those units properly belonging within that department should be placed in it.

The health of our economy and its maintenance at high levels further require that the minimum wage fixed by law should be raised to at least 75 cents an hour.

If our free enterprise economy is to be strong and healthy, we must reinvigorate the forces of competition. We must assure small business the freedom and opportunity to grow and prosper. To this purpose, we should strengthen our antitrust laws by closing those loopholes that permit monopolistic mergers and consolidations.

Our national farm program should be improved—not only in the interest of the farmers, but for the lasting prosperity of the whole Nation. Our goals should be abundant farm production and parity income for agriculture. Standards of living on the farm should be just as good as anywhere else in the country. . . .

We should give special attention to extending modern conveniences and services to our farms. Rural electrification[2] should be pushed forward. And in considering legislation relating to housing, education, health, and social security, special attention should be given to rural problems.

Our growing population and the expansion of our economy depend upon the wise management of our land, water, forest, and mineral wealth. In our present dynamic economy, the task of conservation is not to lockup our resources but to develop and improve them. Failure, today, to make the investments which are necessary to support our progress in the future would be false economy.

We must push forward the development of our rivers for power, irrigation, navigation, and flood control. We should apply the lessons of our Tennessee Valley experience to our other great river basins.

I again recommend action be taken by the Congress to approve the St. Lawrence Seaway and Power project. This is about the fifth time I have recommended it. . . .

The Government has still other opportunities—to help raise the standard of living of our citizens. These opportunities lie in the fields of social security, health, education, housing, and civil rights.

The present coverage of the social security laws is altogether

---

[2]The New Deal began a program of rural electrification in 1935. Government support was necessary because of the unwillingness of private power companies to string lines to remote rural households.

inadequate; the benefit payments are too low. One-third of our workers are not covered. Those who receive old-age and survivors insurance benefits receive an average payment of only $25 a month. Many others who cannot work because they are physically disabled are left to the mercy of charity. We should expand our social security program, both as to the size of the benefits and the extent of coverage, against the economic hazards due to unemployment, old age, sickness, and disability.

We must spare no effort to raise the general level of health in this country. In a nation as rich as ours, it is a shocking fact that tens of millions lack adequate medical care. We are short of doctors, hospitals, nurses. We must remedy these shortages. Moreover, we need—and we must have without further delay—a system of prepaid medical insurance which will enable every American to afford good medical care.

It is equally shocking that millions of our children are not receiving a good education. Millions of them are in overcrowded, obsolete buildings. We are short of teachers, because teachers' salaries are too low to attract new teachers, or to hold the ones we have. All these school problems will become much more acute as a result of the tremendous increase in the enrollment in our elementary schools in the next few years. I cannot repeat too strongly my desire for prompt Federal financial aid to the States to help them operate and maintain their school systems.

The governmental agency which now administers the programs of health, education, and social security should be given full departmental status.

The housing shortage continues to be acute. As an immediate step, the Congress should enact the provisions for low-rent public housing, slum clearance, farm housing, and housing research which I have repeatedly recommended. The number of low-rent public housing units provided for in the legislation should be increased to 1 million units in the next 7 years. Even this number of units will not begin to meet our need for new housing. . . .

The driving force behind our progress is our faith in our democratic institutions. That faith is embodied in the promise of equal rights and equal opportunities which the founders of our Republic proclaimed to their countrymen and to the whole world.

The fulfillment of this promise is among the highest purposes of government. The civil rights proposals I made to the 80th Congress, I now repeat to the 81st Congress. They should be enacted in order that the Federal Government may assume the leadership and discharge the obligations clearly placed upon it by the Constitution.

I stand squarely behind those proposals. . . .

The strength of our Nation must continue to be used in the interest of all our people rather than a privileged few. It must continue to be used unselfishly in the struggle for world peace and the betterment of mankind the world over.

This is the task before us.

It is not an easy one. It has many complications, and there will be strong opposition from selfish interests.

I hope for cooperation from farmers, from labor, and from business. Every segment of our population and every individual has a right to expect from our Government a fair deal.

❖ ❖ ❖

The New Deal was one of the rare seismic upheavals in American politics which, when the dust settled, revealed a new political landscape. It was comparable to the Jacksonian upheaval of the 1820s which made the Democrats the dominant party in the nation until 1860, or to the Civil War crisis which made the Republicans the majority party until the Great Depression. Since the 1930s the Democratic coalition put together by Franklin Roosevelt has dominated American political life. At its peak in 1936 the Roosevelt coalition included the solidly Democratic South, urban ethnic voters, Catholics, Jews, blacks, labor, and much of the midwestern farm belt—a virtually unbeatable combination. Thus, whereas the Republican party controlled the House of Representatives two-thirds of the time between the Civil War and the Depression, in the more than half century since 1932 the Democrats have controlled the House for all but four years. Under a parliamentary system such as Britain's there would not have been a Republican administration in the United States since 1955.

Truman rallied the New Deal coalition to win the election of 1948, but the subsequent history of his administration revealed again that it was neither monolithic nor uniformly liberal. Despite comfortable Democratic majorities in both houses of Congress, very little of Truman's Fair Deal was enacted. Southern Democrats obstructed the civil rights legislation; conservatives in both parties joined forces to defeat the economic programs; Korea and an intensified Cold War produced bipartisan majorities on behalf of American foreign policies, but generated a virulent anti-Communism that sapped liberal purpose and eroded the coalition's strength. In proposing liberal domestic programs, one observer said, "Truman kept asking for all of it and getting none of it." Some have thought that he never really believed he would.

Voters in 1948 indicated that they were unwilling to turn back the clock on the gains they had made since 1932, but they also demonstrated that they were not eager to push reform forward. Minority Republicans, who could not undo New Deal programs nor escape the basic fact of normally Democratic congresses, learned to exploit this ambivalence among the electorate and disagreements among Democrats themselves to obstruct further change. Thus Truman's presidency became one of stalemate, foreshadowing much of the political history of postwar America.

3

The Supreme Court

❖ ❖ ❖

Brown v. *Board of Education of Topeka*
1954

*I*n 1954, the laws of seventeen
states—all the former slave states plus Oklahoma—required the public
schools to segregate pupils according to their race, providing "separate
but equal" facilities for white and black children as sanctioned in 1896 by
the Supreme Court's decision in *Plessy* v. *Ferguson.* (See Part 2.) Four
states permitted racially segregated schools. Fifteen states, mostly in
the Northeast, prohibited them.

   Segregation in education was far from the extent of legal racial
discrimination in the "Jim Crow" states. A complex of laws required
or implied that blacks were banned from hospitals, hotels, and restaurants
serving whites (and vice versa); that segregated seating be provided in
vehicles of public transport and waiting rooms in bus and train stations;
that toilet facilities and drinking fountains be designated "White" and
"Colored"; that beaches, parks, and movie theaters be strictly separate. In
some courthouses in southern states, the tax collector maintained "White"
and "Colored" windows for accepting payment, and trial witnesses were
sworn in on segregated Bibles. Where a community was able to finance only
one gymnasium or swimming pool, and blacks dared to insist on using it,
perhaps one or two days a week were reserved for them. (It was customary
practice to drain and clean pools after "colored day.") The Jim Crow

BROWN v. BOARD OF EDUCATION OF TOPEKA   From *Brown* v. *Board of Education of Topeka*, Supreme Court of the United States, 347 U.S. 483, 1954.

system scarred blacks with a "mark of oppression," constant explicit reminders that they were members of a despised caste which might never cross an omnipresent color line.

Of all these forms of discrimination, it was segregation in education that the National Association for the Advancement of Colored People targeted for what became a long and frustrating campaign in the courts.

In education the mark of oppression was not only spiritual. Nearly everywhere in the South, the inferior quality of black schools condemned blacks, regardless of discrimination, to a lifetime of menial, low-paying jobs. It denied them the equality of opportunity that stood at the center of America's rationale for itself. Moreover, NAACP strategists reasoned that if the courts could be persuaded to forbid segregation in the schools, Jim Crow drinking fountains, bus seating, and the like would fall under their own weight. Others believed that popular racism could best be buried by ending segregation in the arena in which children, in the process of forming their values, spent much of their waking day. If black and white children were allowed to mix with and know one another, it could reasonably be hoped that virulent racial prejudice, like religious prejudice, would wither and die.

NAACP lawyers, headed by Thurgood Marshall, patiently picked away at segregation in education during the late 1940s, beginning at the graduate level. They persuaded the Supreme Court to negate the policy of several states which did not provide law schools for blacks but, instead, paid their tuition to a law school out of state. This did not, the Court ruled, provide a "separate but equal" facility. In 1950 the Court held that the segregated law school the state of Texas provided for blacks was unacceptable under the *Plessy* rule. The prestige of a baccalaureate of law from there was palpably inferior to the prestige of a degree from the whites-only University of Texas law school, they ruled, and was therefore a violation of the equal rights clause of the Fourteenth Amendment.

Despite the fact that neither of these decisions confronted the validity of the "separate but equal" doctrine itself, the Court's willingness to look beyond strict paper equality heartened the NAACP. In 1954, Marshall brought three of the suits (known collectively as *Brown* v. *Board of Education*) to the Supreme Court. These challenged segregation in primary and secondary schools on the grounds that even when schools for blacks were technically the equal of those for whites—identical salaries for the teachers in both, for example—the very fact of separation by race instilled in black pupils a sense of inferiority that crippled them for life. This was not equal protection under the laws.

The tide of sentiment was changing in favor of racial integration in the early 1950s. The NAACP was optimistic of a favorable majority on the Court. Ironically, the jurist who concerned them most was the new Chief Justice, Earl Warren of California. Whereas his predecessor, Fred Vinson (a southerner), had showed signs he was unhappy with the *Plessy* rule, Warren's major brush with racial questions occurred during World War II when, as Governor of California, he had called upon the federal government to intern Japanese-Americans, an unambivalent violation of the Fourteenth Amendment. In 1954, however, Warren himself wrote one of the most important decisions in American judicial history.

❀ In each of the cases, minors of the Negro race, through their legal representatives, seek the aid of the courts in obtaining admission to the public schools of their community on a nonsegregated basis. In each instance, they have been denied admission to schools attended by white children under laws requiring or permitting segregation according to race. This segregation was alleged to deprive the plaintiffs of the equal protection of the laws under the Fourteenth Amendment. In each of the cases . . . [the lower courts] denied relief to the plaintiffs[1] on the so-called "separate but equal" doctrine. . . .[2] Under that doctrine, equality of treatment is accorded when the races are provided substantially equal facilities, even though these facilities be separate. . . .

The plaintiffs contend that segregated public schools are not "equal" and cannot be made "equal," and that hence they are deprived of the equal protection of the laws. . . .

Reargument was largely devoted to the circumstances surrounding the adoption of the Fourteenth Amendment in 1868. It covered exhaustively consideration of the Amendment in Congress, ratification by the states, then existing practices in racial segregation, and the views of proponents and opponents of the Amendment. This discussion and our own investigation convince us that, although these sources cast some light, it is not enough to resolve the problem with which we are faced. At best, they are inconclusive. The most avid proponents of the post-War Amendments undoubtedly intended them to remove all legal distinctions among "all persons born or naturalized in the United States." Their opponents, just as certainly, were antagonistic to both the letter and the spirit of the Amendments and wished them to have the most limited

---

[1]Actually, in one case under the Court's consideration, from the state of Delaware, the lower court had found that segregated schools did deny blacks students their rights under the Fourteenth Amendment, calling on much the same argument as the Supreme Court does herein.

[2]See *Plessy* v. *Ferguson*, Part 2, Selection 4.

effect. What others in Congress and the state legislatures had in mind cannot be determined with any degree of certainty.

An additional reason for the inconclusive nature of the Amendment's history, with respect to segregated schools, is the status of public education at that time. In the South, the movement toward free common schools, supported by general taxation, had not yet taken hold. Education of white children was largely in the hands of private groups. Education of Negroes was almost nonexistent, and practically all of the race were illiterate. In fact, any education of Negroes was forbidden by law in some states. Today, in contrast, many Negroes have achieved outstanding success in the arts and sciences as well as in the business and professional world. . . .

In the first cases in this Court construing the Fourteenth Amendment, decided shortly after its adoption, the Court interpreted it as proscribing all state-imposed discriminations against the Negro race. The doctrine of "separate but equal" did not make its appearance in this Court until 1896 in the case of *Plessy* v. *Ferguson*. . . . In more recent cases, all of the graduate school level, inequality was found in that specific benefits enjoyed by white students were denied to Negro students of the same educational qualifications. . . .

In the instant cases, that question is directly presented. Here, unlike *Sweatt* v. *Painter*,[3] there are findings below that the Negro and white schools involved have been equalized, or are being equalized, with respect to buildings, curricula, qualifications and salaries of teachers, and other "tangible" factors. Our decision, therefore, cannot turn on merely a comparison of these tangible factors in the Negro and white schools involved in each of the cases. We must look instead to the effect of segregation itself on public education.

In approaching this problem, we cannot turn the clock back to 1868 when the Amendment was adopted, or even to 1896 when *Plessy* v. *Ferguson* was written. We must consider public education in the light of its full development and its present place in American life throughout the Nation. Only in this way can it be determined if segregation in public schools deprives these plaintiffs of the equal protection of the laws.

Today, education is perhaps the most important function of

---

[3]In *Sweatt* v. *Painter* (1950), the Court found that although the state of Texas provided a separate law school for blacks, the quality of instruction was "unequal" and that a qualified black applicant must be admitted to the University of Texas law school. In this case, the Court withheld ruling on the applicability of their decision to the public schools.

state and local governments. Compulsory school attendance laws and the great expenditures for education both demonstrate our recognition of the importance of education to our democratic society. It is required in the performance of our most basic public responsibilities, even service in the armed forces. It is the very foundation of good citizenship. Today it is a principal instrument in awakening the child to cultural values, in preparing him for later professional training, and in helping him to adjust normally to his environment. In these days, it is doubtful that any child may reasonably be expected to succeed in life if he is denied the opportunity of an education. Such an opportunity, where the state has undertaken to provide it, is a right which must be made available to all on equal terms.

We come then to the question presented: Does segregation of children in public schools solely on the basis of race, even though the physical facilities and other "tangible" factors may be equal, deprive the children of the minority group of equal educational opportunities? We believe that it does. . . .

To separate [black students from white students] of similar age and qualifications solely because of their race generates a feeling of inferiority as to their status in the community that may affect their hearts and minds in a way unlikely ever to be undone. The effect of this separation on their educational opportunities was well stated by a finding in the Kansas case by a court which nevertheless felt compelled to rule against the Negro plaintiffs:

"Segregation of white and colored children in public schools has a detrimental effect upon the colored children. The impact is greater when it has the sanction of the law; for the policy of separating the races is usually interpreted as denoting the inferiority of the Negro group. A sense of inferiority affects the motivation of a child to learn. Segregation with the sanction of law, therefore, has a tendency to retard the educational and mental development of Negro children and to deprive them of some of the benefits they would receive in a racially integrated school system."

Whatever may have been the extent of psychological knowledge at the time of *Plessy* v. *Ferguson*, this finding is amply supported by modern authority. Any language in *Plessy* v. *Ferguson* contrary to this finding is rejected.

We conclude that in the field of public education the doctrine of "separate but equal" has no place. Separate educational facilities are inherently unequal. Therefore, we hold that the plaintiffs and others similarly situated for whom the actions have been brought are, by reason of the segregation complained of, deprived of the equal protection of the laws guaranteed by the Fourteenth Amendment. . . .

Because these are class actions,[4] because of the wide applicability of this decision, and because of the great variety of local conditions, the formulation of decrees in these cases presents problems of considerable complexity. On reargument, the consideration of appropriate relief was necessarily subordinated to the primary question—the constitutionality of segregation in public education. We have now announced that such segregation is a denial of the equal protection of the laws.

❖ ❖ ❖

The *Brown* decision marked the beginning of the great Civil Rights Movement of the 1950s. However, the Warren Court order that integration proceed with "all deliberate speed" unintentionally provided an excuse for white segregationists to delay compliance. The first black students to attend formerly all-white schools were almost always shunned by their white classmates, often harassed, and sometimes abused. In Little Rock, Arkansas, in 1957, mob violence outside Central High School forced an unenthusiastic President Eisenhower to order the National Guard to enforce the *Brown* decision.

Such resistance led black and white integrationists to launch an extralegal action against racial discrimination on a broad front. In 1955 blacks in Montgomery, Alabama, boycotted the segregated city bus system and won fame for Dr. Martin Luther King, Jr. A young Baptist minister, King became the soul and spokesman in the fight against discrimination through his use of nonviolent civil disobedience. King and his followers violated laws they regarded as immoral, arguing that they could do so and remain good citizens as long as they did not employ violence and submitted passively to arrest. Their strategy was to dramatize the injustice of discriminatory laws and force their repeal through publicity.

In the early 1960s, students at Jim Crow colleges in the South, with help from sympathetic whites, introduced the "sit-in" and the "freedom ride" to the civil rights movement armory. They sat down at lunch counters where they were refused service but would not leave. Unfavorable publicity and economic pressure in time helped them

---

[4]A class action suit is a civil case brought on behalf of all people possessing certain designated characteristics or status (in the case of *Brown*, all black students enrolled in segregated schools). The decision, therefore, applies to all members of the class and not simply to the individual plaintiff.

succeed in their object. This was particularly true when the target was a national chain store such as Woolworth's because in the North, where lunch counters were not segregated, liberal students set up picket lines at local outlets. On the "freedom rides," whites and blacks sat together on interstate buses in violation of state laws. Violent reaction, which was often forthcoming, brought in the federal authorities.

As part of his Great Society program of 1964, President Lyndon B. Johnson sent to Congress and won quick passage of a historic Civil Rights Act that forbade racial discrimination in public facilities, in any endeavor involving interstate commerce, and in all federally financed institutions and projects. The Voting Rights Act of 1965 put the enforcement powers of the federal government on the scene when would-be voters petitioned Washington that they were being denied their right to the suffrage under the Fifteenth Amendment.

Once the campaign began, therefore, legal discrimination on the basis of race was ended in an astonishingly short period of time, in eleven years from the *Brown* decision to the Voting Rights Act of 1965. The extralegal consequences of three hundred years of racism have not, of course, skulked offstage so readily.

4

Lyndon B. Johnson

❀ ❀ ❀

The Great Society
1964

When he ran for President in 1960, John F. Kennedy offered the American people changes in foreign and domestic policy. He claimed that he would close the "missile gap," a Soviet edge in the capacity to deliver nuclear weapons in the event of war. He also offered a "New Frontier" of reform at home, an updating of Harry S. Truman's Fair Deal. However, as the narrowness of his victory over a personally unappealing Vice President Richard Nixon seemed to show, Kennedy was not elected because of a break in the stalemate over reform dating from Truman's presidency. Rather, his wit, good looks, and youthful vigor promised a change of mood and style to a nation which, though prosperous and secure under the aged, avuncular Eisenhower, was also, perhaps, a little bored.

Kennedy also had the political acumen to select as his vice-presidential running mate his principal rival for the Democratic nomination, Senator Lyndon Baines Johnson of Texas. To Johnson, driven to succeed in whatever he endeavored, was assigned the task of winning back the electoral votes of the southern states (particularly Texas), where the Democrats had been slipping and where Kennedy's image of Ivy League sophistication combined with his Roman Catholic religion did not wear as well as it did in the Northeast.

Johnson helped carry most of the South, including the 24 electoral

THE GREAT SOCIETY   From *Public Papers of the Presidents of the United States, Lyndon B. Johnson, 1963–64*, I, 704–707.

votes of Texas, in a election where a shift of 43 votes would have kept the White House Republican. Then, like many vice-presidents before him, he found himself with little to do. It was a gnawing aggravation to a man who was a lifelong doer with a reputation for relentless Texas-style wheeling and dealing, particularly in the game of levering legislation through Congress.

On November 23, 1963, President Kennedy was assassinated and Lyndon B. Johnson found himself President of a grieved nation, for while Kennedy's New Frontier had stalled in Congress, his personal popularity was on the upswing. Johnson may or may not have realized that he could never exude the charisma of his predecessor. President Johnson was a vulgar man, given to embarrassing even the most dignified visitors with raw sexual and scatalogical pranks. Moreover, LBJ was universally insufferable when, in his speeches, he attempted to play the kindly patriarch. Johnson was also torn between envy and scorn for the easy sophistication of Kennedy's northeastern, mostly Ivy League advisors. But the new President knew very well that with the nation distraught, the economic resources for social programs abundant, and his peerless political skills at their height, he could "complete" the New Deal in a way that Kennedy and Harry S. Truman had been unable to do.

A generation of liberals exiled from the halls of power had drafted a broad, bursting agenda of inequities and injustices to be remedied. Johnson voraciously grabbed at the programs labor, liberal intellectuals, and civil rights leaders had devised. While not a well-read historian like Truman, he knew what fame was and hungered after the opportunity to carve for himself a place in history as a great activist President. On May 22, 1964, speaking at the University of Michigan, he proposed a national consecration to the creation of a "Great Society" as the issue upon which he would wage his campaign to win election to the presidency in his own right.

❀ The purpose of protecting the life of our nation and preserving the liberty of our citizens is to pursue the happiness of our people. Our success in that pursuit is the test of our success as a nation.

For a century we labored to settle and to subdue a continent. For half a century we called upon unbounded invention and untiring industry to create an order of plenty for all of our people.

The challenge of the next half century is whether we have the wisdom to use that wealth to enrich and elevate our national life, and to advance the quality of our American civilization. . . . We have the opportunity to move not only toward the rich society and the powerful society, but upward to the Great Society.

The Great Society rests on abundance and liberty for all. It demands an end to poverty and racial injustice, to which we are totally committed in our time. But that is just the beginning.

The Great Society is a place where every child can find knowledge to enrich his mind and to enlarge his talents. It is a place where leisure is a welcome chance to build and reflect, not a feared cause of boredom and restlessness. It is a place where the city of man serves not only the needs of the body and the demands of commerce but the desire for beauty and the hunger for community.

It is a place where man can renew contact with nature. It is a place which honors creation for its own sake and for what it adds to the understanding of the race. It is a place where men are more concerned with the quality of their goals than the quantity of their goods.

But most of all, the Great Society is not a safe harbor, a resting place, a final objective, a finished work. It is a challenge constantly renewed, beckoning us toward a destiny where the meaning of our lives matches the marvelous products of our labor.

So I want to talk to you today about three places where we begin to build the Great Society—in our cities, in our countryside, and in our classrooms.

Many of you will live to see the day, perhaps fifty years from now, when there will be 400 million Americans—four-fifths of them in urban areas. In the remainder of this century urban population will double, city land will double, and we will have to build homes, highways, and facilities equal to all those built since this country was first settled. So in the next forty years we must rebuild the entire urban United States. . . .

A second place where we begin to build the Great Society is in our countryside. We have always prided ourselves on being not only America the strong and America the free, but America the beautiful. Today that beauty is in danger. The water we drink, the food we eat, the very air that we breathe, are threatened with pollution. Our parks are overcrowded, our seashores overburdened. Green fields and dense forests are disappearing.

A few years ago we were greatly concerned about the "Ugly American."[1] Today we must act to prevent an ugly America.

---

[1] *The Ugly American*, by William J. Lederer and Eugene Burdick, was a best-selling novel of 1958 which dealt with the failures of American foreign policy in a fictional Southeast Asian country which, ironically enough, was obviously Vietnam.

For once the battle is lost, once our natural splendor is destroyed, it can never be recaptured. And once man can no longer walk with beauty or wonder at nature his spirit will wither and his sustenance be wasted.

A third place to build the Great Society is in the classrooms of America. There your children's lives will be shaped. Our society will not be great until every young mind is set free to scan the farthest reaches of thought and imagination. We are still far from that goal. . . .

In many places, classrooms are overcrowded and curricula are outdated. Most of our qualified teachers are underpaid, and many of our paid teachers are unqualified. So we must give every child a place to sit and a teacher to learn from. Poverty must not be a bar to learning, and learning must offer an escape from poverty.

But more classrooms and more teachers are not enough. We must seek an educational system which grows in excellence as it grows in size. This means better training for our teachers. It means preparing youth to enjoy their hours of leisure as well as their hours of labor. It means exploring new techniques of teaching, to find new ways to stimulate the love of learning and the capacity for creation.

These are three of the central issues of the Great Society. While our government has many programs directed at those issues, I do not pretend that we have the full answer to those problems. . . .

But I do promise this: We are going to assemble the best thought and the broadest knowledge from all over the world to find those answers for America. I intend to establish working groups to prepare a series of White House conferences and meetings—on the cities, on natural beauty, on the quality of education, and on other emerging challenges. And from these meetings and from this inspiration and from these studies we will begin to set our course toward the Great Society. . . .

Within your lifetime powerful forces, already loosed, will take us toward a way of life beyond the realm of our experience, almost beyond the bounds of our imagination.

For better or for worse, your generation has been appointed by history to deal with those problems and to lead America toward a new age. You have the chance never before afforded to any people in any age. You can help build a society where the demands of morality, and the needs of the spirit, can be realized in the life of the nation.

So, will you join in the battle to give every citizen the full equality which God enjoins and the law requires, whatever his belief, or race, or the color of his skin?

Will you join in the battle to give every citizen an escape from the crushing weight of poverty?

Will you join in the battle to make it possible for all nations to live in enduring peace—as neighbors and not as mortal enemies?

Will you join in the battle to build the Great Society, to prove that our material progress is only the foundation on which we will build a richer life of mind and spirit?

There are those timid souls who say this battle cannot be won; that we are condemned to a soulless wealth. I do not agree. We have the power to shape the civilization that we want. But we need your will, your labor, your hearts, if we are to build that kind of society.

Those who came to this land sought to build more than just a new country. They sought a new world. So I have come here today to your campus to say that you can make their vision our reality. So let us from this moment begin our work so that in the future men will look back and say: It was then, after a long and weary way, that man turned the exploits of his genius to the full enrichment of his life.

❖ ❖ ❖

Johnson went to the polls in 1964 with considerable legislative accomplishments already to his credit. In addition to the Civil Rights Act of 1964, the Economic Opportunity Act provided money and machinery which took the war against inequality beyond political rights into social, cultural, and economic realms. The Republican party put even more power into Johnson's hands by nominating an Arizona Republican, Barry Goldwater to oppose him. Goldwater not only denounced the incipient Great Society, but also spoke of dismantling the New Deal. He even denounced social security and frightened Americans with reckless talk of using nuclear weapons. Johnson not only won a personal landslide, he carried with him a 295–140 Democratic margin into the House of Representatives and a 68–32 edge in the Senate. This included more than forty first term congressmen and women from normally Republican districts who owed their success to his coattails.

The Eighty-ninth Congress enacted Medicare (federal health insurance for the elderly), Medicaid (health care for the poor), low-income housing construction programs, rent help for the urban poor, the Voting Rights Act of 1965, the "War on Poverty" with its dozens of programs to assist both rural and urban poor, federal support for the arts and humanities, and education subsidies, including easy to get, low-cost loans for needy college students.

The Great Society was expensive. Between 1964 and 1970, federal support for social programs tripled. But at its peak the Great Society cost proportionately less than social programs in every other advanced nation. Had the costs of the programs been the whole of the Johnsonian expenditures, the booming economy of the 1960s could well have afforded them. But building the Great Society was not Johnson's only goal as President. Even while he was sending his first bills to Congress in 1964, and the Democrats were attacking Barry Goldwater for reckless bellicosity in foreign affairs, Lyndon Johnson was resolving to win a war in Indochina, a civil war in which the United States had gradually become mired since 1954. The costs of the Vietnam War would rise to $20 billion a year by 1967 (perhaps as much as $676 billion overall). It would leave 57,000 Americans and 1.5 million Indochinese dead, a country bitterly divided, and Lyndon B. Johnson rebuked and reviled by the liberal constituency whose domestic aspirations he enacted in the name of the Great Society.

5

Robert S. McNamara and J. William Fulbright

❖ ❖ ❖

The Vietnam Debate
1964, 1965

*I*ndochina, the pendant belly of Southeast Asia that took its culture from the two great civilizations whose names it combines, was a part of the world in which American interests had never been considerable. In the imperialist scramble of the nineteenth century, most of the peninsula was partitioned between Britain and France, with the French in control of Vietnam on the eastern coast. In 1954, the French were expelled by an anticolonialist force led by Ho Chih Minh, a Communist.

In the Geneva Accords, signed the same year, Vietnam was divided into northern and southern zones. Ho Chih Minh's Viet Minh would govern the north; in the south, an anti-Communist Vietnamese named Ngo Dinh Diem would hold power. Democratic elections to be held in 1956 would determine Vietnam's future as a unified nation. Knowing that his reputation paled before that of Ho Chih Minh, now the symbol of Vietnamese nationalism, Diem sensed defeat and cancelled the elections in the southern half of the country.

President Eisenhower's Secretary of State, John Foster Dulles,

THE VIETNAM DEBATE   From McNamara: Address before the National Security Industrial Association, Washington D.C., March 26, 1964; Fulbright: *Congressional Record*, June 15, 1965.

abetted Diem's action because of Dulles' conviction that the Soviet Union and the People's Republic of China formed a monolithic bloc ideologically bent on "world conquest"; apparent nationalists like Ho were, in his view, mere flunkies, obeisant tools of a monstrous conspiracy. Not even the open rift between the Soviets and Chinese after 1956, or the millennia-old enmity between Vietnam and China, could sway Dulles from his dogma.

In South Vietnam, rebels loyal to Ho launched a guerrilla war of assassination and hit-and-run attacks against the American-financed and equipped army. Diem retaliated with political and military policies that often failed to distinguish between the rebels and that eternal majority of human beings who wish only that the politicians and generals would allow them to pass their daily lives in peace and security.

American involvement grew. After 1961, President John F. Kennedy, advised by young geopoliticians like Harvard professor McGeorge Bundy and Secretary of Defense Robert S. McNamara, had repudiated Dulles' disastrous penchant for threatening "massive retaliation" at every foreign provocation. It was replaced with the policy of "limited response." Kennedy would preserve world peace and simultaneously stem Communist ambitions by responding to provocations with precisely the same kind and degree of aid, covert action, or direct military force that the provocation represented. In Vietnam in 1961, "limited response" seemed to mean massive aid to Diem, including American advisors, civilian and military.

Kennedy and his advisors did not count on the extreme unpopularity of Diem's repressive regime (Diem was assassinated in 1963) nor the determination of the rival National Liberation Front and its North Vietnamese supporters. By November 1963, when Kennedy himself was murdered, the 16,000 American troops in Vietnam were on the losing side of a worsening war.

The new President, Lyndon B. Johnson, was repeatedly misinformed as to the strength of the enemy by his own intelligence and military. He was assured by Bundy, McNamara, and other advisors that the war could be won by "escalating" the American presence, a modification of "limited response." By June 1964, two months after the statement of policy by McNamara which follows there were 21,000 American troops in Vietnam; by mid-1965, the date of Senator J. William Fulbright's call for a negotiated end to the war, there were 50,000. With war-making powers granted to him by Congress in the Tonkin Gulf Resolution of August 5, 1964, Johnson escalated the war into North Vietnam in February 1965 by ordering bombing raids. Still the war went badly and criticism of American policy grew both within Congress and in the nation. In the two documents that follow, Secretary of Defense McNamara explains why the administration believed the war must be fought and won, and a leading critic of the war, the thoughtful and urbane Chairman of the Senate Foreign Relations Committee, J. William Fulbright, calls for the United States to work for a negotiated settlement.

Robert S. McNamara, March 1964

❀ I turn now to a consideration of United States objectives in South Viet-Nam. The United States has no designs whatever on the resources or territory of the area. Our national interests do not require that South Viet-Nam serve as a Western base or as a member of a Western Alliance.

Our concern is three-fold.

First, and most important, is the simple fact that South Viet-Nam, a member of the free-world family, is striving to preserve its independence from Communist attack. The Vietnamese have asked our help. We have given it. We shall continue to give it.

We do so in their interest; and we do so in our own clear self-interest. For basic to the principles of freedom and self-determination which have sustained our country for almost two centuries is the right of peoples everywhere to live and develop in peace. Our own security is strengthened by the determination of others to remain free, and by our commitment to assist them. We will not let this member of our family down, regardless of its distance from our shores.

The ultimate goal of the United States in Southeast Asia, as in the rest of the world, is to help maintain free and independent nations which can develop politically, economically, and socially, and which can be responsible members of the world Community. In this region and elsewhere, many peoples share our sense of the value of such freedom and independence. They have taken the risks and made the sacrifices linked to the commitment to membership in the family of the free world. They have done this in the belief that we would back up our pledges to help defend them. It is not right or even expedient—nor is it in our nature—to abandon them when the going is difficult.

Second, Southeast Asia has great strategic significance in the forward defense of the United States. Its location across east-west air and sea lanes flanks the Indian subcontinent on one side and Australia, New Zealand, and the Philippines on the other, and dominates the gateway between the Pacific and Indian Oceans. In Communist hands, this area would pose a most serious threat to the security of the U.S. and to the family of free-world nations to which we belong. To defend Southeast Asia, we must meet the challenge in South Viet-Nam.

And third, South Viet-Nam is a test case for the new Communist strategy. Let me examine for a moment the nature of this strategy.

Just as the Kennedy Administration was coming into office in January, 1961, Chairman Khrushchev[1] made one of the most important speeches on Communist strategy of recent decades. In his report on a Party conference entitled "For New Victories of the World Communist Movement," Khrushchev stated: "In modern conditions, the following categories of wars should be distinguished: world wars, local wars, liberation wars and popular uprisings." He ruled out what he called "world wars" and "local wars" as being too dangerous for profitable indulgence in a world of nuclear weapons. But with regard to what he called "liberation wars," he referred specifically to Viet-Nam. He said, "It is a sacred war. We recognize such wars . . ."

Communist interest in insurgency techniques did not begin with Khrushchev, nor for that matter with Stalin. Lenin's works are full of tactical instructions, which were adapted very successfully by Mao Tse-tung,[2] whose many writings on guerrilla warfare have become classic references. Indeed, Mao claims to be the true heir of Lenin's original prescriptions for the world-wide victory of Communism. The North Vietnamese have taken a leaf or two from Mao's book—as well as Moscow's—and added some of their own. . . .

The U.S. role in South Viet-Nam, then, is: *first*, to answer the call of the South Vietnamese, a member nation of our free-world family, to help them save their country for themselves; *second*, to help prevent the strategic danger which would exist if communism absorbed Southeast Asia's people and resources; and *third*, to prove in the Vietnamese test case that the free world can cope with Communist "wars of liberation" as we have coped successfully with Communist aggression at other levels. . . .

Our goal is peace and stability, both in Viet-Nam and Southeast Asia. But we have learned that "peace at any price" is not practical in the long run, and that the cost of defending freedom must be borne if we are to have it at all.

---

[1]Nikita Khrushchev was First Secretary of the Communist party of the Soviet Union between 1953 and 1964 and Premier—thus the undisputed Soviet leader—between 1958 and 1964. His policy of "peaceful coexistence" with the western nations marked a significant shift in Soviet foreign policy, but he also earned the suspicion of American policymakers because of his deviousness as a diplomat.

[2]Mao Tse-tung (Mao Zedong), titular head and *de facto* leader of the People's Republic of China between 1949 and his death in 1976, was also a theorist of both the strategy and tactics of guerrilla warfare.

The road ahead in Viet-Nam is going to be long, difficult, and frustrating. It will take work, courage, imagination and—perhaps more than anything else—patience to bear the burden of what President Kennedy called a "long twilight struggle." In Viet-Nam, it has not been finished in the first hundred days of President Johnson's Administration, and it may not be finished in the first 1,000 days; but, in co-operation with General Khanh's[3] government, we have made a beginning. When the day comes that we can safely withdraw, we expect to leave an independent and stable South Viet-Nam, rich with resources and bright with prospects for contributing to the peace and prosperity of Southeast Asia and of the world.

J. William Fulbright, June 1965

It is clear to all reasonable Americans that a complete military victory in Viet-Nam, though theoretically attainable, can in fact be attained only at a cost far exceeding the requirements of our interest and our honor. It is equally clear that the unconditional withdrawal of American support from South Viet-Nam would have disastrous consequences, including but by no means confined to the victory of the Viet-Cong in South Viet-Nam. Our policy therefore has been—and should remain—one of determination to end the war at the earliest possible time by a negotiated settlement involving major concessions by both sides. . . .

The most striking characteristic of a great nation is not the mere possession of power but the wisdom and restraint and largeness of view with which power is exercised. A great nation is one which is capable of looking beyond its own view of the world, or recognizing that, however convinced it may be of the beneficence of its own role and aims, other nations may be equally persuaded of their benevolence and good intent. It is a mark of both greatness and maturity when a nation like the United States, without abandoning its convictions and commitments, is capable at the same time

---

[3]Major General Nguyen Khanh seized control of South Vietnam in a military coup on January 30, 1964. In November of the same year he yielded power to a civilian government led by Tran Van Huong.

of acknowledging that there may be some merit and even good intent in the views and aims of its adversaries. . . .

It seems clear that the Communist powers still hope to achieve a complete victory in South Viet-Nam and for this reason are at present uninterested in negotiations for a peaceful settlement. It would be a mistake to match Communist intransigence with our own. In the months ahead we must try to do two things in South Viet-Nam: First we must sustain the South Vietnamese Army so as to persuade the Communists that Saigon cannot be crushed and that the United States will not be driven from South Viet-Nam by force; second, we must continue to offer the Communists a reasonable and attractive alternative to military victory. For the time being it seems likely that the focus of our efforts will have to be on persuading the Communists that they cannot win a complete military victory; only when this has become clear is it likely they will respond to our proposals for unconditional negotiations.

The short-term outlook is by no means bright but neither is it without hope. It may well be, if we are resolute but also restrained in the conduct of the war, that when the current Viet-Cong offensive has run its course without decisive result the Communists will be disposed to take a different view of our standing proposal for unconditional negotiations. At such time as it becomes clear to all interested parties that neither side can expect to win a complete military victory, I would think it appropriate and desirable for the United States to reiterate forcefully and explicitly its willingness to negotiate a compromise peace and thereafter to join with other countries in mounting a large-scale program for the economic and social development of Southeast Asia.

The possible terms of a settlement cannot now be foreseen or usefully speculated upon. As a general proposition, however, I think there may be much to be said for a return to the Geneva Accords of 1954, not just in their essentials but in all their specifications. Should such a settlement be reached, it is to be hoped that both sides will recall the unrewarding consequences of their past violations of the 1954 Agreements.

Looking beyond a possible settlement of the Vietnamese war, it may be that the major lesson of this tragic conflict will be a new appreciation of the power of nationalism in Southeast Asia and, indeed, in all of the world's emerging nations. Generally, American foreign policy in Asia, in Africa, and in Latin America has been successful and constructive insofar as American aims have coincided with the national aims of the peoples concerned. The tragedy

of Viet-Nam is that for many reasons, including the intransigence
of a colonial power and the initial failure of the United States to
appreciate the consequences of that intransigence, the nationalist
movement became associated with and largely subordinate to the
Communist movement.

In the postwar era it has been demonstrated repeatedly that
nationalism is a stronger force than communism and that the association of the two, which has created so many difficulties for the
United States, is neither inevitable nor natural. In the past it has
come about when, for one reason or another, the West has set itself
in opposition to the national aspirations of the emerging peoples. It
is to be hoped that we will not do so again; it is to be hoped that in
the future the United States will leave no country in doubt as to its
friendship and support for legitimate national aspirations. If we do
this, I do not think that we will soon find ourselves in another
conflict like the one in Viet-Nam.

❊ ❊ ❊

By 1965 the Vietnam debate had gone far beyond the question of
how best to serve the geopolitical interests of the United States. Senator
Fulbright and many others, including several high-ranking generals and
former diplomats (George Kennan among them), continued to argue that
the war effort was misguided, or if not misguided then doomed to failure.
In the country, however, particularly on college and university campuses,
the lengthening casualty lists, corruption in the South Vietnamese
government and army, and the palpable fact that the war had at least
begun as a civil war and not a war of invasion led to mammoth antiwar
demonstrations with up to 500,000 participants.

Some critics argued that in its global rivalry with the Soviet Union
and China, the United States was draining itself materially and morally
while the other superpowers remained untouched. Political radicals said
they opposed the war because the United States simply was on the wrong
side: Ho Chih Minh's forces, whether "Communistic" or an alliance of
anti-imperialist groups, were right. A much larger group of protesters
were grieved by the spectacle of their mighty nation bombing a smaller
country "into the stone age," for whatever reason. They also protested
the fact that the highly technological American war effort inevitably
meant large casualties among innocent civilians.

In the government, one-time liberals responded with emotional
attacks on the loyalty and courage of the critics that seemed more
appropriate to right-wing extremists, who gleefully egged them on. The
Democratic party was torn asunder. Groups that should have been
wedded to it by the Great Society were increasingly in opposition. Careers

and reputations were destroyed. In 1968, with 500,000 American soldiers in Vietnam, President Johnson was forced to withdraw from the presidential election campaign after he was effectively defeated in the first party primary by an obscure antiwar Senator, Eugene McCarthy of Minnesota. The Democrats, overwhelmingly victorious on a Great Society platform in 1964, were narrowly defeated. This defeat was undoubtedly because of the disillusionment of voters opposed to the war, and it began a decline in the popularity of the party that continues to this day.

The war finally ended for the United States when, in March 1973, President Richard M. Nixon called the U.S. defeat a "victory" and withdrew the last of the American troops. In early 1975, following months of skirmishing, the South Vietnamese government crumbled before an attack from the North. Despite attempts by irresponsible political leaders to aggravate old wounds for their personal benefit, the nation's somber, quiet determination not to involve American soldiers in further foreign adventures indicates a popular recognition that the United States underwent one of the greatest tragedies in its history in Southeast Asia.

J. William Fulbright was not rewarded for his prescience. In the Arkansas Democratic primary in 1974, with Vietnam crumbling, the voters denied him renomination to the Senate. After leaving government with President Johnson in 1969, Robert S. McNamara became president of the World Bank.

6

Ronald W. Reagan

❖ ❖ ❖

A Second American Revolution

1985

"*I*f this were any other party in the world," Thomas P. "Tip" O'Neill grumbled about the Democrats in 1979, "we'd be five splinter parties." As Speaker of the House, O'Neill uneasily presided over a fractious majority which had controlled the House of Representatives almost without interruption since 1931—the New Deal coalition assembled by Franklin Roosevelt. However, while Democrats had been indisputably the majority party for fifty years (at one point in the 1970s Republicans claimed only 17 percent of registered voters), Democratic successes in presidential politics had been only erratic.

Every presidential election in the postwar period had been to some extent a referendum on New Deal policies. Successful Republican candidates Dwight Eisenhower and Richard Nixon had promised less government and freer enterprise, while successful Democrats John Kennedy and Lyndon Johnson had campaigned under the banner of continuing liberal reform. Overall the verdict of the electorate had favored moderation. Most postwar presidential elections had been decided by narrow margins. Only when one of the parties ran an extremist candidate—the ultra-conservative Barry Goldwater for the Republicans in

A SECOND AMERICAN REVOLUTION   From Ronald W. Reagan, Annual Message to Congress on the State of the Union, February 6, 1985, *Los Angeles Times*, February 7, 1985, pp. 15–16.

1964 and the ultra-liberal George McGovern for the Democrats in 1972—
had the other party won victories of landslide proportions.

One such landslide—Lyndon Johnson's in 1964—had produced so
great a liberal preponderance that for the first time in the postwar period
the stalemate had been broken, and liberals were able to enact virtually
all of the program sketched out by FDR in 1944 and by Harry Truman in
the Fair Deal. The Great Society thus represented the fulfillment of a
generation of liberal hopes. The Democratic coalition had reached the end
of the liberal agenda which had served as its platform for half a century.
What next?

Perhaps the success of its program would have fragmented the
Democratic party in any case. But during the 1970s American liberalism
became increasingly identified with policies which alienated many of its
traditional constituencies. The purposes of earlier liberal programs had
been to eradicate debilitating poverty, to remedy the inadequate provision
of medical care and education, and to abolish unfair racial discrimination.
After the 1965 Congress, federal agencies and the federal courts began to
use the powers of the federal government for very different purposes,
meddling with local customs and family and sexual mores in ways that
even many liberal observers found troubling.

Court-ordered busing was probably the most disastrous such
experiment. In its *Brown* decision in 1954 the Supreme Court had struck
down artificially *segregated* schools. Busing schemes, however, attempted
to create artificially *integrated* schools by importing white schoolchildren,
often from miles away, to black schools in the inner cities. In many cases the
result was only to hasten the panicked flight of white families out of the
nation's urban centers.

Equally troubling were federally sponsored efforts to discriminate
in favor of minority groups under the euphemistic term "Affirmative
Action." Here the recently won principle of equality before the law
gave way to preferential treatment for racial and ethnic minorities and
women which, however well-intentioned, still amounted to a new kind of
discrimination in federal, municipal, state, and even private employment.

The pestilence of random, violent crime afflicted American
communities to an unprecedented degree in the 1960s and 1970s. By
1980 half the population dared not walk alone at night within a mile of
their homes. Meanwhile the courts were demonstrating exquisite solicitude
for the rights of criminals, hamstringing police departments, reducing
penalities, and subjecting communities to intolerable costs for the trial of
serious crimes. Homosexuals demanded and, in several localities, received
far more than the quiet toleration customarily accorded them. By
extraordinary logic the courts solemnly concluded that pornographic
photographs and even nude dancing constituted free speech protected
by the 1st Amendment. This decision left local communities powerless
to arrest the blight of X-rated movie houses and peep shows. American
liberalism, which had once championed the opportunity for millions of
Americans to lead decent, middle-class lives, seemed to have degenerated

by the 1970s into a kind of special pleading for the flagrantly unjust and unsavory.

In 1980, for the first time in a postwar presidential election, rather than choosing the more moderate candidate, the voters elected the ultra-conservative Ronald Reagan by a hefty majority. Incumbent Democratic President Jimmy Carter tried to rally the New Deal coalition around him as all Democratic candidates had done since World War II. Kicking off his campaign at the Harry Truman Library in Independence, Missouri, he intoned the old litany—Roosevelt . . . Truman . . . Kennedy . . . Johnson . . . New Deal . . . Fair Deal . . . Great Society. But in 1980 it fell on deaf ears; Carter went down to the most humiliating defeat since Herbert Hoover's. Moreover, in 1984 the voters reelected President Reagan by a landslide.

The elections of 1980 and 1984 revealed that, in presidential politics at least, there was virtually nothing left of the Roosevelt coalition.

There had not been a solidly Democratic South since 1948. In 1980 Reagan carried every southern state but one, and in 1984 he won 71 percent of the southern white vote. If there was a solid South at all, it was becoming solidly Republican.

The backbone of the Democratic coalition had been the great urban industrial centers of the Northeast. Here Democratic politics were in shambles. The cities were no longer as powerful as they had been. Many had greatly declined in population as Americans migrated to the sunnier climate of the Southwest or as middle-class whites moved to the suburbs. Of the great urban political machines which had once delivered Democratic votes virtually upon demand, none survived. Chicago mayor Richard Daley's death in 1976 signaled the passing of the last of them.

The great blocs of ethnic voters which the cities had once harbored were dispersed or no longer loyal to the Democratic party. The Irish had merged into the general population years earlier; in 1980, to the extent there was an Irish vote, it was for Reagan. No ethnic group since World War II had enjoyed more spectacular upward mobility than Italian-Americans. In 1980 they were suburbanites, and they voted for Reagan. The Polish and Slavic voters of the Great Lakes region deserted the Democrats in all but three states in 1980. In 1984 Reagan won the Catholic vote by a whopping 56 percent. Even Jewish voters who once had almost unanimously cast Democratic ballots did so by only slender margins. In 1980 and 1984 the Democrats retained the unequivocal loyalty of only one ethnic group—the blacks.

Nor was there a dependable labor vote anymore. Union leaders, who strongly endorsed the Democratic candidates as always, were able to deliver only bare majorities of their members' ballots. Overall, the blue-collar vote went for Reagan.

Americans over the age of 65, most of whom had cast their first ballots for Roosevelt in the 1930s, voted for Reagan in 1984 by 61 percent. And the oldest President in the history of the republic won two-thirds of the 18 to 24-year-old vote! Indeed, younger voters were remarkably indifferent to the old party loyalties. By 1985 voter registration was almost evenly divided between Republicans and Democrats.

Ronald Reagan had been campaigning for the presidency since 1966, passionately arguing that the liberal big-government coalition was leading the country to the dogs. During his first term the President did just what he had always said he would: he slashed federal revenues with a gigantic 25 percent tax cut, sharply reduced support for domestic social programs, and launched a $1.6 trillion military buildup.

In 1985, jubilant over his landslide reelection, he presented Congress with new budget proposals calling for even greater cuts in domestic spending and further tax reductions. During the same week, in his annual message to Congress, he explained that his goal was to make this "Second American Revolution" a permanent one.

❀ Mr. Speaker, Mr. President, distinguished members of the Congress, honored guests and fellow citizens. I come before you to report on the state of our union. And I am pleased to report that, after four years of united effort, the American people have brought forth a nation renewed—stronger, freer and more secure than before.

Four years ago, we began to change—forever, I hope—our assumptions about government and its place in our lives. Out of that change has come great and robust growth—in our confidence, our economy and our role in the world. . . .

Four years ago, we said we would invigorate our economy by giving people greater freedom and incentives to take risks, and letting them keep more of what they earned.

We did what we promised, and a great industrial giant is reborn. Tonight we can take pride in 25 straight months of economic growth, the strongest in 34 years; a three-year inflation average of 3.9%, the lowest in 17 years; and 7.3 million new jobs in two years, with more of our citizens working than ever before. . . .

We have begun well. But it's only a beginning. We are not here to congratulate ourselves on what we have done, but to challenge ourselves to finish what has not yet been done.

We are here to speak for millions in our inner cities who long for real jobs, safe neighborhoods and schools that truly teach. We are here to speak for the American farmer, the entrepreneur and every worker in industries fighting to modernize and compete. And, yes, we are here to stand, and proudly so, for all who struggle to break free from totalitarianism; for all who know in their hearts that freedom is the one true path to peace and human happiness. . . .

We honor the giants of our history not by going back, but forward to the dreams their vision foresaw. My fellow citizens, this nation is poised for greatness. The time has come to proceed toward a great new challenge—a Second American Revolution of hope and opportunity; a revolution carrying us to new heights of progress by pushing back frontiers of knowledge and space; a revolution of spirit that taps the soul of America, enabling us to summon greater strength than we have ever known; and, a revolution that carries beyond our shores the golden promise of human freedom in a world at peace.

Let us begin by challenging conventional wisdom: There are no constraints on the human mind, no walls around the human spirit, no barriers to our progress except those we ourselves erect. Already, pushing down tax rates has freed our economy to vault forward to record growth.

In Europe, they call it "the American Miracle." Day by day, we are shattering accepted notions of what is possible. . . .

We stand on the threshold of a great ability to produce more, do more, be more. Our economy is not getting older and weaker, it's getting younger and stronger; it doesn't need rest and supervision, it needs new challenge, greater freedom. And that word—freedom—is the key to the Second American Revolution we mean to bring about.

Let us move together with an historic reform of tax simplification for fairness and growth. Last year, I asked then-Treasury Secretary Regan to develop a plan to simplify the tax code, so all taxpayers would be treated more fairly, and personal tax rates could come further down.

We have cut tax rates by almost 25 percent, yet the tax system remains unfair and limits our potential for growth. Exclusions and exemptions cause similar incomes to be taxed at different levels. Low-income families face steep tax barriers that make hard lives even harder. The Treasury Department has produced an excellent reform plan whose principles will guide the final proposal we will ask you to enact.

One thing that tax reform will not be is a tax increase in disguise. We will not jeopardize the mortgage interest deduction families need. We will reduce personal tax rates as low as possible by removing many tax preferences. We will propose a top rate of no more than 35 percent, and possibly lower. And we will propose reducing corporate rates while maintaining incentives for capital formation. . . .

Tax simplification will be a giant step toward unleashing the tremendous pent-up power of our economy. But a Second American Revolution must carry the promise of opportunity for all. It is time to liberate the spirit of enterprise in the most distressed areas of our country.

This government will meet its responsibility to help those in need. But policies that increase dependency, break up families and destroy self-respect are not progressive, they are reactionary. Despite our stride in civil rights, blacks, Hispanics and all minorities will not have full and equal power until they have full economic power. . . .

Let us resolve that we will stop spreading dependency and start spreading opportunity; that we will stop spreading bondage and start spreading freedom.

There are some who say that growth initiatives must await final action on deficit reductions. The best way to reduce deficits is through economic growth. More businesses will be started, more investments made, more jobs created and more people will be on payrolls paying taxes. The best way to reduce government spending is to reduce the need for spending by increasing prosperity. . . .

To move steadily toward a balanced budget we must also lighten government's claim on our total economy. We will not do this by raising taxes. We must make sure that our economy grows faster than growth in spending by federal government. In our fiscal year 1986 budget, overall government program spending will be frozen at the current level; it must not be one dime higher than fiscal year 1985. And three points are key:

First, the social safety net for the elderly, needy, disabled and unemployed will be left intact. Growth of our major health care programs, Medicare and Medicaid, will be slowed, but protections for the elderly and needy will be preserved.

Second, we must not relax our efforts to restore military strength just as we near our goal of a fully equipped, trained and ready professional corps. National security is government's first responsibility, so, in past years, defense spending took about half the federal budget. Today it takes less than a third.

We have already reduced our planned defense expenditures by nearly $100 billion over the past four years, and reduced projected spending again this year. You know, we only have a military industrial complex until a time of danger. Then it becomes the arsenal of democracy. Spending for defense is investing in things that are priceless: peace and freedom.

Third, we must reduce or eliminate costly government subsidies. For example, deregulation of the airline industry has led to cheaper airfares, but on Amtrak taxpayers pay about $35 per passenger every time an Amtrak train leaves the station. It's time we ended this huge federal subsidy.

Our farm program costs have quadrupled in recent years. Yet I know from visiting farmers, many in great financial distress, that we need an orderly transition to a market-oriented farm economy. We can help farmers best, not by expanding federal payments, but by making fundamental reforms, keeping interest rates heading down and knocking down foreign trade barriers to American farm exports. . . .

In the long run, we must protect the taxpayers from government. And I ask again that you pass, as 32 states have now called for, an amendment mandating the federal government spend no more than it takes in. And I ask for the authority used responsibly by 43 governors to veto individual items in appropriations bills. . . .

Nearly 50 years of government living beyond its means has brought us to a time of reckoning. Ours is but a moment in history. But one moment of courage, idealism and bipartisan unity can change American history forever. . . .

Every dollar the federal government does not take from us, every decision it does not make for us, will make our economy stronger, our lives more abundant, our future more free. . . .

There is another great heritage to speak of this evening. Of all the changes that have swept America the past four years, none brings greater promise than our rediscovery of the value of faith, freedom, family, work and neighborhood.

We see signs of renewal in increased attendance in places of worship; renewed optimism and faith in our future; love of country rediscovered by our young who are leading the way. We have rediscovered that work is good in and of itself; that it ennobles us to create and contribute no matter how seemingly humble our jobs. We have seen a powerful new current from an old and honorable tradition—American generosity. . . .

I thank the Congress for passing equal access legislation giving religious groups the same right to use classrooms after school that other groups enjoy. But no citizen need tremble, nor the world shudder, if a child stands in a classroom and breathes a prayer. We ask you again—give children back a right they had for a century-and-a-half or more in this country.

The question of abortion grips our nation. Abortion is either the taking of human life, or it isn't; and if it is—and medical technology is increasingly showing it is—it must be stopped. . . .

Of all the changes in the past 20 years, none has more threatened our sense of national well-being than the explosion of violent crime. One does not have to have been attacked to be a victim. The woman who must run to her car after shopping at night is a victim; the couple draping their door with locks and chains are victims; as is the tired, decent cleaning woman who can't ride a subway home without being afraid.

We do not seek to violate rights of defendants, but shouldn't we feel more compassion for victims of crime than for those who commit crime? For the first time in 20 years, the crime index has fallen two years in a row; we've convicted over 7,400 drug offenders, and put them, as well as leaders of organized crime, behind bars in record numbers.

But we must do more. I urge the House to follow the Senate and enact proposals permitting use of all reliable evidence that police officers acquire in good faith. These proposals would also reform the *habeas corpus* laws and allow, in keeping with the will of the overwhelming majority of Americans, the use of the death penalty where necessary.

There can be no economic revival in ghettos when the most violent among us are allowed to roam free. It is time we restored domestic tranquility. And we mean to do just that. . . .

Tonight I have spoken of great plans and great dreams. They are dreams we can make come true. Two hundred years of American history should have taught us that nothing is impossible. . . . Anything is possible in America if we have the faith, the will and the heart.

History is asking us, once again, to be a force for good in the world. Let us begin—in unity, with justice and love.

Thank you and God bless you.

✿ ✿ ✿

APPENDIX

❀ ❀ ❀

The Charter Documents
1776–1971

1

❖ ❖ ❖

The Declaration of Independence
1776

"*B*y every Post and every day," John
Adams exulted in the spring of 1776, "Independence rolls in on us like a
torrent." During the preceding year British troops sent to the colonies to
restore order had met with stubborn resistance—first from local militia,
then from the "Army of the United Colonies" under the command of
General George Washington. There was fighting in Massachusetts,
Canada, and North Carolina. Royal governors, like Lord Dunmore in
Virginia, had fled to the relative safety of British warships anchored
offshore, where they pretended to exercise authority over colonies which
had in fact been self-governing for months.

In May, Virginia, the oldest, richest, and most populous of the
colonies, instructed its delegates to the Continental Congress in
Philadelphia to vote for independence. Therefore on June 7 Richard
Henry Lee introduced in Congress three resolutions calling for
independence, a military alliance with France, and a plan for the
confederation of the colonies. Congress appointed committees to attend
to all three, including a committee to draft a declaration of independence.

It was mostly accidental that Thomas Jefferson became its author.
He was probably the least important member of the Virginia delegation.

THE DECLARATION OF INDEPENDENCE   Reprinted from the facsimile of the original,
engrossed copy in the National Archives.

Young (age 33), shy, and somewhat awkward in appearance, neither especially rich as a landowner nor prominent as a lawyer, Jefferson had been sent to Congress as an alternate and had scarcely opened his mouth during its sessions. Moreover he was only recently married and greatly preoccupied with his eventual masterpiece, the construction of a Palladian villa on an improbable hilltop site, where his bride still kept house in makeshift tents. Jefferson was absent from Congress for four months that spring, buying wine for his cellar and stocking his park with deer. He only chanced to return from Monticello to Philadelphia in time to be appointed to the committee to prepare the Declaration. Jefferson had one important qualification for the assignment. The other colonies deferred to the Virginians, and among the Virginians, a delegation which included splendid orators, superb horsemen and soldiers, opulent committee managers, there was only one with any patience for paperwork. The task fell to the bookish Jefferson by default.

Nor did it call for much originality. Everybody knew how a "declaration" was supposed to go. In law declarations were filed after bringing an action in court; they listed the grounds for complaint. Similarly, in constitutional practice, declarations were issued to explain actions already taken. It was a form followed by, among others, William of Orange when he seized the British throne in 1688 and by Congress itself in 1775 in its Declaration of the Causes of Taking Up Arms. The prescribed form was a modified version of the petition. It required first a brief statement of the just basis of the rights in question, then a detailed list of "grievances," or violations of those rights, and finally the proposed remedy. This form Jefferson followed exactly, borrowing extensively from other documents produced during the revolutionary controversy, not "aiming at originality of principle or sentiment," he afterwards said, but only "to place before mankind the common sense of the subject."

Thus to Jefferson and his contemporaries the most important part of the Declaration was the part we find least interesting—the long list of specific grievances which takes up exactly two-thirds of the document. It was also the least original part. By 1776 the colonists had accumulated a ready supply of these lists, and Jefferson borrowed freely from several of them.

Only the first 300 words of the Declaration make up the "immortal" part of it and these are more properly Jefferson's own. However, even here, as Jefferson himself said, all their "authority" rests on the "harmonizing sentiments of the day." To the student of eighteenth-century moral philosophy they are very resonant indeed. Virtually every phrase evokes long passages from celebrated philosophical works—"self-evident" truths, from John Locke and Thomas Reid; "all men are created equal," the mighty Linnean argument against all kinds of hereditary privilege; "inalienable rights," from Thomas Hutcheson; "the pursuit of happiness," Hutcheson again and Adam Smith; "deriving their just powers from the consent of the governed," the compact theory of John Locke. Into these two brief paragraphs the bookish Jefferson compressed whole volumes, and in doing so he tied a remote colonial rebellion to the highest hopes of the Atlantic world.

It is often said that the grievances enumerated in the Declaration were somewhat arbitrarily directed at the king because the colonists, having already repudiated the authority of Parliament over them, had no one else to declare their independence from. A careful reader of the Declaration will, however, detect a second villain in the piece—the British people. Jefferson had an idiosyncratic theory that Americans had become independent when they left Europe, and had voluntarily allied with the *people* of Great Britain, accepting with them a common sovereign. "We might have been a free and a great people together," Jefferson wrote in a part of his draft which Congress subsequently deleted. Instead "we must endeavor to forget our former love for them, and to hold them as we hold the rest of mankind enemies in war, in peace friends." Here Jefferson addressed, more forthrightly than the version Congress eventually approved, the national meaning of the dissolution of the "political bands" connecting "one people . . . with another."

On July 2, 1776, with Richard Henry Lee's motion before it, Congress formally voted the independence of the United States. For the next two days it debated and amended Jefferson's draft of the Declaration. Someone has counted more than eighty changes made in the text. Old Benjamin Franklin was kind enough to try to divert its fretful young author with a joke or two; even so, Jefferson felt his work had been "mangled." The amended version was adopted by Congress on July 4, promptly printed up, and "submitted to a candid world."

The Unanimous Declaration of the Thirteen United States of America

When in the Course of human events it becomes necessary for one people to dissolve the political bands which have connected them with another, and to assume among the Powers of the earth, the separate and equal station to which the Laws of Nature and of Nature's God entitle them, a decent respect to the opinions of mankind requires that they should declare the causes which impel them to the separation.[1]

---

[1]Paragraphing has been added according to that in Jefferson's draft.

We hold these truths to be self-evident, that all men are created equal, that they are endowed by their Creator with certain unalienable Rights, that among these are Life, Liberty and the pursuit of Happiness. That to secure these rights, Governments are instituted among Men, deriving their just Powers from the consent of the governed. That whenever any Form of Government becomes destructive of these ends, it is the Right of the People to alter or to abolish it, and to institute new Government, laying its foundation on such principles and organizing its Powers in such form, as to them shall seem most likely to effect their Safety and Happiness. Prudence, indeed, will dictate that Governments long established should not be changed for light and transient causes; and accordingly all experience hath shewn, that mankind are more disposed to suffer, while evils are sufferable, than to right themselves by abolishing the forms to which they are accustomed. But when a long train of abuses and usurpations, pursuing invariably the same Object evinces a design to reduce them under absolute Despotism, it is their right, it is their duty to throw off such Government, and to provide new Guards for their future security. Such has been the patient sufferance of these Colonies; and such is now the necessity which constrains them to alter their former Systems of Government. The history of the present King of Great Britain is a history of repeated injuries and usurpations, all having in direct object the establishment of an absolute Tyranny over these States. To prove this, let Facts be submitted to a candid world.

He has refused his Assent to Laws, the most wholesome and necessary for the public good.

He has forbidden his Governors to pass Laws of immediate and pressing importance, unless suspended in their operation till his Assent should be obtained; and when so suspended, he has utterly neglected to attend to them.

He has refused to pass other Laws for the accommodation of large districts of people, unless those people would relinquish the right of Representation in the Legislature, a right inestimable to them and formidable to tyrants only.

He has called together legislative bodies at places unusual, uncomfortable, and distant from the depository of their Public Records, for the sole Purpose of fatiguing them into compliance with his measures.

He has dissolved Representative Houses repeatedly, for opposing with manly firmness his invasions on the rights of the People.

He has refused for a long time, after such dissolutions, to cause others to be elected; whereby the Legislative Powers, incapable of

Annihilation, have returned to the People at large for their exercise; the State remaining in the mean time exposed to all the dangers of invasion from without, and convulsions within.

He has endeavoured to prevent the Population of these States; for that purpose obstructing the Laws for Naturalization of Foreigners; refusing to pass others to encourage their migration hither, and raising the conditions of new Appropriations of Lands.

He has obstructed the Administration of Justice, by refusing his Assent to Laws for establishing Judiciary Powers.

He has made Judges dependent on his Will alone, for the tenure of their offices, and the amount and payment of their salaries.

He has erected a multitude of New Offices, and sent hither swarms of Officers to harass our People, and eat out their substance.

He has kept among us, in times of peace, Standing Armies without the consent of our legislatures.

He has affected to render the Military independent of and superior to the Civil Power.

He has combined with others to subject us to a jurisdiction foreign to our constitution, and unacknowledged by our laws; giving his Assent to their Acts of pretended Legislation:

For Quartering large bodies of armed troops among us:

For protecting them, by a mock Trial, from Punishment for any Murders which they should commit on the Inhabitants of these States:

For cutting off our Trade with all parts of the world:

For imposing Taxes on us without our Consent:

For depriving us in many cases, of the benefits of Trial by Jury:

For transporting us beyond Seas to be tried for pretended offences:

For abolishing the free System of English Laws in a neighbouring Province, establishing therein an Arbitrary government, and enlarging its Boundaries so as to render it at once an example and fit instrument for introducing the same absolute rule into these Colonies:

For taking away our Charters, abolishing our most valuable Laws, and altering fundamentally the Forms of our Governments:

For suspending our own Legislatures, and declaring themselves invested with Power to legislate for us in all cases whatsoever.

He has abdicated Government here, by declaring us out of his Protection, and waging War against us.

He has plundered our seas, ravaged our Coasts, burnt our towns, and destroyed the lives of our people.

He is at this time transporting large Armies of foreign Mercenaries to compleat the works of death, desolation and tyranny, already begun with circumstances of Cruelty and perfidy scarcely paralleled in the most barbarous ages, and totally unworthy the Head of a civilized nation.

He has constrained our fellow Citizens taken Captive on the high Seas to bear Arms against their Country, to become the executioners of their friends and Brethren, or to fall themselves by their Hands.

He has excited domestic insurrections amongst us, and has endeavoured to bring on the inhabitants of our frontiers, the merciless Indian Savages, whose known rule of warfare, is an undistinguished destruction of all ages, sexes and conditions.

In every stage of these Oppressions We have Petitioned for Redress in the most humble terms: Our repeated Petitions have been answered only by repeated injury. A Prince, whose character is thus marked by every act which may define a Tyrant, is unfit to be the ruler of a free People.

Nor have We been wanting in attentions to our British brethren. We have warned them from time to time of attempts by their legislature to extend an unwarrantable jurisdiction over us. We have reminded them of the circumstances of our emigration and settlement here. We have appealed to their native justice and magnanimity, and we have conjured them by the ties of our common kindred to disavow these usurpations, which, would inevitably interrupt our connections and correspondence. They too have been deaf to the voice of justice and of consanguinity. We must, therefore, acquiesce in the necessity, which denounces our Separation, and hold them, as we hold the rest of mankind, Enemies in War, in Peace Friends.

We, therefore, the Representatives of the United States of America, in General Congress, Assembled, appealing to the Supreme Judge of the world for the rectitude of our intentions, do, in the Name, and by Authority of the good People of these Colonies, solemnly publish and declare, That these United Colonies are, and of Right ought to be FREE AND INDEPENDENT STATES; that they are Absolved from all Allegiance to the British Crown, and that all political connection between them and the State of Great Britain, is and ought to be totally dissolved; and that, as Free and Independent States, they have full Power to levy War, conclude Peace, contract

Alliances, establish Commerce, and to do all other Acts and Things which Independent States may of right do. And for the support of this Declaration, with a firm reliance on the protection of divine Providence, we mutually pledge to each other our Lives, our Fortunes and our sacred Honor.

❖ ❖ ❖

The Declaration of Independence did not, immediately at least, set the world on its ear. A leading student of the French Revolution reported after diligent search that the document never "had any particular influence in that country." English radicals also ignored it. More surprisingly, Americans themselves gave it scant attention until several decades later. Its eventual celebrity derived from the happenstance custom of marking the nation's birthday on July 4. John Adams tells us that when the first anniversary of independence rolled around on July 2, 1777, everybody forgot about it until it was too late to make arrangements. The third being spoken for, Congress delayed its celebration until the fourth, the anniversary of the Declaration. Even so, another student has found that few Fourth of July orators ever quoted the language of the Declaration and almost none its preamble.

Only in the years before the Civil War, when the proposition that all men were created equal became the subject of bitter controversy, did the Declaration assume, in the North, the stature of an American creed. Wisconsin in 1848 was the first state to include the language of Jefferson's preamble in its constitution. And Abraham Lincoln made it his mission to recall the nation to "that sentiment in the Declaration of Independence, which gave liberty not alone to the people of this country, but hope to all the world, for all future time." (See Volume 1, Section 5, Reading 3.)

Jefferson kept his original draft of the Declaration, often showing it to visitors at Monticello. It is now in the Library of Congress. Two weeks after the Declaration was adopted, Congress ordered a fair copy to be drawn on parchment and signed by the delegates, a business that stretched into August. This "engrossed" copy was kept for 135 years by the State Department. In 1924 it was encased in a great marble and bronze shrine and, carefully protected from light, heat, and humidity, put on public display. Jefferson, whose journal entry for the day the Declaration was adopted recorded four thermometer readings, would have found in these arrangements much to interest him.

2

❋ ❋ ❋

The American Constitution
1787

When the thirteen colonies declared
that they were independent states in 1776, they were "united" only in the
sense that military allies, before and since, have been united. The only
"political bands" that tied them before 1776 were those that connected
them individually with Great Britain. Consequently, for the first several
years of hostilities, patriot troops fought for their states or, as Ethan Allen
was said to have put it at the battle of Fort Ticonderoga, "in the name of the
Great Jehovah and the Continental Congress."

In November 1777, the Continental Congress adopted a frame of
government that more closely tied the states to one another, the Articles
of Confederation. By no means did the Articles create a united nation. A
confederacy is by definition a league of independent states from which,
implicitly, a member state reserves the right and the power to resign. The
Articles of Confederation ensured the independence and equality of each
of its thirteen members by requiring a unanimous vote of the states to ratify
any tax bill and also to amend this "first American constitution."

From the beginning (the Articles were finally ratified in 1781)
nationally minded Americans were unhappy with mere confederation.
Congress, the sole governing body, was often incapable of providing

THE AMERICAN CONSTITUTION, THE BILL OF RIGHTS, AMENDMENTS TO THE CON-
STITUTION   Reprinted from the fascimile of the original, engrossed copy in the
National Archives.

George Washington with the financial support he needed to keep an army in the field. After independence and peace were established, it was next to impossible to levy a tax. One state delegation or another voted against practically every money bill introduced in Congress. Effective diplomacy was also difficult because, as the British mocked, it was too expensive to send thirteen ambassadors to North America. Congress was unable to settle even petty squabbles between states, such as an argument between Virginians and Marylanders over fishing rights in the Chesapeake Bay. And in 1786 and 1787, when a Revolutionary War veteran, Daniel Shays, led a march of rebellious farmers in western Massachusetts, leaders in that state and elsewhere lamented the fact that there was no national force that could be sent into the Bay State to restore order.

More than any other incident, it was Shays' Rebellion that inspired a series of meetings that led, in the summer of 1787, to a constitutional convention in Philadelphia. This assembly of fifty-five men was officially empowered only to consider amendments that might improve the Articles of Confederation. In fact (and as everyone knew), they immediately set the Articles aside and began writing a new frame of government from scratch. The assembly included so many distinguished leaders, including George Washington and Benjamin Franklin, that it was the focus of attention in the United States even though its meetings were held in secret.

More important than either Washington or Franklin in calling for the convention was Alexander Hamilton of New York. More important than any of them in actually designing the Constitution was James Madison of Virginia. Not yet forty, these young men, together with the other delegates, were nevertheless as expert and as profound in their knowledge of political philosophy and history as anyone in the world.

True to their revolutionary heritage, they were wary of opportunities for tyrants to establish themselves in the government. Thus, for example, they developed the famous concepts of "separation of powers" among executive, legislative, and judicial branches of the government; and "checks and balances," the fact that, among and within the three branches, the exercise of power depended on the concurrence of several arms of the government, not one alone. However, the "Founding Fathers" were not democrats. They were skeptical of democracy, believing that "the mob" was likely to act rashly in times of stress and create, out of a demagogic hero, a tyrant who would suppress the liberties of all.

Indeed, the new Constitution created a strong executive, the president, where there had been no executive at all in the Articles, and the electoral college ensured that there would be at least one "layer" of government between the president and a popular vote. Another momentous departure from Confederation government was the power of Congress to tax nationally. No combination of states in the minority, let alone a single state, could veto such action. In fact, Article I, Section 10, rendered the states almost impotent in economic matters. Internal taxation remained within the states' competence, but all national economic powers, including the regulation of foreign and interstate commerce, was reserved to Congress.

In September, 1787, the Constitutional Convention adjourned and most members returned to their states to urge ratification of the new frame of government. By its own rules, the Constitution would go into effect when nine of the thirteen ratified it. Politically conservative as the document may have been, this provision too was a veritable act of revolution. Under the existing government, the Confederation, unanimity of the states was required to amend, and surely to replace, the Articles.

We the People of the United States, in Order to form a more perfect Union, establish Justice, insure domestic Tranquility, provide for the common defence, promote the general Welfare, and secure the Blessings of Liberty to ourselves and our Posterity, do ordain and establish this Constitution for the United States of America.

Article. I.

Section. 1. All legislative Powers herein granted shall be vested in a Congress of the United States, which shall consist of a Senate and House of Representatives.

Section. 2. The House of Representatives shall be composed of Members chosen every second Year by the People of the several States, and the Electors in each State shall have the Qualifications requisite for Electors of the most numerous Branch of the State Legislature.

No Person shall be a Representative who shall not have attained to the Age of twenty five Years, and been seven Years a Citizen of the United States, and who shall not, when elected, be an Inhabitant of that State in which he shall be chosen.

Representatives and direct Taxes[1] shall be apportioned among the several States which may be included within this Union, according to their respective Numbers, which shall be determined by adding to the whole Number of free Persons, including those bound to

---

[1]Modified by the Sixteenth Amendment.

224 APPENDIX

Service for a Term of Years, and excluding Indians not taxed, three fifths of all other Persons.[2] The actual Enumeration shall be made within three Years after the first Meeting of the Congress of the United States, and within every subsequent Term of ten Years, in such Manner as they shall by Law direct. The Number of Representatives shall not exceed one for every thirty Thousand, but each State shall have at least one Representative; and until such enumeration shall be made, the State of New Hampshire shall be entitled to chuse three; Massachusetts eight; Rhode Island and Providence Plantations one; Connecticut five; New York six; New Jersey four; Pennsylvania eight; Delaware one; Maryland six; Virginia ten; North Carolina five; South Carolina five; and Georgia three.

When vacancies happen in the Representation from any State, the Executive Authority thereof shall issue Writs of Election to fill such Vacancies.

The House of Representatives shall chuse their Speaker and other Officers; and shall have the sole Power of Impeachment.

Section. 3. The Senate of the United States shall be composed of two Senators from each State, chosen by the Legislature thereof, for six Years; and each Senator shall have one Vote.[3]

Immediately after they shall be assembled in Consequence of the first Election, they shall be divided as equally as may be into three Classes. The Seats of the Senators of the first Class shall be vacated at the Expiration of the second Year, of the second Class at the Expiration of the fourth Year, and of the third Class at the Expiration of the sixth Year, so that one third may be chosen every second Year; and if Vacancies happen by Resignation, or otherwise, during the Recess of the Legislature of any State, the Executive thereof may make temporary Appointments until the next Meeting of the Legislature, which shall then fill such Vacancies.[4]

No Person shall be a Senator who shall not have attained to the Age of thirty Years, and been nine Years a Citizen of the United States, and who shall not, when elected, be an Inhabitant of that State for which he shall be chosen.

The Vice President of the United States shall be President of the Senate, but shall have no Vote, unless they be equally divided.

The Senate shall chuse their other Officers, and also a Presi-

---

[2]Replaced by the Fourteenth Amendment.
[3]Superseded by the Seventeenth Amendment.
[4]Modified by the Seventeenth Amendment.

dent pro tempore, in the Absence of the Vice President, or when he shall exercise the Office of President of the United States.

The Senate shall have the sole Power to try all Impeachments. When sitting for that Purpose, they shall be on Oath or Affirmation. When the President of the United States is tried, the Chief Justice shall preside: And no Person shall be convicted without the Concurrence of two thirds of the Members present.

Judgment in Cases of Impeachment shall not extend further than to removal from Office, and disqualification to hold and enjoy any Office of honor, Trust or Profit under the United States: but the Party convicted shall nevertheless be liable and subject to Indictment, Trial, Judgment and Punishment, according to Law.

Section. 4. The Times, Places and Manner of holding Elections for Senators and Representatives, shall be prescribed in each State by the Legislature thereof, but the Congress may at any time by Law make or alter such Regulation, except as to the Places of chusing Senators.

The Congress shall assemble at least once in every Year, and such Meeting shall be on the first Monday in December, unless they shall by Law appoint a different Day.[5]

Section. 5. Each House shall be the Judge of the Elections, Returns and Qualifications of its own Members, and a Majority of each shall constitute a Quorum to do Business; but a smaller Number may adjourn from day to day, and may be authorized to compel the Attendance of absent Members, in such manner, and under such Penalties as each House may provide.

Each House may determine the Rules of its Proceedings, punish its Members for disorderly Behaviour, and, with the Concurrence of two thirds, expel a Member.

Each House shall keep a Journal of its Proceedings, and from time to time publish the same, excepting such Parts as may in their Judgment require Secrecy; and the Yeas and Nays of the Members of either House on any question shall, at the Desire of one fifth of those Present, be entered on the Journal.

Neither House, during the Session of Congress, shall, without the Consent of the other, adjourn for more than three days, nor to any other Place than that in which the two Houses shall be sitting.

Section. 6. The Senators and Representatives shall receive a Compensation for their Services, to be ascertained by Law, and paid out

---

[5]Superseded by the Twentieth Amendment.

of the Treasury of the United States. They shall in all Cases, except Treason, Felony and Breach of the Peace, be privileged from Arrest during their Attendance at the Session of their respective Houses, and in going to and returning from the same; and for any Speech or Debate in either House, they shall not be questioned in any other Place.

No Senator or Representative shall, during the Time for which he was elected, be appointed to any civil Office under the Authority of the United States, which shall have been created, or the Emoluments whereof shall have been encreased during such time; and no Person holding any Office under the United States, shall be a Member of either House during his Continuance in Office.

Section. 7. All Bills for raising Revenue shall originate in the House of Representatives; but the Senate may propose or concur with Amendments as on other bills.

Every Bill which shall have passed the House of Representatives and the Senate shall, before it become a Law, be presented to the President of the United States; If he approve he shall sign it, but if not he shall return it, with his Objections to that House in which it shall have originated, who shall enter the Objections at large on their Journal, and proceed to reconsider it. If after such Reconsideration two thirds of that House shall agree to pass the Bill, it shall be sent, together with the Objections, to the other House, by which it shall likewise be reconsidered, and if approved by two thirds of that House, it shall become a Law. But in all such Cases the Votes of both Houses shall be determined by Yeas and Nays, and the Names of the Persons voting for and against the Bill shall be entered on the Journal of each House respectively. If any Bill shall not be returned by the President within ten Days (Sundays excepted) after it shall have been presented to him, the Same shall be a Law, in Manner as if he had signed it, unless the Congress by their Adjournment prevent its Return, in which Case it shall not be a Law.

Every Order, Resolution, or Vote to which the Concurrence of the Senate and House of Representatives may be necessary (except on a question of Adjournment) shall be presented to the President of the United States; and before the Same shall take Effect, shall be approved by him, or being disapproved by him shall be repassed by two thirds of the Senate and House of Representatives, according to the rules and Limitations prescribed in the Case of a Bill.

Section. 8. The Congress shall have Power To Lay and collect Taxes, Duties, Imposts and Excises, to pay the Debts and provide for the common Defence and general Welfare of the United States; but all

Duties, Imposts and Excises shall be uniform throughout the United States;

To borrow Money on the credit of the United States;

To regulate Commerce with foreign Nations, and among the several States, and with the Indian Tribes;

To establish an uniform Rule of Naturalization, and uniform Laws on the subject of Bankruptcies throughout the United States;

To coin Money, regulate the Value thereof, and of foreign Coin, and fix the Standard of Weights and Measures;

To provide for the Punishment of counterfeiting the Securities and current Coin of the United States;

To establish Post Offices and post Roads;

To promote the Progress of Science and useful Arts, by securing for limited Times to Authors and Inventors the exclusive Right to their respective Writings and Discoveries;

To constitute Tribunals inferior to the Supreme Court;

To define and punish Piracies and Felonies committed on the high Seas, and Offences against the Law of Nations;

To declare War, grant Letters of Marque and Reprisal, and make Rules concerning Captures on Land and Water;

To raise and support Armies, but no Appropriation of Money to that Use shall be for a longer Term than two Years;

To provide and maintain a Navy;

To make Rules for the government and Regulation of the land and naval Forces;

To provide for calling forth the Militia to execute the Laws of the Union, suppress Insurrections and repel Invasions;

To provide for organizing, arming, and disciplining, the Militia, and for governing such Part of them as may be employed in the Service of the United States, reserving to the States respectively, the Appointment of the Officers, and the Authority of training the Militia according to the discipline prescribed by Congress;

To exercise exclusive Legislation in all Cases whatsoever, over such District (not exceeding ten Miles square) as may, by Cession of particular States, and the Acceptance of Congress, become the Seat of the Government of the United States, and to exercise like Authority over all Places purchased by the consent of the Legislature of the State in which the Same shall be, for the Erection of Forts, Magazines, Arsenals, dock-Yards, and other needful Buildings;—And

To make all Laws which shall be necessary and proper for carrying into Execution the foregoing Powers, and all other Powers vested by this Constitution in the Government of the United States, or in any Department or Officer thereof.

Section. 9. The Migration or Importation of such Persons as any of the States now existing shall think proper to admit, shall not be prohibited by the Congress prior to the Year one thousand eight hundred and eight, but a Tax or Duty may be imposed on such Importation, not exceeding ten dollars for each Person.

The Privilege of the Writ of Habeas Corpus shall not be suspended, unless when in Cases of Rebellion or Invasion the public Safety may require it.

No Bill of Attainder or ex post facto Law shall be passed.

No Capitation, or other direct, Tax shall be laid, unless in Proportion to the Census or Enumeration herein before directed to be taken.

No Tax or Duty shall be laid on Articles exported from any State.

No Preference shall be given by any Regulation of Commerce or Revenue to the Ports of one State over those of another: nor shall Vessels bound to, or from, one State, be obliged to enter, clear, or pay Duties in another.

No Money shall be drawn from the Treasury, but in Consequence of Appropriations made by Law, and a regular Statement and Account of the Receipts and Expenditures of all public Money shall be published from time to time.

No Title of Nobility shall be granted by the United States: And no Person holding any Office of Profit or Trust under them, shall, without the Consent of the Congress, accept of any present, Emolument, Office, or Title, of any kind whatever, from any King, Prince, or foreign State.

Section. 10. No State shall enter into any Treaty, Alliance, or Confederation; grant Letters of Marque and Reprisal; coin Money; emit bills of Credit; make any Thing but gold and silver Coin a Tender in Payment of Debts; pass any Bill of Attainder, ex post facto Law, or Law impairing the Obligation of Contracts, or grant any Title of Nobility.

No State shall, without the Consent of the Congress, lay any Imposts or Duties on Imports or Exports, except what may be absolutely necessary for executing its inspection Laws: and the net Produce of all Duties and Imposts, laid by any State on Imports or Exports, shall be for the Use of the Treasury of the United States; and all such Laws shall be subject to the Revision and Controul of the Congress.

No State shall, without the Consent of Congress, lay any Duty of Tonnage, keep Troops or Ships of War in time of peace, enter into any Agreement or Compact with another State, or with a foreign Power, or engage in War, unless actually invaded, or in such imminent Danger as will not admit of delay.

Article. II.

Section. 1. The executive Power shall be vested in a President of the United States of America. He shall hold his Office during the Term of four Years, and, together with the Vice President, chosen for the same Term, be elected, as follows:

Each State shall appoint, in such Manner as the Legislature thereof may direct, a Number of Electors, equal to the whole Number of Senators and Representatives to which the State may be entitled in the Congress: but no Senator or Representative, or Person holding an Office of Trust or Profit under the United States, shall be appointed an Elector.

The Electors shall meet in their respective States, and vote by Ballot for two Persons, of whom one at least shall not be an Inhabitant of the same State with themselves. And they shall make a List of all the Persons voted for, and of the Number of Votes for each; which List they shall sign and certify, and transmit sealed to the Seat of the Government of the United States, directed to the President of the Senate. The President of the Senate shall, in the Presence of the Senate and House of Representatives, open all the Certificates, and the Votes shall then be counted. The Person having the greatest Number of Votes shall be the President, if such Number be a Majority of the whole Number of Electors appointed; and if there be more than one who have such Majority, and have an equal Number of Votes, then the House of Representatives shall immediately chuse by Ballot one of them for President; and if no Person have a Majority, then from the five highest on the List the said House shall in like Manner chuse the President. But in chusing the President, the Votes shall be taken by States, the Representation from each State having one Vote; A quorum for this Purpose shall consist of a Member or Members from two thirds of the States, and a Majority of all the States shall be necessary to a Choice. In every Case, after the Choice of the President, the Person having the greatest Number of Votes of the Electors shall be the Vice President. But if there should remain two or more who have equal Votes, the Senate shall chuse from them by Ballot the Vice President.[6]

---

[6]Superseded by the Twelfth Amendment.

The Congress may determine the Time of chusing the Electors, and the Day on which they shall give their Votes; which Day shall be the same throughout the United States.

No Person except a natural born Citizen, or a Citizen of the United States, at the time of the Adoption of this Constitution, shall be eligible to the Office of President, neither shall any Person be eligible to that Office who shall not have attained to the Age of thirty five Years, and been fourteen Years a Resident within the United States.

In Case of the Removal of the President from Office, or of his Death, Resignation, or Inability to discharge the Powers and Duties of the said Office, the Same shall devolve on the Vice President, and the Congress may by Law provide for the Case of Removal, Death, Resignation or Inability, both of the President and Vice President, declaring what Officer shall then act as President, and such Officer shall act accordingly, until the Disability be removed, or a President shall be elected.[7]

The President shall, at stated Times, receive for his Services, a Compensation, which shall neither be encreased nor diminished during the Period for which he shall have been elected, and he shall not receive within that Period any other Emolument from the United States, or any of them.

Before he enter on the Execution of his Office, he shall take the following Oath or Affirmation:—"I do solemnly swear (or affirm) that I will faithfully execute the Office of President of the United States, and will to the best of my Ability, preserve, protect and defend the Constitution of the United States."

Section. 2. The President shall be Commander in Chief of the Army and Navy of the United States, and of the Militia of the several States, when called into the actual Service of the United States; he may require the Opinion, in writing, of the principle Officer in each of the executive Departments, upon any Subject relating to the Duties of their respective Offices, and he shall have Power to grant Reprieves and Pardons for Offences against the United States, except in cases of Impeachment.

He shall have Power, by and with the Advice and Consent of the Senate, to make Treaties, provided two thirds of the Senators present concur; and he shall nominate, and by and with the Advice and Consent of the Senate, shall appoint Ambassadors, other public Ministers and Consuls, Judges of the supreme Court, and all other

---

[7]Modified by the Twenty-fifth Amendment.

Officers of the United States, whose Appointments are not herein otherwise provided for, and which shall be established by Law; but the Congress may by Law vest the Appointment of such inferior Officers, as they think proper, in the President alone, in the Courts of Law, or in the Heads of Departments.

The President shall have Power to fill up all Vacancies that may happen during the Recess of the Senate, by granting Commissions which shall expire at the End of their next Session.

Section. 3. He shall from time to time give to the Congress Information of the State of the Union, and recommend to their Consideration such Measures as he shall judge necessary and expedient; he may, on extraordinary Occasions, convene both Houses, or either of them, and in Case of Disagreement between them, with Respect to the Time of Adjournment, he may adjourn them to such Time as he shall think proper; he shall receive Ambassadors and other public Ministers; he shall take Care that the Laws be faithfully executed, and shall Commission all the Officers of the United States.

Section. 4. the President, Vice President and all civil Officers of the United States, shall be removed from Office on Impeachment for, and Conviction of, Treason, Bribery, or other high Crimes and Misdemeanors.

Article. III.

Section. 1. The judicial Power of the United States, shall be vested in one supreme Court, and in such inferior Courts as the Congress may from time to time ordain and establish. The Judges, both of the supreme and inferior Courts, shall hold their Offices during good Behaviour, and shall, at stated Times, receive for their Services, a Compensation, which shall not be diminished during their Continuance in Office.

Section. 2. The judicial Power shall extend to all Cases, in Law and Equity, arising under this Constitution, the Laws of the United States, and Treaties made, or which shall be made, under their Authority;—to all Cases affecting Ambassadors, other public Ministers and Consuls;—to all Cases of admiralty and maritime Jurisdiction;—to Controversies to which the United States shall be a Party;—to Controversies between two or more States;—between a State and Citizens of another State;[8]—between Citizens of different States,—between Citizens of the same State claiming Lands under

---

[8]Modified by the Eleventh Amendment.

Grants of different States, and between a State, or the Citizens thereof, and foreign States, Citizens or Subjects.

In all Cases affecting Ambassadors, other public Ministers and Consuls, and those in which a State shall be Party, the supreme Court shall have original Jurisdiction. In all the other Cases before mentioned, the supreme Court shall have appellate Jurisdiction, both as to Law and Fact, with such Exceptions, and under such Regulations as the Congress shall make.

The Trial of all Crimes, except in Cases of Impeachment, shall be by Jury; and such Trial shall be held in the State where the said Crimes shall have been committed; but when not committed within any State, the trial shall be at such Place or Places as the Congress may by Law have directed.

Section. 3. Treason against the United States, shall consist only in levying War against them, or in adhering to their Enemies, giving them Aid and Comfort. No Person shall be convicted of Treason unless on the Testimony of two Witnesses to the same overt Act, or on Confession in open Court.

The Congress shall have power to declare the Punishment of Treason, but no Attainder of Treason shall work Corruption of Blood, or Forfeiture except during the Life of the Person attained.

Article. IV.

Section. 1. Full Faith and Credit shall be given in each State to the public Acts, Records, and judicial Proceedings of every other State. And the Congress may by general Laws prescribe the Manner in which such Acts, Records and Proceedings shall be proved, and the Effect thereof.

Section. 2. The Citizens of each State shall be entitled to all Privileges and Immunities of Citizens in the several States.

A Person charged in any State with Treason, Felony, or other Crime, who shall flee from Justice, and be found in another State, shall on Demand of the executive Authority of the State from which he fled, be delivered up, to be removed to the State having Jurisdiction of the Crime.

No Person held to Service or Labour in one State, under the Laws thereof, escaping into another, shall, in Consequence of any Law or Regulation therein, be discharged from such Service or Labour, but shall be delivered up on Claim of the Party to whom such Service or Labour may be due.

Section. 3. New States may be admitted by the Congress into this Union; but no new State shall be formed or erected within the

Jurisdiction of any other State, nor any State be formed by the Junction of two or more States, or Parts of States, without the Consent of the Legislatures of the States concerned as well as of the Congress.

The Congress shall have Power to dispose of and make all needful Rules and Regulations respecting the Territory or other Property belonging to the United States; and nothing in this Constitution shall be so construed as to Prejudice any Claims of the United States, or of any particular State.

Section. 4. The United States shall guarantee to every State in this Union a Republican Form of Government, and shall protect each of them against Invasion; and on Application of the Legislature, or of the Executive (when the Legislature cannot be convened) against domestic Violence.

Article. V.

The Congress, whenever two thirds of both Houses shall deem it necessary, shall propose Amendments to this Constitution, or, on the Application of the Legislatures of two thirds of the several States, shall call a Convention for proposing Amendments, which, in either Case, shall be valid to all Intents and Purposes, as Part of this Constitution, when ratified by the Legislatures of three fourths of the several States, or by Conventions in three fourths thereof, as the one or the other Mode of Ratification may be proposed by the Congress; Provided that no Amendment which may be made prior to the Year One thousand eight hundred and eight shall in any Manner affect the first and fourth Clauses in the Ninth Section of the first Article; and that no State, without its Consent, shall be deprived of its equal Suffrage in the Senate.

Article. VI.

All Debts contracted and Engagements entered into, before the Adoption of this Constitution, shall be as valid against the United States under this Constitution, as under the Confederation.

This Constitution, and the Laws of the United States which shall be made in Pursuance thereof; and all Treaties made, or which shall be made, under the Authority of the United States, shall be the supreme Law of the Land; and the Judges in every State shall be bound thereby, any Thing in the Constitution or Laws of any State to the Contrary notwithstanding.

The Senators and Representatives before mentioned, and the

Members of the several State Legislatures, and all executive and judicial Officers, both of the United States and of the several States, shall be bound by Oath or Affirmation, to support this Constitution; but no religious Test shall ever be required as a Qualification to any Office or public Trust under the United States.

Article. VII.

The Ratification of the Conventions of nine States, shall be sufficient for the Establishment of this Constitution between the States so ratifying the Same.

done in Convention by the Unanimous Consent of the States present the Seventeenth Day of September in the Year of our Lord one thousand seven hundred and Eighty seven and of the Independence of the United States of America the Twelfth. *In witness* whereof We have hereunto subscribed our Names,

❈ ❈ ❈

If what the Founding Fathers did was revolutionary, the revolution was bloodless. By early 1789, eleven of the thirteen states, including all the large states, had ratified the Constitution. (See Volume 1, Section 2, Reading 5.) North Carolina held out until November, when a Bill of Rights was appended to the Constitution, and little Rhode Island, which, because of its size, feared domination by other states and prized independence of action, remained out of the Union until May 1790.

3

❀ ❀ ❀

The Bill of Rights
1789

*A*t one time, "liberty" meant *privilege,* a special exemption from restraints and restrictions that was granted to certain people. The liberties listed in the English *Magna Carta* of 1215, for example, applied only to the people of the baronial class with whom King John had been disputing. During medieval times, the inhabitants of cities were granted certain liberties not shared by other subjects of the kingdom. Sometimes monopolies and other economic privileges were called liberties. Examples of these liberties included the exclusive right of a baker's guild to set standards regarding the quality and quantity in the baking of bread and the price at which a loaf was sold, or the special privileges enjoyed within the British empire by the East India Company.

Colonial Americans were familiar with all three kinds of liberties. In some contexts, the American tobacco growers' monopoly on the English market was called a liberty. The residents of Connecticut and Rhode Island, corporate colonies until they gained independence, possessed, by virtue of their colonial charters, certain liberties not shared by the inhabitants of other colonies. However, what made being British very special to Britons and colonial Americans was the fact that, unlike people of other nationalities, all free British subjects possessed, because of a law that no lawmaker might alter, wide-ranging guarantees against arbitrary treatment by their rulers.

The personal liberties of *Magna Carta* had long since been extended from the nobility to all English freemen. When King James II was deposed in 1688, his successors, William and Mary, in return for their crowns, signed the 1689 English Bill of Rights, which also extended to Americans. What was special about liberties in the British empire was that they extended to all freemen, and they were no longer privileges but rights.

Indeed, Americans had fought the Revolution because they believed that the King and Parliament were attempting to abridge these rights. Consequently, when they wrote the constitutions of their independent states, nearly every colony included a bill of rights.

The absence of a bill of rights in the federal Constitution of 1787 was, in the minds of many Anti-Federalists, therefore an argument against ratifying it. Several states ratified the Constitution with the provisions or recommendation that a bill of rights be added to the document. North Carolina and Rhode Island remained aloof from the new Union until passage of a bill of rights was assured. In "Federalist No. 84," Alexander Hamilton argued that it was not necessary to include a bill of rights in the Constitution. He pointed out that Anti-Federalists in New York had never complained about the absence of a bill of rights from New York's Constitution. And that was how it should be, he said, for a specific tabulation of rights would have been superfluous. The individual's rights were implicit in or scattered about New York's constitution, and the federal constitution.

Other Federalists argued that a constitutional bill of rights was unnecessary because the states had already provided their own. Nevertheless, sentiment on behalf of a federal bill of rights was so strong that the first Congress adopted ten amendments to the Constitution in September 1789. They were ratified in December 1791.

Amendment I

Congress shall make no law respecting an establishment of religion, or prohibiting the free exercise thereof; or abridging the freedom of speech, or of the press; or the right of the people peaceably to assemble, and to petition the Government for a redress of grievances.

Amendment II

A well regulated Militia, being necessary to the security of a free State, the right of the people to keep and bear Arms shall not be infringed.

Amendment III

No Soldier shall, in time of peace, be quartered in any house, without the consent of the Owner, nor in time of war, but in a manner to be prescribed by law.

Amendment IV

The right of the people to be secure in their persons, houses, papers, and effects, against unreasonable searches and seizures, shall not be violated, and no Warrants shall issue, but upon probable cause, supported by Oath or affirmation, and particularly describing the place to be searched, and the persons or things to be seized.

Amendment V

No person shall be held to answer for a capital or otherwise infamous crime, unless on a presentment or indictment of a Grand Jury, except in cases arising in the land or naval forces, or in the Militia, when in actual service in time of War or public danger; nor shall any person be subject for the same offence to be twice put in jeopardy of life or limb; nor shall be compelled in any criminal case to be a witness against himself, nor be deprived of life, liberty, or property, without due process of law; nor shall private property be taken for public use, without just compensation.

Amendment VI

In all criminal prosecutions, the accused shall enjoy the right to a speedy and public trial, by an impartial jury of the State and district wherein the crime shall have been committed, which district shall have been previously ascertained by law, and to be informed of the nature and cause of the accusation; to be confronted with the witnesses against him; to have compulsory process for obtaining witnesses in his favor, and to have the Assistance of Counsel for his defence.

Amendment VII

In suits at common law, where the value in controversy shall exceed twenty dollars, the right of trial by jury shall be preserved, and no fact tried by a jury, shall be otherwise reexamined in any

Court of the United States, than according to the rules of the common law.

Amendment VIII

Excessive bail shall not be required, nor excessive fines imposed, nor cruel and unusual punishments inflicted.

Amendment IX

The enumeration in the Constitution, of certain rights, shall not be construed to deny or disparage others retained by the people.

Amendment X

The powers not delegated to the United States by the Constitution; nor prohibited by it to the States, are reserved to the States respectively, or to the people.

❂ ❂ ❂

For more than a hundred years, Americans had little doubt about what the Bill of Rights said. The brief amendments seemed crystal clear, their meaning established through centuries of precedent in England. Comparatively few cases testing the interpretation of them came before the Supreme Court. (By comparison, the Fourteenth Amendment was a snarl of interpretive difficulty from the beginning.)

In the second half of the twentieth century, however, many rights listed in the first ten amendments became the object of intensive scrutiny that, under the liberal Warren Court of 1953–1969, usually meant a vast broadening of their meaning. For example, the guarantees of freedom of speech and freedom of the press in the first amendment were extended to permit publication of pornography which previous generations of Americans had seen as no abridgement of liberty to prohibit. Curiously, Alexander Hamilton had argued against trying to specify freedom of the press as a right because of the snares he saw in attempting to interpret it: "What is the liberty of the press? Who could give it any definition which would not leave the utmost latitude for evasion? I hold it to be impracticable; and from this I infer, that its security, whatever fine declarations may be inserted in any constitution respecting it, must altogether depend on public opinion, and on the general spirit of the people and of the government."

The broad reinterpretation of the Bill of Rights in our own time, whether in allowing almost any kind of public expression, in making very specific the procedures that guarantee the rights of persons accused of crimes, or even in temporarily abolishing the death penalty under the "cruel and unusual punishments" provision of the eighth amendment, reflects well Hamilton's shrewd insight and the wisdom of the "Founding Fathers" in providing a clear means of amendment within the Constitution.

4

❋ ❋ ❋

Amendments to the Constitution
1795–1971

*A*mericans have amended the Constitution twenty-six times, or, on the average, about once every seven years. However, the Bill of Rights was ratified so soon after the ratification of the Constitution, and almost as a condition of ratification, that the first ten amendments may reasonably be considered part and parcel of the original document—in which case it can be said that the Constitution has been amended only about once every twelve years.

Moreover, the most important amendments have come in two bunches. These are the "Civil War Amendments" (the 13th, 14th, and 15th), ratified between 1865 and 1870, and the "Progressive Amendments" (the 16th, 17th, 18th, and 19th), ratified between 1913 and 1920.

One of these Progressive Amendments, the 18th—or Prohibition—Amendment, which made it illegal to import, manufacture, sell, or transport intoxicating liquors, was revoked by the 21st—or Repeal—Amendment fourteen years after Prohibition went into effect. The 18th is generally conceded to have been a colossal blunder. The Constitution is intended to be a instrument of *basic* law, not a hodgepodge of ordinances to be modified according to the opinion, mood, or whim of the people on a very specific matter at a particular time. Only two "frivolous" amendments over almost two hundred years is not a bad record. In fact, since 1789 more than 6000 amendments have actually been proposed in Congress. Of these, only thirty-three have been passed and sent to the states for ratification.

Amendment XVIII[1]

Section. 1. After one year from the ratification of this article the manufacture, sale, or transportation of intoxicating liquors within, the importation thereof into, or the exportation thereof from the United States and all territory subject to the jurisdiction thereof for beverage purposes is hereby prohibited.

Section. 2. The Congress and the several States shall have concurrent power to enforce this article by appropriate legislation.

Section. 3. This article shall be inoperative unless it shall have been ratified as an amendment to the Constitution by the legislatures of the several States, as provided in the Constitution, within seven years from the date of the submission hereof to the States by the Congress.

Amendment XXI[2]

Section. 1. The eighteenth article of amendment to the Constitution of the United States is hereby repealed.

Section. 2. The transportation or importation into any State, Territory, or possession of the United States for delivery or use therein of intoxicating liquors, in violation of the laws thereof, is hereby prohibited.

Section. 3. This article shall be inoperative unless is shall have been ratified as an amendment of the Constitution by conventions in the several States, as provided in the Constitution, within seven years from the date of the submission hereof to the States by the Congress.

❋ ❋ ❋

The 11th Amendment may also be passed over lightly. Enacted by Congress in 1794 and ratified the next year, it provides that no one may sue a state government in the federal courts. The 11th was inspired by the ruling of the Supreme Court in *Chisholm* v. *Georgia* that citizens and foreigners did indeed possess this right. It was ratified very quickly by state governments anxious to assure themselves of this exemption and is chiefly notable as an example of a "check" on the power of the Supreme Court. That is, just as the impeachment of existing Justices or

---

[1]Passed December 18, 1917. Ratified January 16, 1919.

[2]Passed February 20, 1933. Ratified December 5, 1933.

appointments of new Justices to the Court are "checks" (see Volume 2, Section 1, Reading 4), an unpopular Court interpretation of the Constitution may be "checked," or nullified, by Constitutional Amendment.

Amendment XI[1]

The Judicial power of the United States shall not be construed to extend to any suit in law or equity, commenced or prosecuted against one of the United States by Citizens of another State, or by Citizens or Subjects of any Foreign State.

❁ ❁ ❁

The Civil War/Civil Rights Amendments

*A*fter the ratification of the 12th Amendment in 1804, the Constitution was unchanged for sixty years. By 1864, however, the agony and turmoil of the Civil War, then near the end of its third year, dictated that at least one significant amendment was in order. By the end of 1864, it was clear to all, including Confederate leaders who did not delude themselves, that American Negro slavery was dead. By 1865, even Jefferson Davis was prevailed upon to pledge manumission for slaves who donned Confederate gray. In the North, opposition to abolition virtually ceased to exist. When Congress approved the 13th Amendment on January 31, 1865, only a handful of men voted nay. In less than a year, the amendment was ratified.

It was soon clear, however, that neither President Andrew Johnson, the courts, nor many of the whites of both the South and North regarded freedom as tantamount to citizenship. Southern state governments set up with Johnson's approval wrote the "Black Codes" which gave a decidedly inferior status to the freedmen. In several northern states, laws preventing blacks from voting were reinstituted or reaffirmed. Such discrimination was all quite constitutional. Defining citizenship was, in 1866, clearly the prerogative of individual state governments.

The Radical Republicans, who won control of Reconstruction policy after the Congressional elections of 1866, were determined that full

---

[1]Passed March 4, 1794. Ratified January 23, 1795.

citizenship be accorded to the freedmen. Even extreme idealists like Thaddeus Stevens had earlier expressed their reluctant willingness to allow discrimination against blacks in the North, but there was no way, under the Constitution, that full citizenship could be accorded in some states and not in others. So, the 14th Amendment forbade all states from abridging the rights of or denying equal legal protection to any United States citizen.

There were exceptions, detailed in Section 3 of the amendment. For example, Confederates who had earlier taken an oath of loyalty to the Constitution of the United States were to be deprived of their civil rights until pardoned by Congress. Also, Section 4 forbade the repayment of Confederate debts.

The 15th Amendment forbade states to deny the right to vote to anyone on the basis of race, color, or previous condition of servitude—in other words, the former slaves. It was adopted by Congress shortly after the presidential election of 1868 when a careful analysis of the results showed that, even this soon after the Civil War, the Republican candidate Ulysses S. Grant might not have won except for the almost solid support of southern blacks. Had blacks been able to vote in several northern states, Grant's plurality would not have been so slender in the North. The Republicans had no intention of yielding control of the federal government to the Democrats, whom they associated with treason, so soon after the dreadful war. The 15th Amendment, while surely motivated by idealism as well, was very much motivated by the political situation in 1869.

Amendment XIII[1]

Section. 1. Neither slavery nor involuntary servitude, except as a punishment for crime whereof the party shall have been duly convicted, shall exist within the United States, or any place subject to their jurisdiction.

Section. 2. Congress shall have power to enforce this article by appropriate legislation.

Amendment XIV[2]

Section. 1. All persons born or naturalized in the United States, and subject to the jurisdiction thereof, are citizens of the United States and of the State wherein they reside. No State shall make or enforce any law which shall abridge the privileges or immunities of citizens

---

[1]Passed January 31, 1865. Ratified December 6, 1865.
[2]Passed June 13, 1866. Ratified July 9, 1865.

of the United States; nor shall any State deprive any person of life, liberty, or property, without due process of law; nor deny to any person within its jurisdiction the equal protection of the laws.

Section. 2. Representatives shall be apportioned among the several States according to their respective numbers, counting the whole number of persons in each State, excluding Indians not taxed. But when the right to vote at any election for the choice of electors for President and Vice-President of the United States, Representatives in Congress, the Executive and Judicial officers of a State, or the members of the Legislature thereof, is denied to any of the male inhabitants of such State, being twenty-one years of age, and citizens of the United States, or in any way abridged, except for participation in rebellion, or other crime, the basis of representation therein shall be reduced in the proportion which the number of such male citizens shall bear to the whole number of male citizens twenty-one years of age in such State.

Section. 3. No person shall be a Senator or Representative in Congress, or elector of President and Vice-President, or hold any office, civil or military, under the United States, or under any State, who, having previously taken an oath, as a member of Congress, or as an officer of the United States, or as a member of any State legislature, or as an executive or judicial officer of any State, to support the Constitution of the United States, shall have engaged in insurrection or rebellion against the same, or given aid or comfort to the enemies thereof. But Congress may by a vote of two-thirds of each House, remove such disability.

Section. 4. The validity of the public debt of the United States, authorized by law, including debts incurred for payment of pensions and bounties for services in suppressing insurrection or rebellion, shall not be questioned. But neither the United States nor any State shall assume or pay any debt or obligation incurred in aid of insurrection or rebellion against the United States, or any claim for the loss or emancipation of any slave; but all such debts, obligations, and claims shall be held illegal and void.

Section. 5. The Congress shall have the power to enforce, by appropriate legislation, the provisions of this article.

Amendment XV[3]

Section. 1. The right of citizens of the United States to vote shall not be denied or abridged by the United States or by any State on

---

[3]Passed February 26, 1869. Ratified February 2, 1870.

account of race, color, or previous condition of servitude—
Section. 2. The Congress shall have power to enforce this article by appropriate legislation.

With the end of Reconstruction in 1877, the 15th Amendment was effectively allowed to lapse in the southern states. At first, through terrorism of the Ku Klux Klan and then through economic pressures (most blacks were tenant farmers, dependent on landowners for their living), blacks were informally disenfranchised. They were kept from voting in a number of legal ways. For example, requiring voters to pass a literacy test did not deny anyone's right to vote on the basis of race, color, or previous condition of servitude, but when administered by local officials it could easily serve that purpose. Simpler tests were given to whites, or grading was done on a double standard. Charging would-be voters a "poll tax," a fairly substantial sum, disqualified many blacks, to whom a few dollars could mean the difference between hunger and minimal comfort. "Grandfather clauses" in some states' electoral laws provided that people whose grandfathers had been eligible to vote were exempted from literacy tests and poll taxes. These contrivances, strictly construed, were not in violation of the 15th Amendment, but they kept blacks away from the polls. No black man's grandfather had been eligible to vote during his lifetime.

Such palpable evasion of the spirit of the 15th Amendment was possible only with the connivance of the courts. The Supreme Court's decision in the case of *Plessy* v. *Ferguson* in 1896 (see Volume 2, Section 2, Reading 4) was a signal to white southern racists that they could evade the Civil War Amendments with impunity. Not until the 1940s and 1950s did the courts begin to enforce the 14th and 15th Amendments with any consistency. One historian has correctly described the Civil War Amendments as the nation's "deferred commitment" to its black citizens. In fact, it required another constitutional amendment, the 24th, ratified in 1964, to eliminate the poll tax as a means of disenfranchising the poor, whatever their race.

Amendment XXIV[1]

Section. 1. The right of citizens of the United States to vote in any primary or other election for President or Vice President, or for Senator or Representative in Congress, shall not be denied or

---

[1]Passed August 27, 1962. Ratified January 23, 1964.

abridged by the United States or any State by reason of failure to pay any poll tax or other tax.

Section. 2. The Congress shall have power to enforce this article by appropriate legislation.

❖ ❖ ❖

The Progressive Amendments

*T*he so-called "progressive movement" was in reality a mélange of reform impulses that swept the country during the first two decades of the twentieth century, some of them quite in conflict with others. Nevertheless, the demand for change was real and formidable and resulted in the ratification of four amendments within six years.

The Prohibition Amendment, the 18th, has already been noted. The 16th, ratified in 1913, made a graduated income tax constitutional. Previously, as the Supreme Court ruled in 1895, Congress could not levy a direct tax on individuals because it would mean taxing different states at different rates. The Constitution required that direct taxes be apportioned equally among the states, that is, at a rate proportionate to a state's population. However, the income tax was based on wealth. For example, in 1890 Alabama had a greater population than New Jersey but the per capita income of New Jersey was double and perhaps as much as triple that of Alabama. This meant that a federal income tax would raise at least two times as much in New Jersey as in Alabama—a situation which was not constitutional. Thus, the 16th Amendment became the basis of our income tax today.

The 17th Amendment removed the power to elect United States Senators from the state legislatures and required that senators be elected by popular vote. This amendment marked one of the most significant philosophical departures from the intentions of the Founding Fathers. They had put election of senators in the hands of state legislators deliberately and explicitly to remove senators a step from "the democracy," the people. One of the underlying beliefs of many progressives was that the more democracy there was in government, the less likely it was that government would be corrupt and beholden to special interests.

Any number of similarly democratic amendments were proposed during the progressive years, and their objects—the recall and the referendum—were enacted in many states. At the constitutional level, however, only the direct election of senators was enacted. One of the progressive proposals is still periodically proposed in Congress: the abolition of the electoral college and the direct popular election of the president. The electoral college too was seen by the Founding Fathers as a device to remove the president several steps from direct democracy.

The 19th Amendment prohibits states from denying citizens the right to vote on the basis of their sex. It is commonly known as the Woman Suffrage Amendment.

Amendment XVI[1]

The Congress shall have power to lay and collect taxes on incomes, from whatever source derived, without apportionment among the several States, and without regard to any census or enumeration.

Amendment XVII[2]

The Senate of the United States shall be composed of two Senators from each State, elected by the people thereof, for six years; and each Senator shall have one vote. The electors in each State shall have the qualifications requisite for electors of the most numerous branch of the State legislature.

When vacancies happen in the representation of any State in the Senate, the executive authority of such State shall issue writs of election to fill such vacancies: *Provided*, That the legislature of any State may empower the executive thereof to make temporary appointments until the people fill the vacancies by election as the legislature may direct.

This amendment shall not be so construed as to affect the election or term of any Senator chosen before it becomes valid as part of the Constitution.

Amendment XIX[3]

The right of citizens of the United States to vote shall not be denied or abridged by the United States or by any State on account of sex.

---

[1]Passed July 12, 1909. Ratified February 3, 1913.

[2]Passed May 13, 1912. Ratified April 8, 1913.

[3]Passed June 4, 1919. Ratified August 18, 1920.

Congress shall have power to enforce this article by appropriate legislation.

In 1972, Congress approved another feminist amendment, the ERA or Equal Rights Amendment, which read: "Equality of rights under the law shall not be denied or abridged by the United States or by any State on account of sex." At first, the ERA sailed through almost enough state legislatures to be incorporated into the Constitution. But anti-ERA forces mobilized and ended the trend toward ratification. By 1979, the deadline for ratification, ERA was still three votes short of acceptance. In the meantime, Congress extended the cut-off date to June 30, 1982.

When three states rescinded their ratification, there was some question as to whether or not these reversals were constitutional. Anti-ERA forces argued they were, because of the unprecedented action of Congress in modifying the terms of ratification. In any case the issue was moot because ERA failed to win the approval of a single additional state during the three-year extension.

To date, therefore, the final amendment to the Constitution is the 26th, which extends the right to vote to all citizens over the age of eighteen. It has been called the "Baby Boom Amendment." Ratified with extraordinary haste in 1971, it was designed to appeal to the huge baby boom generation who were then reaching their maturity and who had been a source of considerable social tumult during the 1960s. Ironically, no sooner was the amendment ratified than the apparently intense interest of youth in politics evaporated. Statistically, the 18- to 21-year-old age group is by far the least likely to participate in or even express an interest in political issues and the right to vote.

Amendment XXVI[1]

Section. 1. The right of citizens of the United States, who are eighteen years of age or older, to vote shall not be denied or abridged by the United States or by any State on account of age.
Section. 2. The Congress shall have power to enforce this article by appropriate legislation.

❋ ❋ ❋

---

[1]Passed March 23, 1971. Ratified July 5, 1971.

The Presidential Amendments

*T*he 12th, 20th, 22nd, 23rd, and 25th Amendments deal with presidential elections, terms, and succession. Each has its roots in specific historical circumstances.

The 12th Amendment, ratified in 1804, was written to ensure that the events of the election of 1800 would not be repeated. The Founding Fathers had assumed that the United States would be home to no political parties. Therefore, they reasoned, every four years the Electoral College would select the nation's best qualified person to be president. Because the vice-president succeeded to the presidency in case of a vacancy, it was assumed that the vice-president should be the second best qualified person. So, under the original Constitution, the person receiving the most electoral votes became president, the person receiving the second most vice-president.

Already in 1796, the inadequacy of the scheme in an age of political parties was made clear. Federalist John Adams and Republican Thomas Jefferson, representing different parties and running against one another, received, respectively, 71 and 68 electoral votes, with the intended Federalist vice-presidential candidate, Thomas Pinckney, running third with 59 votes. Adams' vice-president was, therefore, his chief political rival, Thomas Jefferson. Had Adams died in office, the representative of the opposition would have become president, not exactly what the Founding Fathers had in mind.

Adams did not die in office. Instead, in 1800 he was roundly defeated by the Republican ticket of Jefferson and Aaron Burr. However, no Republican elector was assigned to "throw away" a Burr vote so that Jefferson would have a majority. Instead, the two were locked in an electoral college draw. When that happens (and this is still the case), the power to break the tie goes to the House of Representatives. Finally, in 1801, the House chose Jefferson and he moved into the Executive Mansion. But he and his party were determined that the colossal snafu would not occur again. Their 12th Amendment required electors to distinguish their votes for president from their votes for vice-president.

The 20th Amendment changed Inauguration Day from March 4th to January 20th. Ratified in 1933, this amendment in part represented a recognition of the transportation and communications revolution of the nineteenth and twentieth centuries. It was no longer necessary to allow a president-elect four months to prepare for the presidency and travel to the national capital. The long interregnum seemed even longer in 1933 because the country was entrapped in the greatest crisis since the Civil War, the Great Depression. In November 1932, the electorate emphatically voted against the incumbent, Herbert C. Hoover, who was perceived as paralyzed by the economic disaster, and voted in the Democratic candidate, Franklin D. Roosevelt. Because the depression had assumed the character of an emergency, Hoover's four remaining months in office seemed like an eternity. The 20th amendment assured that there would not again be such an interminable period of "lame-duck" government.

The 22nd Amendment was inspired by FDR's historic presidency. Elected to the office four times, Roosevelt was so much a symbol of Republican disarray that in 1947 they used their control of Congress to draft an amendment to ensure that no future president would serve more terms than the two established as traditional by Washington, Jefferson, Madison, Monroe, and Jackson. Harry S. Truman, president in 1947, was exempted from the 22nd Amendment but wisely chose not to stand for re-election in 1952 when his second term ended. He would surely have been defeated.

By 1960, a majority of the population of Washington, D. C., was black, and the decision taken years before—that the District would not be self-governing—had become a civil rights question. This was the rationale for the 23rd Amendment, ratified in 1961, which enfranchises the residents of the District of Columbia in presidential elections. Previously, citizens of the District were not permitted to select Electoral College representatives.

The 25th Amendment enables the president to appoint a vice-president when there is a vacancy in the vice-presidency. As of 1965, this had happened twelve times—seven times when a president died in office and the vice-president assumed the position, and five times when the vice-president died in office, or, in the case of John C. Calhoun, resigned. At those various times, either the Secretary of State or the Speaker of the House of Representatives was next in line of succession. However, this state of affairs presented somewhat the same situation as had held between 1797 and 1801, when the president and vice-president represented different political parties. During those years, had an "accident of history"—the death of the president—occurred, the administration would have fallen to the political opposition. Likewise, were the vice-presidency vacant and the House of Representatives under the control of the opposition when the president died or resigned, the executive would change parties despite the fact that no such wish had been expressed by the electorate. Thus, the 25th Amendment, while giving the president substantial power to choose a successor, is actually a further reinforcement of our nation's principle of rule by majority.

Amendment XII[1]

The Electors shall meet in their respective States and vote by ballot for President and Vice-President, one of whom, at least, shall not be an inhabitant of the same State with themselves; they shall

---

[1]Passed December 9, 1803. Ratified June 15, 1804.

name in their ballots the person voted for as President, and in distinct ballots the person voted for as Vice-President, and they shall make distinct lists of all persons voted for as President, and of all persons voted for as Vice-President, and of the number of votes for each, which lists they shall sign and certify, and transmit sealed to the seat of the government of the United States, directed to the President of the Senate;—The President of the Senate shall, in the presence of the Senate and House of Representatives, open all the certificates and the votes shall then be counted;—The person having the greatest number of votes for President, shall be the President, if such number is a majority of the whole number of Electors appointed; and if no person have such majority, then from the persons having the highest numbers not exceeding three on the list of those voted for as President, the House of Representatives shall choose immediately, by ballot, the President. But in choosing the President, the votes shall be taken by states, the representation from each state having one vote; a quorum for this purpose shall consist of a member or members from two-thirds of the states, and a majority of all the states shall be necessary to a choice. And if the House of Representatives shall not choose a President whenever the right of choice shall devolve upon them, before the fourth day of March next following, then the Vice-President shall act as President, as in the case of the death or other constitutional disability of the President.—The person having the greatest number of votes as Vice-President, shall be the Vice-President, if such number be a majority of the whole number of Electors appointed, and if no person have a majority, then from the two highest numbers on the list, the Senate shall choose the Vice-President; a quorum for the purpose shall consist of two-thirds of the whole number of Senators, and a majority of the whole number shall be necessary to a choice. But no person constitutionally ineligible to the office of President shall be eligible to that of Vice-President of the United States.

Amendment XX[2]

Section. 1. The terms of the President and Vice-President shall end at noon on the 20th day of January, and the terms of Senators and Representatives at noon on the 3d day of January, of the years in which such terms would have ended if this article had not been ratified; and the terms of their successors shall then begin.

---

[2]Passed March 2, 1932. Ratified January 23, 1933.

Section. 2. The Congress shall assemble at least once in every year, and such meeting shall begin at noon on the 3d day of January, unless they shall by law appoint a different day.

Section. 3. If, at the time fixed for the beginning of the term of the President, the President elect shall have died, the Vice-President elect shall become President. If a President shall not have been chosen before the time fixed for the beginning of his term, or if the President elect shall have failed to qualify, then the Vice-President elect shall act as President until a President shall have qualified; and the Congress may by law provide for the case wherein neither a President elect nor a Vice-President elect shall have qualified, declaring who shall then act as President, or the manner in which one who is to act shall be selected, and such person shall act accordingly until a President or Vice-President shall have qualified.

Section. 4. The Congress may by law provide for the case of the death of any of the persons from whom the House of Representatives may choose a President whenever the right of choice shall have devolved upon them, and for the case of the death of any of the persons from whom the Senate may choose a Vice-President whenever the right of choice shall have devolved upon them.

Section. 5. Sections 1 and 2 shall take effect on the 15th day of October following the ratification of this article.

Section. 6. This article shall be inoperative unless it shall have been ratified as an amendment to the Constitution by the legislatures of three-fourths of the several States within seven years from the date of its submission.

Amendment XXII[3]

No person shall be elected to the office of the President more than twice, and no person who has held the office of President, or acted as President, for more than two years of a term to which some other person was elected President shall be elected to the office of the President more than once.

But this Article shall not apply to any person holding the office of President when this Article was proposed by the Congress, and shall not prevent any person who may be holding the office of President, or acting as President, during the term within which this Article becomes operative from holding the office of President or acting as President during the remainder of such term.

---

[3]Passed March 12, 1947. Ratified March 1, 1951.

Amendment XXIII[4]

Section. 1. The district constituting the seat of Government of the United States shall appoint in such manner as the Congress may direct:

A number of electors of President and Vice President equal to the whole number of Senators and Representatives in Congress to which the District would be entitled if it were a State, but in no event more than the least populous State; they shall be in addition to those appointed by the States, but they shall be considered, for the purposes of the election of President and Vice President, to be electors appointed by the State; and they shall meet in the District and perform such duties as provided by the twelfth article of amendment.

Section. 2. The Congress shall have power to enforce this article by appropriate legislation.

Amendment XXV[5]

Section. 1. In case of the removal of the President from office or of his death or resignation, the Vice President shall become President.

Section. 2. Whenever there is a vacancy in the office of the Vice President, the President shall nominate a Vice President who shall take office upon confirmation by a majority vote of both Houses of Congress.

Section. 3. Whenever the President transmits to the President pro tempore of the Senate and the Speaker of the House of Representatives his written declaration that he is unable to discharge the powers and duties of his office, and until he transmits to them a written declaration to the contrary, such powers and duties shall be discharged by the Vice President as Acting President.

Section. 4. Whenever the Vice President and a majority of either the principal officers of the executive department or of such other body as Congress may by law provide, transmit to the President pro tempore of the Senate and the Speaker of the House of Representatives their written declaration that the President is unable to discharge the powers and duties of his office, the Vice President shall immediately assume the powers and duties of the office of Acting President.

Thereafter, when the President transmits to the President pro

[4]Passed June 16, 1960. Ratified April 3, 1961.
[5]Passed July 6, 1965. Ratified February 11, 1967.

tempore of the Senate and the Speaker of the House of Representatives his written declaration that no inability exists, he shall resume the powers and duties of his office unless the Vice President and a majority of either the principal officers of the executive department or of such other body as Congress may by law provide, transmit within four days to the President pro tempore of the Senate and the Speaker of the House of Representatives their written declaration that the President is unable to discharge the powers and duties of his office. Thereupon Congress shall decide the issue, assembling within forty-eight hours for that purpose if not in session. If the Congress, within twenty-one days after receipt of the latter written declaration, or, if Congress is not in session, within twenty-one days after Congress is required to assemble, determines by two-thirds vote of both Houses that the President is unable to discharge the powers and duties of his office, the Vice President shall continue to discharge the same as Acting President; otherwise, the President shall resume the powers and duties of his office.

The 25th Amendment was called upon under the first president elected after its ratification. Republican Richard M. Nixon was elected president in 1968 and re-elected in 1972. In October 1973, under fire for taking bribes while governor of Maryland, Vice-president Spiro T. Agnew was forced to resign. Less than a year later, President Nixon himself resigned as a result of the "Watergate" scandal. Had the 25th Amendment not been in effect, Thomas P. "Tip" O'Neill, the Democratic Speaker of the House, would have become president, representing a major switch of parties and political philosophies. However, under the terms of the 25th Amendment, President Nixon had named as vice-president a member of his own party, Gerald Ford of Michigan. Curiously, when Ford named Nelson A. Rockefeller as vice-president, the two highest offices in the land were held by people who had never even stood as candidates in a national election.